YOU'RE NOT AS CRAZY AS I THOUGHT

(BUT YOU'RE STILL WRONG)

Related Titles from Potomac Books

New Common Ground: A New America, a New World
—Amitai Etzioni

The Politics of Gratitude: Scale, Place & Community in a Global Age
—Mark T. Mitchell

YOU'RE NOT AS CRAZY AS I THOUGHT

(BUT YOU'RE STILL WRONG)

**Conversations between a Die-Hard Liberal
and a Devoted Conservative**

PHIL NEISSER AND JACOB HESS

Potomac Books
Washington, D.C.

Published in the United States by Potomac Books, Inc. All rights reserved. No part of this book may be reproduced in any manner whatsoever without written permission from the publisher, except in the case of brief quotations embodied in critical articles and reviews.

Library of Congress Cataloging-in-Publication Data
Neisser, Philip T., 1957–
    You're not as crazy as I thought (but you're still wrong) : conversations between a die-hard liberal and a devoted conservative / Phil Neisser and Jacob Hess.
    pages cm
    Includes bibliographical references and index.
    ISBN 978-1-61234-461-4 (hardcover : alk. paper)
    ISBN 978-1-61234-462-1 (electronic edition)
1. Conservatism—United States—Anecdotes. 2. Liberalism—United States—Anecdotes. 3. Neisser, Philip T., 1957—Anecdotes. 4. Hess, Jacob (Jacob Z.)—Anecdotes. I. Hess, Jacob (Jacob Z.) II. Title.
    JC574.2.U6N45 2012
    320.50973—dc23

                                                                    2012000669

Printed in the United States of America on acid-free paper that meets the American National Standards Institute Z39-48 Standard.

Potomac Books
22841 Quicksilver Drive
Dulles, Virginia 20166

First Edition

10 9 8 7 6 5 4 3 2 1

Contents

Acknowledgments

Phil: I know that authors routinely write glowing accolades about their partner in the preface, but I really mean it: Eudora Watson—my partner and my sweetheart—is a great person, a great writer, and a great editor, and I am lucky to live with her (in sin, or so my coauthor might say). My other words of praise are for Jackie Rush, the secretary of the Department of Politics at SUNY Potsdam. Jackie helped a great deal with references in this book and (more importantly) is a wonderful person. I have been very lucky to work with her.

Jacob: To my parents, Paul and Martha, and my sweetheart, Monique: thank you for being patient with my writing and supportive with my dreams. To Elaine Shpungin, Nicole Allen, Wendy Heller, Julian Rappaport, Carol Diener, Mark Aber, Edelyn Verona, Gregory Miller, Howard Berenbaum, and other life-changing faculty in the Clinical-Community Division of the Psychology Department at the University of Illinois, Urbana-Champaign. To Joe Minarik and Joycelyn Landrum-Brown with the Illinois Program on Intergroup Relations and cofacilitators, Danielle Rynczak and Lance Wright. To Mariolga Reyes-Cruz, Eric Clausell, Ben Hidalgo, Rebecca Levin, Sarah Sass, Simone Barr, Kelly Watt, Adrienne Abramowitz, Nausheen Masood, Shabnam Javdani, Melissa Milanak, Megan Radek, Lili Qin, and other remarkable classmates. To dear friends Lori Hendricks, Niti Pandey, and Kostas Yfantis. And to my political narrative research "podner," Nathan Todd. It was in conversation with each of you, that this conservative kid from Utah fell hopelessly in love with dialogue. For welcoming me authentically, teaching me deeply, and loving me profoundly, thank you with all my heart! My life will never be the same since crossing each of your paths. To you, I dedicate this book.

Phil and Jacob: Thanks also to those who offered feedback on drafts of this book: Elaine Shpungin, Mikhail Lyubansky, Monique Hess, Daniel Hess, Paul Hess, Martha Hess, John Thompson, Bill Moore, Daniel Bell, Eudora Watson, and Jackie Rush.

Introduction

It's been a long day. On your way home, you flip through radio channels:

"These liberal activists are kooks. They are loony tunes. And I'm not going to apologize for it. . . . There's going to be a retard summit at the White House." —Rush Limbaugh[1]

Finally home, you sit down and pick up the newspaper:

"As a Democrat who loves the president, I am downright giddy [with the Republican candidates]. There ain't no way we can lose to them idiots." —Charles Barkley[2]

Hmm . . . what's on television?

"I think a good chunk of the Republican caucus is either stupid, crazy, ignorant, or craven cowards." —Bruce Bartlett[3]

How about a book?

"Liberals are always against America. . . . They hate flag-wavers, they hate abortion opponents; they hate all religions except Islam." —Anne Coulter[4]

Over weeks and months, thousands of such rapid-fire put-downs, accusations of treachery, and intimations of bad faith are served up to a watching, listening American public. Some citizens grow weary of the rhetorical barrage, others become cynical, and still others start to jam with the beat. The net result is that millions of Americans fear, distrust, or hate millions of other Americans whom they've never even met.

Do we have to live this way?

We have our doubts. Allow us to introduce ourselves:

Phil: I'm Phil Neisser, a political science professor at a university in New York, an atheist, and on the left on most political issues.

Jacob: And I'm Jacob Hess, research director at a charity for abused children in Utah, a practicing religious man, and a committed social conservative.

Some might think that two individuals as different as we are should not be spending time together—let alone writing a book. Certainly neither of us anticipated ever collaborating at length with a political opponent. Our paths eventually crossed, however, at a point in time when a shared concern outweighed the many other things dividing us. Americans, Phil had concluded in a previous book, were losing the capacity to disagree with one another in healthy ways, especially when it came to their liberal-conservative differences.[5] Indeed, it seemed that one rarely witnessed a liberal and a conservative talking to each other about their disagreements without engaging in some degree of name-calling, attacking, or political posturing.

More than simply sharing this general observation, we also noted that when it came to talking openly and productively with those who held views orthogonal from our own, neither of us had had much personal experience. Thus we agreed to test ourselves by talking at length about what most divided us, and see what came of it. This book is a record of that encounter.

Obstacles to Dialogue

Why is it especially challenging for staunch conservatives and die-hard liberals to converse? One reason is the degree to which we are inundated with voices in the media suggesting there's little point in talking to "them idiots."

Another obstacle is the way government officials from different parties routinely treat one another. One political science research team goes so far as to say that the national political establishment is "dominated by activists and elected officials who behave like squabbling children in a crowded sandbox."[6] Hyperbole aside, the nation's public figures do indeed routinely serve their opposition a steady stream of disparaging and besides-the-point insults. And the media take those harsh words, along with any poor judgments made and slight missteps taken, and amplify them to the point where the sandbox of squabbles becomes a centerpiece of daily entertainment in living rooms across the nation. In the words of comedian Jon Stewart:

> The country's 24-hour politico-pundit-perpetual-conflictinator did not cause our problems, but its existence makes solving them that much harder. The press can hold its magnifying glass up to our problems, bringing them into focus, illuminating issues heretofore unseen, or they can use that magnifying glass to light ants on fire, and then perhaps host a week of shows on the sudden, unexpected flaming ant epidemic. If we amplify everything, we hear nothing. . . . The press is our immune system . . . [but] if we overreact to everything we actually get sicker.[7]

This phenomenon is described by sociologist James Davison Hunter more broadly when he asserts that the "culture war" has become institutionalized by the work of "special-purpose organizations, denominations, [and] political parties," and "further aggravated by . . . the technology of public discourse."[8] However one describes it, the frequent deployment of demonization and misrepresentation is clearly effective in creating perceptions of extreme conflict, standoff, and crisis at epidemic levels across the nation. Hunter elaborates:

> Clearly, entire populations are not divided at anywhere near the level of intensity of the activists and the rhetoric, but because issues are often framed in such stark terms, public choices are forced. In such circumstances, even communities and populations [that] . . . prefer other options and [would like to see] much greater reason and harmony in the process, find themselves divided.[9]

We have thus reached a point where many conservatives are more interested in what Bill O'Reilly says about liberals than what their own liberal neighbors say about themselves. Likewise, many liberals "know" about conservatives from reading updates on the *Huffington Post* as opposed to getting to know actual conservative acquaintances.

To be clear, the problem is *not* "partisanship," if by that word one means the attitude a person has simply by virtue of being firmly committed to a particular political party or cause. Such adherence is natural and often positive. The problem is instead what could be called "empty polarization," meaning a partisanship so full of disdain and harshness that it distracts us from our real, legitimate differences.

The resulting black-and-white (red-and-blue) sociopolitical atmosphere, according to researchers D. Conor Seyle and Matthew L. Newman, tacitly encourages citizens to "see themselves as members of a unified group opposed by people with fundamentally different perspectives."[10] Conservatives are, for example, portrayed by some as the ones who care about individuals making personal changes for the better, family well-being, and the preservation of tradition. Liberals, conversely, are portrayed by others as the ones who care about the well-being of marginalized populations, respect for diversity, and broader social change attempting to improve upon tradition. It's not surprising, then, that when liberal and conservative citizens do try to talk to each other about social issues, the questions are often framed as brute dichotomies:

- Preserving tradition vs. changing it
- Promoting openness vs. opposing it
- Embracing diversity vs. being prejudiced
- Valuing common standards vs. having *no* standards
- Encouraging internal change vs. a do-what-you-want culture
- Supporting families vs. not supporting them
- Holding larger institutions accountable vs. letting them walk all over us

As Seyle and Newman point out, dichotomous frames such as these reinforce a "winner-take-all approach to public judgment" and predispose people to engage in political action that "does not allow other perspectives to be incorporated into the final decision."[11]

Is there a way out of this highly polarized situation? We believe there is and that it begins with—a different way of talking across deep social and political differences.

How Our Conversation Started

Dialogue is, of course, not our personal discovery or invention. In 2002, a number of individuals gathered to launch an organization: the National Coalition of Dialogue and Deliberation. The NCDD includes hundreds of individual citizens, professionals, and groups (from fields as diverse as philosophy, social work, psychology, linguistics, computer science, and physics[12]), all of whom share a commitment to rich conversation across differences that help people tackle complex issues. The techniques developed to support these aims are increasingly being put to use in settings ranging from high schools, colleges, and work places to community settings and individual homes.[13] Literally dozens of deliberative "methodologies" have emerged at this point, all of which involve individuals from "multiple, conflicting perspectives coming together to compare, weigh and carefully consider different views, interpretations, and options."[14] Some of these approaches have led to documented successes in high-intensity contexts such as the interfaith acrimony that arose after 9/11,[15] the war in Northern Ireland,[16] and the Palestinian-Israeli conflict in the Middle East.[17]

In 2008, the NCDD convened a conference in Austin, Texas, and it was there that we met. Almost immediately we realized that together we could go beyond our prior academic work to experience the intensive liberal-conservative exchange for ourselves.[18] Thus we hatched our plan to talk carefully over the course of many months about our deepest disagreements, and to see where that led.

Our Conversation Process

We first made a list of the issues that most deeply divided us: morality, power, authority, gender roles, sexuality, race, big government, big business, and big media. We then wrote and exchanged brief essays on each subject. After responding to each essay in writing, we went another round: addressing the questions the other had posed and reviewing our respective answers further, sometimes with the help of extensive telephone conversations. And when discussion of one issue felt "saturated," we moved on to another.

Thus layer upon layer of disagreement and agreement were explored, fleshed out, and sometimes turned on their heads. Along the way, we were able to observe larger patterns and themes, take note of how our conversation connected to what others in society were saying, and consider the many practical implications of our clashing interpretations.

It's perhaps worth noting that the process just described was unlike what usually goes by the name of "debate." With no audience judging us as we went along, neither of us faced in-the-moment pressure to perform well, represent "our side," or prove something to someone. Nor did we feel compelled to prepare retorts and comebacks for every point the other person raised. Instead, we were free to focus on (a) seeking to understand where the other person was coming from, (b) trying to articulate our thinking in the clearest and most compelling manner, and (c) looking for any common ground we could find. Our conversations were also unlike traditional debate in that they took place over an extended period of time (from June 2009 to December 2010, to be exact). That gave us each room to reflect on what we had shared previously and to think at length about what the other person had been saying, and how to best respond.

The Results

When it was all over, we still disagreed intensely in much the same ways we had at the start. On the other hand, we were heartened to discover some patches of newly uncovered common ground. And we were excited to find that we had each been led away, over and over, from the simple either/or dichotomies of difference mentioned earlier toward more nuanced differences that offered possibilities for compromise, or at least for mutual understanding. For example, instead of arguing about whether to preserve tradition, we found ourselves disagreeing about what *exactly* should be preserved. Instead of positioning ourselves "for" or "against" tolerance, we found ourselves discussing what we each *meant* by tolerance, openness, and acceptance. Instead of debating whether or not "diversity" should be supported, we explored what *sort* of diversities and commonalities are helpful and what sort are harmful.

And, instead of one of us positioning himself as "for" family well-being while the other stood "against" it, we found ourselves arguing about what family means in the first place and exactly what should be done to support families.

Each chapter of this book summarizes our dialogue about one issue area. The three chapters in part one deal with broad-brushstroke, foundational topics, including morality, power, religion, big media, big business, and big government. The three chapters in part two deal with more specific issues holding particular relevance in the current national climate. These include gender roles, race, sexuality, gay and lesbian rights, marriage, and diversity. And the concluding chapter reviews the results of other dialogues that cross ideological and/or religious borders, summarizing what we each learned from our conversations, and offering thoughts about what our experience might mean for society more broadly. All in all, we are able to confirm a number of concrete and positive results flowing from dialogue, even when those involved continue to strongly disagree.

Purple America

Naturally, there are many important issues we do not deal with and worthwhile points of view we do not adequately represent (e.g., libertarian views). Rather than speaking as a "typical" liberal or conservative (if there are such things), we each speak as a unique individual who belongs to a diverse political community. Phil, for example, sees himself as more of a leftist than a liberal,[19] as an environmentalist, and as a no-resentment, man-friendly feminist. And Jacob, while sharing the same core values as other religious conservatives, has been influenced by his Mormon community in how he understands those convictions.[20]

Are these idiosyncrasies a problem? Only if one assumes that the nation is "divided into two unified camps"[21] with look-alike liberals (living in "blue" states) and look-alike conservatives (living in "red" states) amassed into warring factions. And by many indicators, that assumption is patently false. In the words of the aforementioned researchers Seyle and Newman, the U.S. political divide is not so much "red vs. blue" as it is a battle of many shades and hues of purple.[22]

A Few Misconceptions about Dialogue

Do you wonder about the value of dialogue between people with strongly opposing viewpoints? Certainly some skepticism is warranted, given the lack of publicly visible, successful examples of that kind of conversation in our society. But from our observations, the hesitancy many people experience results, at least in part, from misconceptions about what dialogue is all about.

Dialogue as Manipulation

The first misconception many people have is that dialogue is an attempt to persuade or convince them of something new, thereby potentially encouraging them to compromise deeply held beliefs. Conservative-leaning citizens, for example, sometimes see public calls for dialogue as part of a hidden "liberal agenda" for changing society. In the words of David Davenport, cochair of Common Sense California, "some conservatives fear that the tools of citizen engagement [such as dialogue] come only from the progressives' tool box."[23] Such fears are not without merit. Many dialogue advocates are, in fact, liberal, and some do, indeed, frame dialogue as an "educational tool" that should be used to "promote diversity, social justice, and social change."[24] Thus Pete Peterson, a pro-dialogue conservative who is also a member of Common Sense California, argues that dialogue opportunities should be designed and presented to citizens as ends in themselves, not as a means to this or that particular end.[25]

Conservatives are not the only ones with suspicions. Many liberal-leaning citizens likewise see dialogue as reinforcing the status quo in subtle ways.[26] And that suspicion is also understandable, given the many historical instances whereby a simple invitation to "talk" has functioned to placate angry victims, subvert intended action, or muffle dissent.

By definition, however, authentic dialogue is the free, unmanipulated engagement of at least *two* persons, *two* unique perspectives, and *two* distinct agendas. Thus Alison Kadlec and Will Friedman, from New York–based Public Agenda, a nonpartisan educational organization, warn of the need to ensure, in the design of every dialogue setting, that "no single entity with a stake in the substantive outcome of the deliberation . . . be the main designer or guarantor of the process."[27] (This may have been a damning flaw of some of the Democrat-sponsored town hall meetings held in recent years on the subject of health care.) Even in the presence of good intentions, the moment a conversation becomes a site for unilateral or one-directional communication, it *ceases* to be "dialogue" in any meaningful sense. As Brazilian educator Paulo Freire writes, "Dialogue cannot be reduced to the act of one person's 'depositing' ideas in another, nor can it become a simple exchange of ideas to be 'consumed' by the discussants."[28]

Dialogue as Relativism or Compromise

A second misconception sees participation in dialogue as a reflection of weakness, "caving in," or lacking strong conviction. Thus many of the Jewish and Palestinian participants in conciliatory Middle East dialogues found themselves criticized as "collaborators with the enemy" or "traitors to the cause."[29]

At the heart of such reactions is the presupposition that hearing out others in dialogue is to some degree synonymous with accepting or validating their ideas—or somehow signals agreement with the idea that truth is "relative," and that any point of view is as good as any other. From this viewpoint, dialogue becomes a sort of group hug or parade of self-expression, as in "you have your feelings and I have mine, so let's share with each other so we feel better."

Adjoining such perceptions is the conviction that dialogue and civil discourse are weak, let's-try-to-avoid-offending-each-other exercises. Thus Mark DeMoss, when attempting to explain why U.S. government leaders largely ignored his "civility pledge," writes that "too many people equate civility in public life with unilateral disarmament." To illustrate, he then cites *Fox News'* Bill O'Reilly's analysis: "I wouldn't sign [the civility pledge] if I were in Congress. . . . I'd be afraid that if my opponent attacked me I wouldn't be able to attack him back."[30]

To those who harbor such concerns, know that a conversation asking participants to give up their point of view or accept all ideas as equally valid is anything but dialogue. And anyone attempting to strip you of your convictions or silence your point of view (whatever it might be), is pursuing aims very different than our own.

Indeed, we enjoyed the degree of freedom our conversation gave us to speak our minds and raise tough questions. Throughout the conversation we challenged each other again and again, with unusual vigor. And in the end, we each found ourselves able to express our respective views with new force. Ultimately, our political positions, rather than becoming watered down and soft, were clarified and solidified through the experience.

We also gained a new degree of understanding and appreciation of each other and of our political opponents more generally. Consistently, professor Thomas Schwandt had this to say about the process and outcomes of genuine deliberation:

> Parties to the encounter are not viewed as opponents who seek to expose the weaknesses in each other's arguments. Rather, the conversation begins with the assumption that the other has something to say to us and to contribute to our understanding. The initial task is to grasp the other's position in the strongest possible light. . . . The other is not an adversary or opponent, but a conversational partner.[31]

Dialogue as Wasted Time

The group most likely to see this text with disinterest might be those who are confident they *already know* what the other side thinks and believes. Such certainty is often accompanied by settled convictions on the worth, value, intelligence, and morality (or lack thereof) of others. From that point of view, a dialogue such as ours is simply wasted time. After all, why talk with someone from a different sociopolitical community, when you could hear from others who, like you, already have those other people "figured out"?

Rather than pigeon-holing individuals in a particular way, dialogue participants proceed based on an implicit belief that those who disagree with them on an issue are reasonable and complex human beings, not unlike themselves. And in doing so, they outsmart those self-proclaimed experts on liberals or conservatives (especially those using big words like "idiot" or "liar" in their book titles) who offer final, condemnatory descriptions of the other side. What those experts have figured out is how to make a lot of money by feeding the public's morbid fascination with bitter accusations and dramatic attacks.

Can we compete with that kind of an action-packed show? If you're looking for Phil to get Jacob in a headlock or Jacob to pull a kidney punch, you'll have to wait for the sequel: *You're Crazy and Wrong . . . And Dumb, Too!* On the other hand, if you're looking for new insight, additional knowledge, fresh questions, and a few surprising realizations, then we can compete.

What's the Point?

So why deliberately engage in something as difficult as dialogue with someone you know you stand against in some fundamental ways? One conservative religious student in Jacob's dialogue course asked herself that question after feeling a great deal of initial discomfort. The gay marriage dialogue, for example, pushed her "out of her comfort zone" to the point where she went home in tears. In her final evaluations, while she said she "gained a lot," she also said she would "never do it again in the future" because the pain was so intense. By the time another semester had gone by, however, she did an about-face and decided to enroll in training to become a dialogue facilitator herself. Why? Because the pain and discomfort of intense conversation had been worth it. The experience had pressed her to see more people in the world as deeply similar to her, and as deserving of respect, even while retaining crucial differences. That in turn had expanded her world and gave her a new degree of optimism and hope.

Like Jacob's dialogue class, this book might occasionally elicit some discomfort in readers. Certainly, what follows is not simply an aggregation of warm fuzzies designed to make liberals and conservatives feel good and like each other. Phil will press and stretch some conservative readers with his questions and views, and Jacob will bother and frustrate some liberal readers with his own queries and perspectives. But, as we each learned for ourselves, being stretched, challenged, and frustrated can, in the context of a dialogue, lead a person to gain a new appreciation of the value his or her political opponents offer toward the project of living together well in a good society.

If, then, you don't mind some discomfort and frustration, stretching and challenge; if you're not too fearful of relativism and compromise, manipulation or conversion; and most of all, if you don't mind learning something new . . . welcome to the book! We're delighted to have you. In the chapters that follow, you will find old and new questions, diverging convictions and common aspirations, compelling proposals of change, and the defense of es-tablished ways. We've been working hard to make sure your time with us is enjoyable and productive. As you join us, do your best to remain open to new insights and fresh understanding, even (and especially) when you find yourself disagreeing passionately. Finally, if you experience any uncomfort-able moments, try following the advice offered by dialogue trainer Joycelyn Landrum-Brown: "sit with your discomfort" instead of reacting. As you ride out those feelings, wait and watch to see what emerges.[32] You might be surprised by what you find out.

PART I
FOUNDATIONAL ISSUES

1

DIFFERING TAKES ON POWER
AND AUTHORITY

When Jacob was in graduate school, some of his classmates raised concerns during a student-faculty meeting. The issues they raised were legitimate, but the immediate tone of the exchange was adversarial. A larger group of students soon banded together to confront what they saw as injustices perpetrated by the faculty as a whole—taking for granted that the professors' authority needed to be challenged and their motives held suspect. And thus during the span of just a few weeks, the students and professors became enemies.

Events of this kind often happen in communities across the country in response to exercises of power by those in authority. From national measures on health care and the economy, to state policies on marriage and abortion, to local school action on tuition or prayer, some citizens lament a particular decision as totally unjustified, irresponsible, and even despotic. At the same time, other citizens might declare the same exercise of power justified, necessary, and even inspired. Ensuing discussion of the policy tends to follow accordingly: either the exercise of power was *simply* good (i.e., "crucial," "indispensable," "long overdue") or *simply* bad (i.e., "wrong-headed," "destructive," "ignorant," "evil," "hateful").

To be clear, the problem is not that people take opposing positions. It's that when those positions are cast as placing tyranny against noble duty, public exchanges are likely to devolve into mere accusation and acrimony: "Who gave you the right to tell me what to do?" "How dare you impose your values on us!" "We need to take the government back from those idiots!"

Laying aside the wearying quality of such slash-and-burn exchanges, other consequences exist that are more subtle and more serious. Because the dramatic fury of a few draws the collective attention of many, other meaningful questions tend to remain largely untouched, let alone thoughtfully explored. Relevant to the previous example, for instance: Is there a danger in so quickly assuming that those with power are *inevitably* self-interested and largely motivated by personal agendas? Alternatively, is it naïve to trust or respect leaders in power generally, or should that courtesy be reserved for those with whom we especially agree? What is power, anyway? And what exactly does it mean to exercise power in helpful (right, liberating) as opposed to unhelpful (wrong, oppressive) ways?

The two of us began our series of conversations by tackling these questions, because we see them as fundamental. And sure enough, by the time we were done we found ourselves better understanding exactly where we disagreed. We also found—somewhat to our surprise—that a good deal of fresh commonality now lay under our feet.

How should we evaluate power and authority?

Phil: To begin, Jacob, let me offer some definitions: *Power* in the simplest sense is the ability to create or prevent outcomes or to accomplish something. In the lexicon of political and social theory, this is referred to as "power to." The kind of power those on the left and right usually argue about, however, is "power over," meaning power exercised by some people (or by a system) over other people, thereby reducing the power or freedom of the latter.

Authority, conversely, is the shared belief or social recognition that someone—either because of who they are or because of a position they occupy—has a right to exercise power of some kind.

Jacob: Would you agree that "power over" could also potentially *increase* the power and freedom of those being led, rather than reducing it? That would, of course, depend on how the leaders use their power. I've noticed, however, that academics often speak of "power" in a stand-alone, abstract sense—

without a modifier attached. In contrast, religious conservatives typically qualify the term with reference to the intention and purpose of the exercise of power, for instance, divine or righteous power aiming to bless people's lives, and malicious or evil power aiming to oppress. And, we consider certain authority associated with sacred positions of power to also be inherently valid and legitimate, having been conferred by a higher authority than collective belief.

Rather than thoughtfully making these kinds of distinctions between healthy and unhealthy uses of power, however, it seems people are increasingly quick to question whole categories of authorities in one swoop—suspecting the motives of *any* political or religious leader who holds some power.

Phil: Thanks, Jacob. I certainly agree that neither power nor authority is bad in and of itself. Indeed, one meaning of "authority" is power granted, acknowledged, or accepted for a good reason. By my lights, the most important question about a claim to authority is whether or not a legitimate, important purpose is served by granting that authority. For example, is a legitimate purpose served by giving police officers authority? My personal answer is a qualified yes, in that humans need to agree on some rules to live together successfully. And, in complex societies that include thousands of people, some of those rules won't work unless someone is charged with enforcing them.

Jacob: Unless individuals voluntarily obey, that is? No one is "making sure" I follow the rules of my faith; rather, we freely share updates together in ways that provide a healthy collective accountability. But I do like your emphasis again, Phil, on "to what end" power is being exercised. If we agree that authority and power have the potential to both bless *and* oppress depending on its purposes, then we ought to go beyond blanket accusations (or rejections) of particular authorities or amounts of power, to a more qualitative question: "To what exact end is power/authority being exercised here, in this case?" As a question of interest across the political spectrum, this calls for more thoughtful attention to the nature, kind, and purpose of the specific power being exercised. At the same time, we may better acknowledge respect for authority as an idea valued across the political spectrum to some degree (as reflected in your police comments, Phil).

Phil: Yes, humans need authority, and authority deserves a degree of respect. On the other hand, in my view the authority conferred by democracy (or by any other process) is provisional, partial, and imperfect. And sometimes it's highly imperfect or downright unjust. Those who enforce the law (e.g., police officers) don't always enforce the law properly and fairly, and recourse for those mistreated is not always available or effective. Still, when I pull my car over to heed those flashing lights it's not simply because I feel compelled to do so. It's also because I know that police need to be vested with authority to do their job. On the other hand, I am typically "liberal" in my belief that one should question authority, as the bumper sticker says. All in all, I side with Henry David Thoreau, Martin Luther King Jr., and Socrates: if one is going to challenge authority, one should do so nonviolently and with respect for the idea of authority (except when violence is needed to save lives).

To yield to authority: right, wrong, or it depends?

Jacob: Picking up from your last comment, Phil, let me ask you this. I sometimes get a sense from liberal-leaning friends that "questioning authority" is an unmitigated good—and that, correspondingly, a willingness to "yield to authority" is more often than not dangerous. Conversely, my own conservative community holds essentially the reverse set of views—that following authority is generally good and questioning is often problematic. And it seems to me that either of these patterns can lead to problems in practice—namely, liberals being driven by their credo to question benevolent authority, and conservatives being driven by their credo to obey oppressive authority.

Phil: Jacob, how can you know if authority or power is oppressive or not if you don't question it? To "question" does not mean to attack without reason, nor does it mean to assume that one knows the right answer already.

Jacob: I think conservatives would be more willing to ask and field pointed questions regarding traditions and faith commitments if we felt more assurance that doing so wouldn't necessarily require opening oneself to suspicion, cynicism, or a different agenda. The British philosopher Charles Taylor defined "pseudo-questions" as asking something *without* actual openness to hearing an answer. The point of such a "question," obviously, is not really to find out anything at all.

Phil: With openness to hearing your answer then, Jacob, let me ask you this: Do we agree that authority does not exist in and of itself or as something absolute, except as a means to one or more ends?

Jacob: Yes and no. I, like all religious conservatives, see God's authority as absolute in terms of power to act. For me, however, this does not mean that God has radically unlimited power, irrespective of the laws, and realities of the universe. In other words, the God I worship, unlike Zeus or Jupiter, cannot suddenly decide one day, "Hmm, I want to have an affair with that mortal woman . . . she is good-looking." Instead, God's power and authority are linked to His inherent commitment to what is true and best for the welfare of all. The omnipotence possessed by God, then, is not a power to change the fundamental truths of the universe or to alter "laws of heaven"—from chastity to gravity. It is, rather, a power that relies upon God's willingness to work in harmony with these laws and principles, alongside an unconditional commitment to help others do the same. This, at least, is the view of my own faith community, and something many other conservatives may likely resonate with as well.

What this means, in part, is that we don't place our trust in God simply "because He is God"—but also because of what we understand about God's character and the nature of His work—both of which are fully oriented to help us. For all these reasons, we can and do seek to trust Him absolutely!

Phil: If I understand, what you're saying is that you see God's power as absolute, but still dependent on him doing work that is in fact beneficial to humankind? I agree that your God offers some advantages over Zeus, but then again the ancient Greeks could blame their Gods for social problems, famines, and the like, and who knows, maybe that helped keep them from blaming one another. Anyway, your language of absolute trust makes me uncomfortable. Absolute trust is dangerous, is it not?

Jacob: Given the numerous examples of oppressive rulers (including religious ones) who have wreaked havoc with the help of large, compliant followings, it is understandable why "obedience" has become a scary word to some—seen as synonymous with a kind of mindless caving-in, something one has to be duped into as in a religious cult. But mind control aside, Phil, whatever happened to simply *hearing counsel* and *taking advice* from someone with more experience or wisdom? In the kids we work with at our agency, there is often a striking disregard for authority of any kind in their home or community. Given similar trends nationally, what's wrong with actively promoting thoughtful, mindful listening to those who *do*, we trust, actually "know better"—be they parents, professors, or God.

And sure, there will be moments like God's test of Abraham, when a kind of blind faith is needed to "try out" tough counsel initially—but even then, the promise is that a personal assurance of peace eventually comes. We believe, moreover (as do many other religious conservatives), that God provides confirmation on multiple levels—through living leaders, written scripture, and the peaceful whisperings of the Spirit—levels which together add up to a kind of built-in "concurrent validity" check. Thus, if something harmful were taught by a particular spiritual leader, its contradiction to written scripture, the voice of the Spirit, and the reality of one's own lived experience should (and would) show it to be so. Other patterns, such as manipulative mind control and the restriction of real agency, are also obvious red flags that someone is being misled.

So to address your question, Phil, yes, if not accompanied by personal critical thinking and exploration, total trust and obedience *can* become something scary.

Phil: When it comes to authority, Jacob, I am looking for validity, not for a "personal assurance of peace" (which seems to me a separate subject entirely). But I understand what you are saying, and I think your basic idea of looking for confirmation is a good one.

Jacob: Let me relate something, Phil, to bring the question of trust and yielding into a more familiar context. As you know, I do research for a child welfare charity that helps kids who have been "out of control" find safe placements in group homes and foster care. On one visit to a residential treatment facility, I spoke with two of the kids soon to graduate from the program and move on with their lives. What struck me most about this teenage boy and girl was the aura of *humility* they each conveyed. In contrast to the defiance and aggression they showed before entering the program, they carried a gentle spirit of listening, openness, and malleability. I concluded that that was because our program emphasizes receiving feedback, learning to accept no for an answer, and disagreeing in healthy ways. And I came away from the visit thinking that maybe the best thing we do for such kids is help them regain a basic sense of humility toward trustworthy leaders and mentors as something crucial to their future lives.

Phil: Hmm . . . About those kids: my thought is that perhaps their initial defiance was a call for help, and thus when they came to believe that the adults around them cared about them and could be counted on, they dropped that defiance and revealed their vulnerability and need. Perhaps they also learned at that time that it's often safe to trust, and maybe that led to the humility of listening to and treating other people respectfully. I agree that kids who get to that point are more likely to grow into adults who possess the ability to trust and who know something about when and how to be humble. But to me, that does not mean they (or anyone) should be humble all the time, or in every way. Indeed, children who have positive experiences trusting adults might (ironically) be thereby enabled as adults to be assertive and to question authority when such questioning is called for.

Thus I wonder: Are you, Jacob, lumping together children's behavior and citizen behavior as if they were one category of problem? I see them as very different. Also, you seem to be presuming that people can't question authority and be appropriately obedient at the same time. Don't more distinctions need to be made? How about this: As children we need love, care, and responsibility in order to respond with trust and obedience to the rules that caretakers use (we hope) to protect and teach us. But as grown-up citizens we should, by contrast, use the confidence and reasonableness that (hopefully) our upbringing gave us in order to be somewhat watchful and suspicious of our leaders, bosses, and elected officials. After all, one job of a citizen is to exercise oversight of the actions that leaders engage in and the statements they make in their official capacity.

To be clear, citizen suspicion of leaders need not entail suspicion of their motives. I can respect my representatives without thinking that I should elect them and leave the rest up to them. I am as ready as any conservative to criticize people who criticize their leaders just because it feels good to do so, or in order to avoid responsibility. In other words, it's one thing to be a watchdog and another thing to be a brat. Leaders are imperfect like the rest of us and sometimes need to be put on the right track. But we shouldn't act like spoiled kids demanding the impossible and whining when we don't get it. If what I imagine is in the right direction, then it follows that what our kids need is reliable care and appropriate responsibility first and foremost, and appropriate forms of humility can be left to develop as a result. Does that make sense? Have I now put us in disagreement?

Jacob: No, you're right on . . . and I like how your response is pressing me—introducing, it seems, another frame within which humility (like power) can be valued in a less abstract and absolute sense. You're suggesting that humility is inherently linked with being cared for and taught responsibility, rather than a stand-alone virtue—e.g., "It is good to accept counsel." And in this way, you are insisting there are times when "humility" is simply inappropriate. This is all right on—as is, of course, a sensible age distinction in terms of what is appropriate humility for adults vs. children.

When defending my dissertation on depression treatment, I was asked why so many people in Utah were (reportedly) on anti-depressants. The explanation preferred by many outsiders is that elements of Mormonism drive the trend—this in spite of multiple studies showing practicing Latter-day Saints (LDS) men and women less depressed than the general population. My primary answer to the committee was that conservatives simply trust authority more than usual—including that of their doctors. I've seen situations where a neighbor or friend had a bad feeling about the advice of a physician, but heeded it dutifully anyway. Can conservatives learn to be a little less humble in situations like this? I think so.

We do, however, maintain a natural deference and humility in relation to someone whose authority we believe comes from God. Christ Himself on several occasions spoke of the importance of "becoming as a little child."[1] This doesn't mean that Jesus was encouraging us to regress to an infantile state or cry when we don't get our way—but rather, to take on the positive attributes of children at their best, including openness, love, and trust. That is the kind of sincere faith we believe God expects of us, His children.

Phil: Don't many people trust ecclesiastical leaders when they shouldn't, Jacob? And isn't the abuse that sometimes happens in part a result of an excessive grant of trust and authority?

Jacob: Sure, and that highlights the fact that, even in regard to the authority of religious leaders, it is important that we think for ourselves and have space to question and verify teachings in our own lives. Brigham Young once wrote:

> I am more afraid that this people have so much confidence in their leaders that they will not inquire for themselves of God whether they are led by him. I am fearful they settle down in a state of blind self-security, trusting their eternal destiny in the hands of their leaders with a reckless confidence that in itself would thwart the purposes of God in their salvation.[2]

Any community (religious or otherwise) that discourages questions and personal inquiry, once again, should raise a red flag. I admire the Jewish community for how much questioning is built-in as an inherent part of their religious and cultural practice. And I think conservatives are sometimes rightly criticized for essentially questioning the value of questioning.

This caution regarding questions likely comes from our acknowledgment of ultimate authorities of some kind—be they sacred books or persons vested with power. In any case, I think you're right that sometimes we conservatives overemphasize obedience and humility—or at least talk about it in decontextualized ways that don't acknowledge its linkage with love sufficiently. And certainly there are those who mistake their community's call for obedience to authority as a green light to get their way—e.g., batterers, abusive parents, and pushy leaders.

Given this, I like your suggestion that learning to trust and receive love may be the more fundamental dynamic than simply "becoming humble." I think I agree. Indeed, if it were not connected to an awareness of love and trust, the humility I value would not be quite what I signed up for. Instead, it would start to look like mere subservience, compliance, or being pressured. Also, I like that this same trust and love could be the basis for both appropriate humility *and* appropriate resistance in the future. . . . Good stuff, Phil!

Can questioning authority be taken too far?

Jacob: Phil, let me return to my initial comment to ask you this: If it is true that conservatives can sometimes overdo obedience and submission, I wonder if you would see the opposite tendency among more progressive communities—namely, sometimes overemphasizing *questions and resistance* and thinking of them in absolute terms. I've spoken with some people who are so into questioning that they are overtly uncomfortable with any conclusion that appears too stable or "truthy."

Phil: To answer your question: no, I don't see a problem with excessive questioning and I have not observed widespread love of questioning for its own sake in those communities that call themselves "progressive." Sure, in grad school I had many friends who, as you put it, challenged everything that seemed "truthy" and did so to a fault. But those folks were then engaged in an intense program of critical thinking, and in a way their job was to challenge everything. So in my view there's no society-wide problem of people making "too many" challenges to truth.

By the way, who (or what philosophy) actually says all power or all authority is oppressive or inherently suspect? Granted, some individuals seem to imply as much, and some clearly do so in certain situations—e.g., some Tea Party libertarians say it when they rail against all new government action as if it marks the onset of a second Nazi regime, and some anarchists denounce authority whenever it takes the form of law.

It seems to me, moreover, that conservatives are as likely as liberals—or more likely—to denounce power and authority, to be distrusting, or to fail to give people in positions of authority a chance. It seems to be all about *which* positions of authority those people occupy and whether or not they are perceived by conservatives to be fellow conservatives.

Jacob: Fair enough. There is enough suspicious questioning to go around. I'm intrigued, though, with your comment that there's no legitimate problem with overquestioning itself. I admit the longer I spent with progressive friends, the more I came to appreciate their penchant for questioning the world around them. It has been those willing to question and even revolt against old ways who, after all, started many positive things in this world, including the rebels behind our good ol' U.S.A. Perhaps my observation, then, has more to do with the *type* and *kind* of questions asked than it does with the *amount*. In other words, maybe we can never have too many *sincere questions*, while still being mindful of a societal glut of don't-you-think advocacy questions—or, more accurately, statements masquerading as questions.

Phil: This talk of a progressive penchant for questioning calls upon me to point out that political progressives do in fact believe things; also, they own up to believing those things without apology. They believe, for example, that free market economies, while necessary as instruments of wealth production and as vehicles of individual choice, create unjust inequities and concentrations of economic power unless regulated in the public interest and balanced by a social safety net provided by government.

That said, I can only agree that American culture includes strong anti-authority beliefs and inclinations. Sometimes they appear in the form of a graduate student's critical exuberance, but more often they appear in the form of a hostility to government so gut-level that millions of Americans became convinced that the health-care reform legislation enacted in 2010 amounted to a radical expansion of government, an attack on individual freedom, and the beginning of the end of the private sector—despite the fact that the legislation was actually quite moderate. Thus there's nothing inherently "liberal" about hostility to authority.

Jacob: And from what you're saying, neither is there anything inherently "conservative" about strong convictions, Phil. It does seem we agree there are patent problems with either categorically trusting or distrusting authority.

Taking either to its logical extreme seems to pose a danger in minimizing and dismissing important realities—whether actual instances of oppressive power (for authority trusters) or instances of beneficent power (for authority distrusters).

In light of this, perhaps we ought to pay more attention as politically diverse Americans to the nature and quality of the power/authority being exercised—i.e., when is power good, when is it bad, and what is a good way to know? Instead of stand-alone statements about submission or rebellion, what about more carefully exploring together *when* should we submit, and when perhaps rebellion or resistance is called for? *Whom* should we trust? And *how* (in what way) should we submit (if at all)?

Phil: Jacob, you have, I think, listed the right questions. And we agree, it seems, in believing that ethical order is not possible without the presence of bonds of trust. But, as you mention, we nonetheless disagree on the level and kinds of humility that are appropriate, as well as on which settings call for what sorts of humility, obedience, and/or resistance. In short, it seems that you believe that adults should determine which authorities are trustworthy and then offer them general trust and support. In contrast, I believe that adults should demand that all authority justify itself, but also respect the idea of authority and do their best to begin each inquiry with friendly assumptions about the motives of all concerned.

Jacob: Almost. I, too, expect justification from the authorities I trust, Phil—but with criteria that wouldn't likely satisfy you (e.g., peaceful assurance of the Spirit). That aside, I am seeing that some degree of distrust for authority is common to our communities, even as we share concern when that distrust is taken to an extreme.

Phil: Yes, I agree that people can be too distrusting, sometimes even rebelling in shallow or childish fashion just for the sake of it, possibly based on some unrealistic concept of total freedom akin to a simplistic version of "do your own thing." On the other hand, when it comes to the cause of the problem, I am guessing that we disagree.

For example, is the tendency to reject authority that we see in some young people caused by liberal doubts about "truth" (as many conservatives say), or is it instead (or for the most part) caused by the way capitalism breeds the notion that truth is really just a matter of preference? It seems to me the latter. To briefly explain: market societies depend on high levels of consumer spending, and that tends to cultivate the idea that individual choice and preference should rule. Also, new *real* needs are routinely created by individualistic systems of consumption (e.g., first many people buy a car, next community geography comes to assume that people have cars, and eventually every household needs a car—or needs more than one). And, to sum it up, the capitalist celebration of individual choice and preference sends the message to people that they shouldn't necessarily heed the word of their parents, elders, or teachers.

Another question: Is the weakness of parental authority the result of permissiveness, relativism, and lack of religion (as many conservatives say), or is it instead caused by the lack of useful skills parents have to offer children in today's market society, where the keys to "success" are being "attractive," dominating in one's peer group, and knowing how to use the latest technology, rather than knowing what one's parents knew? It seems to me that it's the latter more than the former.

Jacob: Per your first question, you set up a dichotomy as if only one argument could be valid—either the economic or the moral/religious explanation of societal distrust of authority. Yet the celebration of individual, immediate preference is clearly encouraged by our economic system, and surely plays a role in trends of receding respect for authority. Is this, then, merely an economic phenomenon? Are you assuming that truth or religion operate in a different realm than sermons preached by the marketplace or the teaching passed down (or not) by parents? My religion and truth have something to say about individual preference as well—offering encouragement and direction to go beyond immediate indulgence and prioritize family, service, sacrifice, and so on. If you have minimized the possible relevance of religion as an institution, however, I must confess doing the same for capitalism—something about which I have not been thoughtful enough for sure.

Phil: You're right, Jacob. The celebration of immediate preference is not simply an economic phenomenon. Nor can one entirely separate what happens in the economy from what is said by religion or taught by parents and teachers. And we can and should counter consumer mentality with ethical teaching. Where I think we disagree is on whether or not "respect authority" is the ethical teaching that's truly needed. I see it as risky, and I also think the more important lessons are "respect each other as equals," "respect limits," "respect nature," and "respect community."

Jacob: Interesting. It sounds like we ought to further explore the question of what authority deserves to be legitimately trusted. We obviously differ in our views on the subject. So, who deserves our trust, and how should we determine that?

One of my assumptions is that everyone has to place their trust somewhere. Some like to poke fun at religious people for deciding to believe, or to put faith in something, as if they were not themselves directing their own core belief and trust someplace as well. Would you agree that having some kind of trust—directed somewhere—is fairly inescapable, Phil? If so, I wonder if I could ask where you place your own faith and confidence?

Phil: First, I promise that I don't poke fun at people for placing trust somewhere; quite the contrary. More to the point, I agree that there's no avoiding trusting something or someone. As for me, I enjoy relationships of trust with many of my friends and family members; I place a good deal of trust in the power of clear, honest thinking; I trust that each person is essentially another version of myself; and I trust that all human beings are bearers of compassion and love (however squelched, layered over, or misdirected their compassion and love might be). On the other hand, I know that there's no guarantee my trust is well placed. I know I could be mistaken. And so I must (I believe) accept questioning by others and also ask hard questions of myself, so as to keep my hubris in check, and perhaps catch and repair errors.

Jacob: Thank you, Phil. I've heard other conservatives speculate on this question, but never asked someone with your beliefs myself. Do you want to hear what you are supposed to be trusting, Phil, as a secular dude? Money, sex, power, and popularity . . . or some combination of these objects of societal worship and adoration. Yet I hear you saying that you trust loving relationships, honest exploration and learning, and the underlying goodness and potential of human beings. Wow. You almost sound like the conservatives who were speculating about you!

Yes, we still disagree about whether Someone else is supervising this whole affair . . . but it's interesting how much your objects of trust are also things highly valued among my community. There are, I should say, religious conservatives who believe that mankind is inherently depraved and evil. These individuals will feel less resonance with what you have just said. The real depravity and evil of humanity, according to my faith community, emerge when individuals yield to and give themselves over to the fallen ways of the world around them. That is, something happens when an individual senses something is right (or wrong), but acts contrary to that sense because of influences and invitations outside of himself/herself. As that occurs, any otherwise positive tendency (to love, seek truth, etc.) can truly be, as you put it "squelched, layered over, or misdirected." Yet, again, perhaps the most important point is that the struggling individual himself or herself, as a child of God, still has goodness at his or her core and not inherent evil. (While humans are thus often poisoned or corrupted by the toxicities/temptations of the surrounding world, this is different than saying they are fundamentally rotten.) And that points to what we ultimately believe Christ intended by His message of redemption—that He will help "restore our souls" to who we really are, in our deepest, truest sense of self.

What authority should we trust, and why?

Jacob: The discussion thus far makes me want to further explore where the inclination toward (or away from) trusting authority originates in the first place. For religious conservatives, their views of authority surely derive, in part, from their belief in centering their lives around the teachings of a sovereign God. It seems, moreover, that one defining feature of conservative thoughts across faiths is a consistent emphasis on *particular guidelines* for personal action that are given by God. And that clearly distinguishes them from my progressive friends who are also religious. While these friends care deeply about spirituality as well, they nonetheless think differently about their relationship with God.

In college, I participated in an educational club to raise awareness about the dangers of pornography. As we approached different campus ministries to seek support, I noticed an interesting split between the various faiths. In the more conservative ministries, the emphasis was on (a) embracing one God—especially Jesus—and (b) following a set of standards for personal behavior (His commandments, rules, etc.). In contrast, the more progressive ministries emphasized belief in (a) unconditionally accepting all people and (b) taking action to eliminate inequality and injustice in the world. Those differences came to a head during our local commemoration of the national Pornography Awareness Week. In the context of that event, the more conservative religious ministries, like my friend Pastor Wayne Wagner's Illini Life Christian Fellowship, were comfortable supporting the message that God's will extends to sexuality, and that there are particular messages and materials that are toxic to one's spiritual health. Alternatively, liberal-leaning ministries seemed much more focused on addressing institutional, structural problems than on advocating for certain personal standards or guidance—at least when it came to sexuality.

Phil: What I find entirely unconvincing is the idea that a sacred text does (or could) provide "particular guidelines for personal action." Granted, humans clearly need systems or traditions that invest certain people with a degree of authority when it comes to making and teaching rules, but in my view no being (including "God") gets to decide what's right by decree. Also, I don't believe that what counts as right and wrong can ever be adequately captured in a list of rules for all to heed. Instead, actual moral rules flow from the application of general principles to complex (and always historical) situations that real people live in. In sum, the Bible surely contains some good advice, but it's up to me to use reason and consult my compassion so as to decide which advice is good and when. I see no way around that.

Jacob: You speak as if clear teaching disallows individual adaptation and complex variation in application, Phil. We would say both exist and both have value. Indeed, if you've never met a liberal who hates all authority, I've never met a conservative that relishes rigidity or rules—staying up late, poring over tomes of life directives just for the heck of it. Instead, we see scriptural teachings as helpful guides and road signs—a God-given atlas on what to cherish and what to reject. You'll have to help me better understand what's so scary about this kind of clear teaching and direction about life, Phil.

That said, I have to say it's pretty exciting (and unusual) to be able to have this kind of a conversation about morality in spite of deep religious differences. I've never before experienced such a thing. We can delve into that subject more in chapter three, but for now we will have to agree to disagree as to whether the danger lies in looking toward or away from scripture. I do think you would be surprised, Phil, at the complexity with which we talk about scriptural applications and the need for moment-by-moment wisdom in how to act.

To try to sum up for now, we clearly differ in *who* we believe we should trust and *how much* we think we ought to accept others' claims of authority (parents, clergy, God) to provide guidelines for us. While many of my liberal religious friends genuinely love and trust God, they do not see His role in counseling humans on matters of personal behavior in quite the same way that I do. It is these differences that I think we sometimes see playing out in the broader cultural debates: "How dare you suggest we make a change like that!" "Keep your values to yourself!"

Phil: To add to that, Jacob, you and I seem to hold different views on where humility comes from. For you it comes from acceptance of divine truth and divine sanction for some forms of authority. For me, on the other hand, humility comes from (a) my firm belief that every person is as valuable as myself, and (b) my acceptance of uncertainty as unavoidable. And it's that acceptance of uncertainty that leads me to put limits on how much I trust. No matter what authority someone has, they could be wrong, just as I might be.

I feel the need to repeat something I mentioned earlier, which is that many conservatives seem highly selective when it comes to their willingness to trust someone. It depends on what position that other person occupies (e.g., it helps if they are a cleric rather than a college professor), what political "side" they're perceived to be on (i.e., perceived liberals are actively distrusted whereas perceived conservatives are taken at their word), and whether or not their position of authority is governmental. Many conservatives approach people in government with striking distrust (unless of course those people are able to pass themselves off as infiltrators of government who aim to "take government back" from liberal government-lovers).

Jacob: Aren't liberals equally selective, Phil, in who they are willing to trust?

Phil: I don't think that's a characteristic flaw of liberals, no. Many are fairly consistent in their questioning, even to the point where they—and leftists all the more so—hammer one another with criticism. But there's no denying that some of us are more consistent than others. Many liberals, for example, root for a political party, point of view, or politician, in the same way that they root for their favorite sports team, as in "my team is right because they're my team."

It seems to me that many conservatives hold a unique (and questionable) assumption about the nature of social and political problems—namely, that all would be right with the world if only each person were in the position they deserve to be in and everyone were following the line of command and otherwise doing their duty. In my view, difficult problems—sometimes insoluble problems—are going to arise no matter what, even in societies that feature perfect systems of authority, leaders with nothing but good intentions, and Godliness on the part of all. They will arise because of flaws in structural arrangements, dilemmas, costs that couldn't be anticipated, natural disasters, resources that run out, and so on. And that means that those who believe that human problems can be solved by granting trust and obedience to those rightfully in authority are likely, when awful problems arise, to denounce those currently in power as impostors, as not deserving of authority, or as fundamentally immoral. In my view, that's why so many conservatives went beyond disagreeing with President Clinton to hating him, to speak as though he did not deserve to be president and had somehow betrayed the nation. In other words, excessive trust tends to lead to excessive distrust and demonization, and even to visceral hatred and distrust.

Jacob: Once again, Phil, hasn't this same demonization happened on both sides? I mean, really . . . did conservatives hate Clinton any more than liberals came to hate Bush Jr.? But I suppose your argument is still that conservatives are prone to greater distrust and dislike for some kinds of roles—especially if leaders do not share their values?

Phil: Yes, Jacob, on both counts. Some liberals do indeed vilify George W. Bush. But others—and most leftists—do the opposite: they criticize oppressive aspects of systems and discourses and express at least some sympathy for people—such as Bush—who are caught up in those systems and discourses to the point where they act as their agents.

Where does oppressive power come from?

Phil: On that note, let me say something more about power—specifically "power over." On one side, cultural discourse (ways of speaking and representing) and institutional structures have power over everyone. They have this power by shaping the nature and number of opportunities available to people and the credentials needed to experience success, and they also reach deeper to shape people's desires, conceptions of success, ideas of beauty, levels of self-esteem, and personal identities. On the other side, institutional structures and cultural discourse do not have, and cannot have, *total* power. Keeping both these sides of the situation in mind, one can see that no one is all-powerful and also that no one is entirely without power of any kind. Every individual lives within, and is limited and enabled by, webs of power.

My observation, moreover, is that many liberals and conservatives share a tempting but naïve view of power very different than the one just sketched. They think power to be more or less conspiratorial in form. They think that the possession of power means being free from the power of anyone else, as if those who rule are not themselves subject to rule, and as if they possess total control over specified events and outcomes. Likewise, it's often assumed that the world is the way it is (whether good or bad) for the sole reason that someone wants it that way and made it that way (God, the Devil, or some stand-in for the Devil such as liberals, Jews, whites, blacks, conservatives, and so on). What the world needs, according to this view, is to get those malevolent, self-interested people out of power and replace them with leaders of benign intention. In other words, the good guys just need to ride into town and throw out the bad guys, and all will be well.

This idea of power makes for a compelling story line. The web idea of power, on the other hand, makes better sense of real-world complexities and ambiguities. After all, when people have power they have it as an artifact of the positions they occupy in organizations, the identities they form in their different cultural and organizational locations, and the ideas that circulate to offer justifications for those organizations and attach authority to those positions. Also, good people often have power they shouldn't have, and good people sometimes exercise power poorly or wrongly. Power, moreover, is not all secrecy and violence. More important to power is the generation of belief, especially about what's legitimate and what's not. And everyone is ruled by belief to one degree or another; everyone is influenced by ways of talking, depicting, and imagining themselves and the world. Thus, all forms of power come with built-in limits, and those who benefit most from a given set of power structures are in their grip just as much—or more—than those who benefit minimally or do not benefit at all.

Jacob: So "power" goes beyond simply individual or collective desires to the larger narratives and institutions within which we all are embedded and operate. There was a time when I would have found this idea threatening— to posit anything against the individual will. But my experience studying depression narratives changed my mind quite a bit. First of all, many depression survivors share sorry tales of friends and family telling them essentially to just "buck up" and "choose to be happy"—reflecting people not understanding how other forces from body and life narrative can constrain one's power to choose tangibly. More to your point, the influence of the multibillion-dollar pharmaceutical industry extends to medical schools, researchers, and even public educational organizations—in turn, constraining patient and practitioner narratives about whether full recovery is even possible.

I used to think of the philosopher Michel Foucault as just another crazy relativist in his claim that "truth" could be produced by power,[3] until I saw evidence of that happening via this corporate influence. This research experience thus reminded me of the need to attend to larger systematic forces that constrain and shape "truth" (in some cases) and human choices (in many more). And on that note, I find your model of power consistent with our belief that evil can operate in subtle ways that blind many otherwise good people—for example, through unethical influence from powerful institutions, as the apostle Paul put it, "spiritual wickedness in high places."[4]

Instead of talking about the problem as one of "structures of social injustice," however, we frame those external forces as reflections of the "fallen world." And that makes me wonder: could it be that both liberal and conservative communities are authentically concerned with the scope of real oppression in the world, but simply use dramatically different lingo, definitions, and "frames"?

Phil: In case our readers want a definition: a "frame" is a set of basic interpretive concepts used to organize and understand the information provided by human perception. No one freely chooses the frames they use, and no one can avoid framing altogether, but what people can do is "reframe," meaning adjust or change their frame in a significant way. To reframe is to see the world—and thus the options it presents—in new ways. That happens for many reasons: because existing frames cease to make sense, competing ideas hit just the right chord, people make an effort in dialogue to figure out someone else's frame, or someone makes a personal commitment to self-examination. Such reframing can go so far as to change an entire culture, if it happens to a lot of people at the same time.

As for your question, Jacob, I do indeed believe that both liberals and conservatives are authentically concerned about oppression. And yes, I think they sometimes fail to notice that commonality because of the different terms and frames that they use.

Jacob: The point might seem too obvious to be revelatory—but it was for me: both liberal and conservative communities recognize something wrong happening systematically, but have different ways of framing it! To review, the prevailing liberal frame includes the idea that individuals are oppressed by hostile institutional structures, whereas the frame common to many religious conservative includes the idea that individuals are enslaved by sin in a fallen world. While the language used by the two communities is distinct, it also potentially reflects some common cause (see chapter three). Of course, reframing issues certainly can't resolve everything. . . . I think that in some cases it can actually make differences loom larger. On the other hand, if we (liberals, conservatives, etc.) could more effectively translate between our native "tongues," we could perhaps thereby better harness our shared concern about external forces, so as to prompt some powerful collaborations.

Phil: One reason I think that the collaboration you speak of is possible, Jacob, is that I don't see conservatives as malevolent people. And that point gets back to what I said earlier about power. If power is in part a result of systemic forces, then there are forms of malevolent power that are *not* the result of malevolence as a character trait. Thus the people with whom I disagree are in all likelihood worth talking to.

How should we respond to oppressive power?

Phil: It seems to me that oppression—whether emanating from a system, oppressive individuals, or some combination—needs to be countered in an *ongoing* way: not by the good guys riding into town, but by democratic institutions, democratic forms of discourse, and a democracy-friendly economy. And that ongoing work must include cross-border discussions that continually correct misunderstandings, build community, and temper demonization. That is what builds democratic people power in a diverse society.

To say it another way, benevolent leadership cannot be an adequate answer to the problem of how to create and maintain a good community or make good public policy. History is replete with examples of people of good character who were wrong about something, and who did the wrong thing. Sure, good character is important, but we also need leaders who get input from people who disagree with them. And that means that we need to challenge leaders, not defer to them out of respect for their authority.

Jacob: We seem to disagree, Phil, about the role of benevolent leaders, and how followers should approach them. But I'm seeing we do agree that knee-jerk conspiracy stories about deliberate malevolence and deceit at a corporate level often go too far, for some of the reasons you are pointing out. Namely, well-intentioned people can be operating in systems that shape their own personal views and choices—to the point that they really believe in what they are doing.

But, I find it curious that you seem to minimize the intention and character of those behind these power matrices. On the most basic level of an abusive family, it seems clear that living, breathing human intention is behind the oppressive power and authority in the home. Why would it be any different on a larger scale?

Also, while I like the idea of leaders listening to their opponents and citizens who are willing to pose questions to their leaders, I wonder if those deliberations will ever happen (or make a difference if they do happen) without leaders who are pure of heart, honest, etc.?

Phil: Yes, good leaders are important. But who is pure of heart? Everybody is moral to a degree or has a moral sense, but everybody is also impure. Also: Why *wouldn't* it be different on a larger scale? Why should we assume that institutions are just like individuals, only bigger? Consider excessive institutional growth and the resulting monopoly power (e.g., banks that are "too big to fail") or wasteful spending and onerous taxation (e.g. "big government"). Those forms of growth are mostly the result of the accumulation of individual actions that are quite reasonable in and of themselves—measures meant to improve performance in certain divisions of a business, efforts to increase efficiency, people defending programs they helped create with good intention, people calling for new programs because a new approach is needed, one division of an institution competing with another division for resources, and so on. Consider also corporate malfeasance. It's often caused by individual actions undertaken out of loyalty to the boss, reasonable conceptions of what it means to "do one's job," and pressure to do what's already being done by the competition. Other factors include inhumane working conditions, a need to be liked by peers, and a dare culture, all of which can push honest, good-hearted people into zones of behavior they themselves don't fully understand and would not approve of as individuals (e.g., abuse of prisoners by prison guards who have been encouraged to dehumanize prisoners, who must enforce inhumane rules, and who cannot get to know the prisoners as individuals). All of these problems have to do with factors introduced by the nature of groups and/or organizations, and are not simply the result of the aggregate features of the individuals involved.

Jacob: The corporate executive who undertakes deceitful actions influenced by cultural pressures is still ultimately rationalizing what he or she surely senses to be wrong. I suppose your point is that all the external institutional trappings are as responsible for creating the situation as he/she is. In that case the difference between us is that in my view those institutional aspects still bear the moral imprint of individual actions as much as the reverse—i.e., individuals do not merely play out institutional forces.

Beyond this, however, what I hear you saying is *not* that benevolent leaders are not important, but that they are not enough—that we need to be acknowledging external forces and make sure that associated examination is happening as well. Is that right?

Phil: Yes! I'll attempt a summary: for you, humans need humility before God to check common impulses to abuse power over others. By accepting His authority, we are held accountable to a higher power in the manner in which we relate to others. For me, humans need humility when it comes to the possibility of absolute truth in order to properly check abuses of power and authority and to discourage us from abusing power and authority our-selves. And to me, the idea of one God with a good plan can and sometimes does lead believers in the direction of abusing power and authority, in part because it encourages them to put themselves on a pedestal compared to oth-ers, because they see themselves as enjoying God's sanction.

And, to bring us full circle, you believe that people who see hidden motives and harmful power could benefit from a dose of the humility that comes from accepting God's ways of being (e.g., charity, respect for benevo-lent authority), whereas I believe that they need a dose of the humility that comes from more fully accepting the idea that humans lack access to truth with any certainty. How's that?

Jacob: A fine summary, Phil. Thanks. You're pointing also toward another key difference we will have to explore later—namely, the core belief of re-ligious conservatives that humans really do have access to some important truths and certainties.

Phil: I'll bet that feels good.

Jacob: It feels great. . . . Can't wait to show Brother Phil the light! (smile)

2

BIG GOVERNMENT, BIG MEDIA, BIG BUSINESS, AND BIG RELIGION

As our book-writing process intensified, the 2012 Republican presidential nomination contest began to likewise heat up, to the point where there seemed to be a candidate debate more than once a week. Because we were ourselves engaged in discussion, we could not help but compare our experience with theirs. In these and other debates, what especially struck us was how often the debaters offered all-or-nothing claims even about complex subjects like the role of government and the importance of religion. Making matters worse, those claims were often bound up with the denunciation of others, as in "Everything in the media is distorted," "These corporate leaders can't be trusted," and "Government is the root of our problems." It was as if the candidates were obeying a reversed version of that old rule for children: if you can't say anything disparaging, don't saying anything at all. Certainly they were not offering much by way of actual analysis or competing visions when it comes to the things Americans often argue about.

In our own discussions, conversely, we have sought to explore competing views of major institutions like government and the media without also unilaterally denouncing the key players involved. Yes, we strongly disagree. But we also, it turns out, share small patches of common ground. What, then, are the complexities? What are the commonalities? And what assumptions or worldviews lie behind our points of view? These are the subjects of this chapter.

Large-scale systems: good, bad, or it depends?

Jacob: Why don't you kick us off, Phil. From your experiences studying politics, you've come to embrace some leftist ideas, an unbecoming word to conservatives, as you know. Can you say more about that, and help me understand some of your concerns with institutional size along the way?

Phil: Sure. Let's start with the idea that systems, institutions, organizations (especially those large in scale) are impersonal forces. To say it another way, they are not merely the sum of their parts; instead they have *tendencies* based on how all their parts work together. Many organizations, for example, tend to self-replicate, grow, and do what they can to increase their budgets. Moreover, those tendencies are to one degree or another independent of the motives and desires of the individuals involved. Bigness, in other words, brings "system imperatives," meaning things that need to be done *from the point of view of the system.*

But how, one might ask, could such "needs" possibly have power over the people who are in charge? Isn't it the other way around? One reason it's not the other way around is that systems and organizations usually act in the ambit of—and depend on—other systems and organizations that are even larger or more encompassing. The management of a given company, for example, might be committed to putting their customers and workers ahead of profit, but might nonetheless end up putting profit first, thanks to pressure about the "bottom line." Elected officials who want to shrink government might face defeat in the next election unless they vote in favor of making government bigger. And those who wish to reduce unemployment might run up against the fact that today's economies (supposedly) work best when five or six percent of the workforce is officially unemployed. In sum, meta-organizational imperatives have real power.

Often, these imperatives contradict each other. An economy might fall into recession unless people increase their level of consumption, but might also benefit if the same people were to save more. Likewise, a government, in order to support economic growth, might need to spend a lot of money on infrastructure and economic stimulus, but that same cause might also call upon the government to lower its deficit and debt. Likewise again, large organizations need procedures and specialization (to, e.g., protect people from arbitrariness, increase fairness, and enhance efficiency), but those same features can also reduce room for personal inspiration, inventiveness, peer-to-peer accountability, and motivation by love.

All in all, bigness tends to move society in the direction of certain values and away from others. Bigness has, for example, made efficiency and growth seem inherently good. It has also led people to feel less individual responsibility for outcomes, in part because it does in fact reduce their power in that regard. And bigness has increased the power of technology (e.g., for weapons building) without likewise increasing the ability of people to shape and constrain that power (e.g., with ethics, democracy, and community).

Jacob: Interesting, Phil. It's only in graduate school that I began to think explicitly about the power and influence of systems. Like many Americans, I grew up assuming the systems around us—for food production, medical treatment, education—were largely beneficial and indispensible, a backdrop for daily living as natural as our Rocky Mountain skyline. This embrace of existing institutions and systems (with some exceptions) is perhaps especially typical of conservatives. Across conventional medicine, public schools, corporate America, and traditional religious institutions, this seems to be the case. Alternatively, liberals seem to embrace those institutions less warmly. My progressive friends, for instance, seem far more inclined to critique conventional medicine and explore naturopathic, complementary alternatives than are my conservative friends. And for most of my liberal-leaning friends, stepping foot into a more traditionally religious service is not anything they would seriously consider.

While there are clear exceptions to this pattern—e.g., liberals often trust government, and conservatives often raise hard questions about public schools, welfare, and other forms of social spending—this general pattern seems to hold. Why is that? Is it the trust that religious conservatives often hold in God's oversight over their affairs? We do frequently hint that American institutions and values, for instance, reflect God's blessing and interest in our nation. To be sure, we conservatives are not ignorant of system problems and some institutions whose net influence is outright harmful. Since we've both brought up institutional influence, Phil, perhaps the right question is how best to differentiate between institutions that provide more value and benefit to society and those that provide less. In religious conservative language, this would be a question of which institutions best serve God's purposes on earth (or not)—identifying systems that are helping people live thoughtful, disciplined lives and cultivating love and service. Where an institution/system is seen to be doing that, religious conservatives will typically embrace it! Where an institution seems to be doing the reverse, we will likely resist and even condemn it.

Phil: Hmm . . . Are you too nice to conservatives here, Jacob? The way I see it, many conservatives have a tendency (a need, a hankering) to see the world in terms of a grand battle between absolutes, such as the Devil and God. And to support those narratives they often decide to hate some institutions and love others, and to place themselves squarely on the side of what they have deemed totally good. For example, "America is in its intrinsic nature great in every way, but completely evil infiltrators have taken over institution x (the media, art, teachers' unions, and the like)."

Jacob: The only thing I have a need or "hankering" for is frozen custard . . . and maybe a good nap (in that order). I see the world as it actually appears to me, Phil—not in order to fulfill a subconscious need for an exciting Wild West showdown between good and evil. . . . But then again, if my needs are subconscious, I wouldn't even know it, right?

Phil: That was a poor choice of words on my part. What I meant to say is that when conservatives *do* criticize the *current* performance of an institution they often imply that the problem is some sort of takeover by forces of unrighteousness (as in "we have to take back our government"). And in my view that way of thinking flies in the face of what I tried to explain at the beginning of the chapter: institutional problems are connected to the design of the institutions themselves, how institutions connect to one another, and tradeoffs inherent in the human dependence on institutions. They're not the result of unrighteousness (though for sure people often could step up and do better).

Jacob: Okay. Thanks, that helps. I would add, though, don't mistake our belief in a real battle between absolutes for a belief that everything is absolute. The conservative evaluation of a given institution is more complex than "those black-and-white thinkers" are often given credit for, with most institutions understood as doing a mixture of some good and some bad. My own community, for instance, regularly acknowledges and talks about how the media is both (a) a tool to spread truth and goodness in some ways and (b) the reverse in significant other ways.

Phil: Excellent, but maybe then you and your community are not as conservative as you think!

Jacob: Or maybe you are being too hard on conservatives, Phil. Are you perhaps getting to know more of who we really are? You've certainly shaken up my own stereotypes of liberal thinking. The larger point I see is this: the discussion that prevails in our society about institutions and systems often seems centered on whether they are "good" or "bad"—big government "bad," local government "good," religion "good" (or "bad"), big business "bad" (or "good"), and mass media "extremely bad" (or "mind-blowingly awesome, man!"). These kind of absolute, blanket judgments, however, defy the complexity of the ethical space in which we inevitably dwell—a space in which the same institution can serve very different moral ends depending on the specific actors involved and their motives, desires, and personal actions. Is federal government good or bad? Is religion a good idea or a bad idea? Is the media a blessing or a curse? From this perspective, the answer is neither and both! Or, more accurately, it depends!

In this way, maybe we could stop asking oversimplified, all-or-nothing questions that set up and predispose the exploration of certain territories while overlooking others. And instead, we could insist on new questions that frame more fresh and productive discussions.

Phil: When it comes to better questions, Jacob, do you have any suggestions?

System problems, character problems, or a little of both?

Jacob: Yes, but first I am interested to hear a little more from you, Phil, about business and government, because what you have said so far on those topics seems to stretch both my own understanding of these institutions and my views of what liberals are "supposed to think" about them.

Phil: Yes, I think what you are referring to is the fact that my "post-socialist" leftism is open to critiques of big business *and* big government. I agree, in other words, with James Madison, that while we humans need government, we also need to protect ourselves from its potentially abusive power. And that means we must continually champion individual rights, strictly adhere to due process, insist on government transparency, maintain independent courts, and implement radical dialogue democracy.

Madison was wrong, however, when he famously said that if "men were angels" they wouldn't need government, because he had too narrow a view about *what* government is for. Even angelic humans would need to collaborate so as to manage the economy, support transportation, subsidize education, and protect the environment. And since they are angelic they would know enough to limit the scope and power of the large for-profit institutions that are inevitably generated over time by the workings of capitalist markets and private property. Also, they would sensibly choose to minimize the swings of the business cycle. What besides government can do those things?

There's no denying that government has coercive power and also often does a bad job, wastes money, etc. The same is true, however, of businesses. The vaunted competition of the "free market" is, moreover, hardly adequate as a control. For one thing it's not always present, in part because some little companies get big and use that bigness to crush smaller businesses. For another thing, competition can only prevent some ills—others it makes worse (e.g., firms competing with one another to offer lower prices for the same products might forgo spending money on environmentally friendly forms of production).

All in all, I am baffled by the conservative argument that the "free market" is a realm of freedom that will bring a solution to virtually every problem without the application of so much as a whiff of coercion. Supposedly a truly free market (one not distorted by foolish government "intervention") would brilliantly provide prosperity and simultaneously cultivate personal responsibility. Supposedly, that market's practices of buying, selling, hiring, firing, and renting would add up to a realm of ethics even though those practices rely on the pursuit of self-interest. I don't think so.

Jacob: It does seem that complete "freedom" in the marketplace does sometimes reward the achievement of corporate profit as much as it does the needs of consumers—whether we are talking about the pharmaceutical industry, agribusiness, or the media. Even so, Phil, don't you think there's something to the market "working itself out" through the free choices of consumers?

Phil: To work well markets need to serve the needs humans have as workers and stewards of the environment, not just as "consumers." But that aside, by my lights it begs credulity to assume that individual freedom and independence are compatible with a situation where many of the marketplace's "exchangers" are enormous firms and where most individuals live by virtue of dependence on such firms (and, I might add, possess zero ownership control of those firms, even if they happen to own some stock). To me, one interesting aspect of this situation is how many Americans (left, right, and center) don't fully grasp this situation. Is it that they don't want to? Do they prefer to think about public problems as if the national economy were composed of small family farms, mom-and-pop businesses, and firms that are just like small businesses, only bigger? I think many people do indeed prefer to see the world in that way, and I think that they likewise prefer to think of government as it if were just another household managing its money. Thus one often hears platitudes like "households have to balance their budgets, so the government should as well."

In reality the situation is much more dilemma-bound. What we call the "economy" is not—and will never be—distinct from the government. It can operate only by virtue of coexistence with government, with the latter needed as (e.g.) a buyer, a manager of the money supply, and a provider of business subsidies, research funding, and infrastructure. Moreover, today's economy is inherently oligopolistic (i.e., it leads to the development of very large firms that dominate in their business area), not to mention highly dependent on enormous financial firms that juice the system by making profits through betting on price fluctuations and engaging in other nonproductive activities. But, hey, call me a leftist.

My main point here is that people often imagine the world falsely in order to wish away dilemmas and replace them with simple, implementable, and fully conclusive solutions. Also—and I now stick my neck out a bit—I think that conservatives fall prey to that sort of thinking more often than do liberals. And I think that's because conservatives often want to understand the problems posed by society and by systems in the same way they understand the problems posed by individuals: as a matter of character. Thus many conservatives refer to those who even hint at dilemma as "wishy-washy" and "indecisive."

Jacob: "Wafflers, relativists" . . . yes, that's sometimes what we say.

Phil: Let me add, however, that the conservative interest in character gives them an inkling of the tremendous cost humans pay for their dependence on large-scale systems. It enables them, for example, to see that our reliance on bureaucracies and endless growth tends to take power away from morality and personal responsibility. What makes a conservative a conservative, however, rather than a revolutionary, is that they back away from this truth and instead simplify the world so that character *still* reigns—i.e., bad character is still to blame and good character is the answer. Consider, by way of example, the following selection from an essay by Charley Reese, entitled "545 People Responsible for All of America's Woes":

> Have you ever wondered why, if both the Democrats and the Republicans are against deficits, we have deficits? Have you ever wondered why, if all the politicians are against inflation and high taxes, we have inflation and high taxes? . . . One hundred Senators, 435 congressmen, one president and nine Supreme Court justices—545 human beings out of 235 million—are directly, legally, morally and individually responsible for the domestic problems that plague this country. . . . What exists is what they want to exist. . . . Do not let them con you into the belief that there exist disembodied mystical forces like "the economy," "inflation" or "politics" that prevent them from doing what they take an oath to do. . . . They and they alone should be held accountable by the people who are their bosses—provided they have the gumption to manage their own employees.[1]

This pithy statement is appealing, yes? It makes our problems clear and easily comprehensible. It blames them on a small number of people, to the point of explicitly rejecting the idea that forces beyond their control play even a small role. It declares those people blameworthy because they lack character rather than expertise or adequate information. It allows us to scoff at the idea that legislators (and government in general) are caught between a rock and a hard place. What if, however, many of the things that are genuinely needed by individuals and families can only be had at enormous cost? What if those things won't ever be adequately provided by pure free markets? It's not hard to come up with a list: affordable education, instant communication, affordable medicines, a finance system that reliably provides investment funds for projects that will bring no immediate profit but will support future economic growth, and so on. In my view, no amount of rectitude and righteousness in the government can make those needs go away, and none of those needs can be met by the private sector alone. And that means Reese is way off the mark.

Jacob: Phil, even if "no amount of . . . righteousness" on the part of our leaders can make those needs go away—wouldn't a larger amount still make a difference? Yes, I do believe that truly righteous leadership makes a tremendous difference. And by "true righteousness" I mean that which would be seen as righteous by us all—e.g., respect, honesty, and kindness.

Phil: I agree; good character *does* matter. Or, to put it another way, we each need to do our part, rather than look to others, or to systems, to do things for us. That's part of what it means to have character. Taking responsibility is healthy, even a key element of happiness. This means—as conservatives often point out—that people need to be allowed to fail sometimes. Without the possibility of failure the meaning of success and the satisfaction of achievement are necessarily diminished. Sometimes, then, we need to refrain from rescuing one another.

Having said that, I don't believe society in fact suffers from a shortage of good character. I believe there are plenty of reasonably good people (and a much smaller number of stellar people) in every political party, every community, and every nation, in roughly equal proportions. Moreover, I don't believe that good character is enough, in and of itself, to make people do the right thing. People also need to figure out *what* the right thing *is*, and the way I see it, that's often complicated and many-sided. We need, for example, to figure out how to make large organizations more human, we need better public policies and programs, and we need to design and implement new forms of collaborative decision making to counter the irrationalities of public and private institutions. In other words, it's not enough to mind your own business, do your duty, take your lumps, play by the rules, obey the law, stand up strong, obey the Ten Commandments, and so on.

Jacob: That makes sense. Rather than denying the importance of character, you're just saying it isn't everything. Most religious conservatives would have no problem signing off on that, since good character or righteous acts are seen as insufficient to any end, without divine grace anyway. In other words, few conservatives really believe good character is enough.

Even so, just this shared acknowledgment of the basic worth of character, Phil, were it to become more widely recognized, could perhaps help ease the one roadblock currently dividing liberals and conservatives. There is still some disagreement about emphasis, however. Whereas you are questioning the centrality of personal change, in order to allow more attention to larger system issues, a conservative christian focus reverses the priorities. One leader of our faith wrote the following:

> The Lord works from the inside out. The world works from the outside in. The world would take people out of the slums. Christ takes the slums out of people, and then they take themselves out of the slums. The world would mold individuals by changing their environment. Christ changes individuals, who then change their environment. The world would shape human behavior, but Christ can change human nature.[2]

It's not that we don't believe God cares about changing the slums, to be sure—only that this depends on change in us first, in order to make that happen. As Mahatma Gandhi once said, "be the change you want to see in the world."

Even while highlighting this difference in emphasis, I do wish there was more common language by which liberal and conservative citizens could better see their common stake in character and basic morality. Language differences can really get in the way of working together. During one conversation, a progressive individual objected to my use of the word "evil" to describe rape. Other words were okay—oppressive, unjust, patriarchal—but even the hint of moral wrongness was uncomfortable for him.

Phil: I agree that differences in language often get in the way of understanding between liberals and conservatives. The tricky thing is that the differences in language reflect different worldviews, and thus it's not possible for people to speak in a fully common language without keeping some people from saying everything they want or need to say. For me to call something "evil," for example, is to say not only that it's immoral and unacceptable but also that it stems from a desire to do wrong for the sake of doing wrong. And it thereby invokes the idea that harmful and unacceptable actions and events are caused by an independent and willfully evil force. In my view, then, evil is a religious concept, and one I reject. I do, however, believe in right and wrong (see chapter three). What I suggest, then, is that liberals and conservatives try to understand each other's language, try to appreciate it for what it really means, and see what common language emerges out of dialogue (much as we are doing).

To get back to the "bad institutions vs. bad character" issue, I want to reiterate that, as far as I'm concerned, humanity's current dependence on large organizations is limiting and destructive but also beneficial and unavoidable. Consider agribusiness, for example. Big farming disconnects people from land, seasons, and natural limitations. It contributes to today's high incidence of chronic diseases, and it thereby makes life less worth living for many. It causes problems that cost taxpayers billions of dollars. But on the other hand big farming of some kind is needed to feed the world's enormous population and to sustain millions of people in nonagricultural livelihoods. Thus, we have a dilemma on our hands. Unfortunately, many people ("on both sides of the aisle") wish away that dilemma so they can believe in what seem to be easily implementable and fully conclusive solutions.

Jacob: Okay, my complex friend. Let me try the reverse direction: Can't wishful thinking just as often create dilemmas when the reality is indeed simple? Are you seeing relatively simple answers as inevitably flawed? Some of your comments hint in that direction—"there they go again, staking out simple answers . . . can't those conservatives see that reality is complex?" Are you opposed to simple and comprehensible explanations by virtue of their being that way? Or, are you open to the possibility that simple, direct answers might actually exist but are overlooked? Consider, for instance, the practice of dialogue. In essence, we are proposing that people listen intently and try to understand before sharing their own views and reasons. Not rocket science! Likewise, I find many clear, simple, and powerful insights emerging from the dialogue we are having right now.

And, of course, even as I ask the question, I know that you are not actually opposed to simplicity or comprehensibility in explanation so much as to some of the particular proposals now being disseminated in society that you think too simple.

Phil: Yes, that's right. I'm reacting to the particular proposals that I see as simplistic, rather than as merely simple. And yes, some truths are simple, including the central moral rules of human life. But even simple rules come with a catch; they have to be applied to mean anything, and that often brings complexity. Consider a rule like "take good care of the elderly." The rule itself is simple, but for many of us there's no simple, obviously correct, bureaucracy-free, and trade-off-free way to follow it. After all, we live in a society of millions where resources are limited, where many elderly people want or need to live on their own, where many elderly people do not have children, and where the children of many elderly people have to work full-time jobs and thus can't look after their parents all day. Hardly simple.

I concede, Jacob, that liberals and leftists can be as simplistic as conservatives, if not more so. In past centuries, for instance, many leftists envisioned a fully utopian, easy-to-manage, and dilemma-free society of the future—one that would "flower" automatically when capitalism was finally "abolished" (whatever that means), thereby bringing harmony and cooperation, and putting an end to nationalism and patriotism. How naïve those visions seem now! More recently, when President Obama ran for office in 2008, many of his followers attached their own meanings to his campaign slogan "change," and many concluded as well that whatever change they had in mind would come overnight if Obama were elected. It seemed that those followers believed that a leadership team with good heart and vision is the only thing needed to sweep away major social problems quickly (much like Reese, eh?). I myself knew going in to the election that U.S. presidents don't in fact possess great power (thanks in part to the institutional structure of the U.S. government, it having been designed precisely to make wholesale change difficult). I also knew that the problems Obama said he would tackle were many-sided and deeply rooted, and would not be easy to solve. Thus, I was not one of those liberals disappointed by the slow pace of results during his first years in office.

Jacob: Aha! So you people *do* want to abolish capitalism. Wait until Bill O'Reilly gets a hold of this!

Organized religion: good, bad, or does it depend?

Jacob: Enough about government for a while. Let's turn to a topic closer to the conservative heart: religion. In discussions with friends who have concerns about religion, it's interesting to see how often religion is portrayed as one single entity that can and should be explored as such. For example: "*Religion* has been the reason for so many wars throughout history." "*Religion* shouldn't be mixed with public or political activities." And: "*Organized religion* really isn't necessary to connect with God." I sometimes wonder whether meaningful differences between various religions even matter to people, I once asked a neighbor hostile to religion, "Are you open to the possibility of an organized religion that actually blesses and lifts its members, rather than the reverse?" His answer was no. They were all "religions," and that was all that mattered.

But, of course, the religious inspiration for Mother Teresa to give her life for the poor is of a fundamentally different kind than the religious motives of the popes who commissioned slaughter during the Crusades. I would argue these different kinds of religious manifestations shouldn't be clumped together or glibly spoken of in the same breath. Doing so would be like classifying rotten junk food together with healthy nutritious food and then condemning all "food" as problematic.

Phil: I agree with you, Jacob, that religions are not all the same, that the forms taken by religious belief are not all the same, and that the sects of any given religion are not all the same. There are even important differences between individual churches that belong to the same sect. I agree as well that religion in general has brought, and still brings, many benefits to humanity, along with plenty of harm. But I wonder if the people you mentioned believe two things simultaneously, that there's something similar about all religions (such that some generalizations are justified) and also that religions differ greatly from one another in important ways (too much generalization is wrong).

Jacob: Yes, I think your description is a more nuanced characterization that fits. Thank you for hearing me out, Phil. It's a little eye-opening for me to realize atheism does not have to mean animosity toward religion. You defy what many religious people might think. Turning from the anti-religion sentiment now, I'm wondering if we can discuss a little the differences between conservative and liberal "believers" in their interpretation of religious faith.

Phil: Yes, many liberals believe in God. And yes, religious conservatives are much more likely to go to church, synagogue, or mosque than religious liberals.[3] Religious liberals, it seems, more often believe in God in ways that are private and/or individualistic. Also many progressives believe in God but consider religious institutions to be mere human creations that tend to serve organizational goals rather than the best human goals, much less divine goals, for example by focusing their efforts on protecting the jobs of their leaders, raising money, getting new adherents, and competing with other religious organizations. Isn't that a wise distinction, Jacob? And aren't all institutions merely things made by humans that can then control those humans, at least to a degree? Don't all institutions face system imperatives to a degree?

Jacob: Who's to say that system imperatives and organizational goals cannot also reflect human and even divine needs? No, I would not call every institution human-created. I believe that some institutions are divinely created and organized with a purpose to guide and edify humans, rather than control them. When Christ walked the earth, He organized a church to do just that—with the many Christian churches existing today attempting to hearken back to that model.

Are there mundane organizational imperatives operating within churches? Of course. But in my view there is nonetheless something special and divine in the institution itself—a question that continues to divide Christians across different traditions, regardless of their political orientation.

Phil: Then maybe we can agree that one thing many conservatives and liberals could productively talk about is their respective ways of being religious.

Jacob: Yes! Conversations could be reframed and reoriented to address how religion is framed, approached, and pursued in different ways by liberals as opposed to conservatives. For example, what different religious "stories" do they each tell, when it comes to the purpose of life and God's role in human affairs, including the place of His counsel, authority, direction, and books? This is not the place to make that comparison in any depth, but I will mention that the religious narratives of faith-minded liberal/progressive friends are distinct from those of fellow conservative individuals. The "plan" the progressives speak of is much more open-ended, "the truth" is much more relative to era and epoch, and "salvation" is much more open to anyone, as in "all paths lead to God" (except perhaps, the path of those intolerant conservatives who insist on a salvation conditioned by specific truths and laws set in place).

Phil: Your half-joking remark at the end is actually a good point. Too often tolerance and inclusion are offered "to all" in ways that don't in fact include everyone and that are insulting to some people. If you believe that salvation is real and conditioned, then that's your belief, not your "intolerance."

Let me ask this: is there a place for atheists in a liberal-conservative dialogue about religion? Of course it's not as if every person has to take part in every conversation. I know that. But don't atheists have something to contribute to discussions about "God's role in human affairs"?

Jacob: For sure. The idea that atheists are not welcome in discussions of religion might be a mistaken artifact of a simple assumption, namely—if you are not religious, then you have no conception of God or theology. But you do have such conceptions, don't you, Phil?

Phil: Hmm . . . Is that a trick question, meant to convert me? My conception is that God is a mythical being most people believe in, even if the ideas they have about God vary widely. Also, I understand theology as the theories people have about God, the divine, and so on. And, because I do not believe "God" actually exists, I'm not (I confess) all that interested in discussing conceptions of theology. But you're right that if one frames a conversation as about the *conception* of God rather than about whether or not a given institution truly reflects God's will, then I might have a good deal to say. We could, for example, talk about *which* conceptions of God, and *which* religious institutions, do more to serve the good, compared to others. Is that what you're getting at?

Jacob: Yes. That's just what I'm thinking. Why not open the conversation up?! Brigham Young taught that a fundamental principle of true religion is to accept truth from whatever source it comes. Over the last couple of years, I fell in love with my evangelical friends' fresh exuberance for their faith. More recently, I also have found immense reservoirs of peace and additional support via meditative techniques of the Buddhist mindfulness tradition. And so rather than seeing someone like you, Phil, as irrelevant to a discussion of spirituality and religion—why not give place as religious conservatives to questions, insights, and concerns from you and others as a way to teach us more about ourselves? You've done a lot of that for me so far.

In addition to teaching us more about ourselves, perhaps this kind of an open conversation could clarify stereotypes in the reverse direction (e.g., "Wow, these conservative folks aren't the goons the media makes them out to be").

Phil: Nice.

Jacob: To sum up, the dialogue we propose could foster greater collective awareness of (a) specific conditions present in religious organizations that lead to healthy individual growth and well-being and (b) other conditions that lead to the reverse.

Phil: I agree once again.

Maybe this is a good time for us to talk about another institution that can get liberals and conservatives hot under the collar: the mass media. I'll pick the opening question.

Is the mass media dominated by a "liberal elite"?

Phil: I feel compelled to make a speech: Many conservatives, like James Dobson, Robert Bork, Rush Limbaugh, and William J. Bennett, argue that the worlds of journalism, entertainment, higher education, and art ("the media") have for decades been dominated by liberals who are, to use Bennett's words, "nihilist," "hedonist," "atheist," "relativist," and "ideological." These liberals—collectively dubbed "the liberal elite"—are said to use their influence to infect the nation with bad values and bad character.[4] Bennett is especially brilliant in his rhetorical tactics—for example, by frequently constructing sentences that refer to "the liberal elite" as having one position on an issue and "Americans" as having another, and thereby stamping the reader's mind with the message that U.S. citizens who are liberal are not fully and truly American. He also states his claims in ways that take for granted—rather than demonstrate—that reporters and actors are the ones who decide what news gets reported, which dramas get produced, how often sex gets depicted, and so on. In general, he speaks as if everyone "knows" that professors, news anchors, and actors are liberal, have more power than they should, are arrogant and "out of touch" with "Americans," and possess an "agenda" that they attempt to implement. Where are the names of these hedonists? How do we know they are hedonist? Where are the notes taken from secret liberal meetings and leaked by converts to conservatism, in which liberals can be found saying they stand for nothing, believe in nothing, live only for personal pleasure, and are pleased with the progress of their plan to take over journalism? Such details are not provided.

One reason that rants against liberals so often fail to offer evidence is that there isn't any to be found. But let's say there is evidence somewhere: why would conservatives bother to dig it up? They don't need to, for several reasons: First, since the liberal villains often act in secret (or so the thinking goes), any lack of evidence of their existence can count as evidence of their great deviousness. Second, many people sign on to the conservative cause because they find its anti-liberal narrative very satisfying, rather than because of the evidence. They find in conservatism a way to allocate blame for society's problems that validates how they see themselves, how they see society, and what they believe in. Hard work, faith, and moving up, for example, are supposed to be enough. At one time they were enough, weren't they? You work hard, don't you? The conservative narrative reassures many people that the good old days were what we would like to think they were and that society can get back to those days without any major institutional reform. (And of course the conservative story also generates plenty of funny jokes about liberals.)

Jacob: To counterbalance the glut of jokes about conservatives, right? But I appreciate your speech, Phil—and can readily see in the emotion of your words that these attacks on "liberal elites" have human, breathing targets behind them (professor Phil, et al.). Although sympathetic to some of the conservative material you reference, you're also helping me see some of its excesses. Allow me to point out, however, that progressives have their own narratives that they likewise find satisfying as a way to, as you say, "allocate blame for society's problems that validates how they see themselves [and] society," etc. Everyone has a story they believe in. And again, ours includes a belief in what Paul called "spiritual wickedness in high places."[5]

Can one find evidence of deliberate, malicious intent on the part of media figures? Perhaps not. Then again, you don't have to be conscious or aware of the harm you are doing, to be doing it. If you want evidence of hedonism, nihilism, and celebrity delusion, just turn on the television.

Phil, I think you are responding to the venom of some conservative critics more than the broader message. And maybe that is why our dialogue has been so refreshing—a chance to share and hear key ideas, while checking any venom we might have at the door: "Please remove all fangs before entering the dialogue. Thank you."

And sure, I can acknowledge a tendency among some conservatives for oversimplistic rhetoric—a rhetoric that positions all virtue and rectitude on our side, while condemning the other side absolutely. Those who are spewing the venom, stirring everyone up, rallying the troops to fight the evil liberals. . . . Something is not right in their heart and character; they seem to need a good war story to justify their feelings of resentment.

Phil: I appreciate that. I also think, however, that you have not quite understood all that I'm saying. To start with, I'm very much responding to the conservative message, not just to the venom. And even though you reject the venom (of which I'm very glad) I see you buying at least some of the message. For example (and this is perhaps a minor point) you use language in some of same ways as the conservatives of which I speak. Can you, for example, define the "nihilism" you say is easy to find on television? Do you really mean the belief in *nothingness*? That is, after all, what the word nihilism means. Also, can you connect the appearance of the footage you take to be nihilist with any actual nihilist beliefs of a liberal reporter, scriptwriter, ad writer, story writer, or editor? And finally: Did that supposed nihilist put the footage on the screen with the intention to promote nothingness—actually *hoping* that the messages sent by the media do harm to people and society? Is that really your vision, Jacob? I don't think so.

Jacob: You're right in one way: the writers, actors, and distributors are clearly saying something particular—something more than "nothing." I'm also sure that most do not consciously wish to cause harm. In their minds, I'm sure they have lots of great reasons for what they are doing—from "I'm just entertaining" to "I'm giving people what they want." On the other hand, the messages conveyed by many voices in the media fly in the face of basic, foundational principles that protect society. Take a 2011 blockbuster movie, *No Strings Attached*, that details one couple's decision to have sex as many times as possible, with no commitment required. Or check out season one of *Skins*, a show recently canceled on MTV. As someone who has worked directly with teenagers who have followed the party life glorified and promulgated by such productions (and many others), I cannot stay silent about the destructive path it invites. Are these examples of nihilism? Well . . . anyone (whether liberal or conservative) who values committed relationships, spousal loyalty, and basic health can legitimately find such a "whatever you want goes" philosophy as reflecting chaos, meaninglessness, and, yes, even nothingness—consisting of literally *nothing* of redeeming value.

Phil: Okay. I think we can at least agree that plenty of the footage in the media is downright objectionable (for me it's the "trailers" that often precede the features at movie theaters, which are composed of one quickly displayed violent scene after another). But what if that footage is put in front of us because some media executives think it's their job to do whatever it takes to get more viewers, and might get fired if they don't think that way? What if political ideology has nothing to do with it? What if the real issue is the profit imperative of large media institutions? That's how I understand things. As far as I'm concerned there's no such thing as the "liberal elite." Liberals do not "run" the media, much less the nation.

Jacob: Good point. So political philosophies in the media run the gamut. And the story is more complicated than devious writers and producers spreading evil—with financial incentives, competing visions of artistic merit, and so forth, all playing a role. All that you share could shape a much more thoughtful societal discussion of media messages.

Phil: Sounds good. So why has it been so difficult for people to talk across party lines about this issue? I'm sure liberal and conservatives could find plenty of common ground.

Can we agree on any concerns with the media?

Jacob: I used to believe that liberal-leaning citizens didn't think media influence was an issue of any concern. Then I went to school with some progressive professors and classmates who had plenty of concerns regarding the "hyper-sexualized" media, and I also encountered an extensive report issued by the American Psychological Association on the "sexualization of young girls in society as reflected in the media."[6] Those experiences prompted me to consider a more meaningful frame: In what ways do liberal and conservative concerns with the media interrelate? A basic problem I see is that what goes by media "entertainment" has become a primary and powerful means of literal mass public education in our society. When I worked as a part-time educator at several middle schools on behalf of an organization that focused on sexual health, my coteachers and I would go into health classes to make a presentation to kids. It shocked me to see how extremely sexualized the seventh and eighth graders were. On certain days it felt something of a farce that we were "educating them" about sexuality when they seemed to already have been exposed to hundreds, if not thousands, of presentations by exciting celebrities on TV *teaching* them how to think about sex, relationships, men, women, love, beauty, and so on. This observation is, moreover, backed up by research that documents the alarming degree to which the media has overtaken peers, family, and religion as the dominant influence in children's lives today.[7]

And it's not just kids who are "under the influence." The dictionary defines "religion" as "a specific fundamental set of beliefs and practices generally agreed upon by a number of persons or sects . . . concerning the cause, nature, and purpose of the universe . . . usually involving devotional and ritual observances, and often containing a moral code governing the conduct of human affairs."[8] By this definition, I would argue that the connection many people have to the media has become almost religion-like. A columnist for the *Dallas Morning News*, for example, described the ferment around Super Bowl XLV as having the "feel of a pagan ritual. . . . I'm torn between feeling like I'm watching a modern form of Baal worship and wanting to exult in the excitement."[9] And eating disorder researcher Sharlene Hesse-Biber, compared some American women's relationship with the mainstream media to classic patterns within actual cults:

> The basic behavior associated with being in a cult—ritualistic performance and obsession with a goal or ideal—is also characteristic of many modern women. . . . The body rituals women practice, and the extent to which they sacrifice their bodies and minds to this goal [of thinness], seem to create a separate reality for its followers. . . . The object of worship is the "perfect" body. . . . The advertising industry and the media provide plenty of beautiful-body icons. There are plenty of guides and gurus along the way. . . . Some of the most revered oracles—Kirstie Alley, Jessica Simpson, Oprah Winfrey, and Anna Nicole Smith—are among those who advise their fans on the virtues or pitfalls of certain diets and exercises. Other sages have medical qualifications and have produced "sacred texts," including Dr. Atkins's diet, the South Beach Diet, etc.[10]

You get the picture, Phil. The media do more than just entertain and model. They invite an adoration and literal veneration of certain people, ideas, and practices, and as such can be said to represent a quasi-religion in most every important sense: adherents, regular services at set times with attention devoted to one's preferred icon (e.g., Sunday football, Saturday golf, Friday *Oprah*), invitations to change behavior in certain directions, and so on. The Bible refers to many ancient traditions that competed with worship of the "one true God"—systems that invited human adoration of objects of nature, humans, and most often, sex.

Phil: I agree with you, Jacob, that many people who do not see themselves as "religious" are often nonetheless worshippers of a kind. We are all believers in something, and so we are all prone to cultlike thinking. But what exactly is a cult? Can we make clear distinctions between healthy brands of faith and those forms of worship that depend on and then create excess dependency, a loss of critical thinking, a giveaway of autonomy, and/or an insistence on the demonization of someone or something? Also, can we grasp what sorts of media, and what media content, tend to lead people toward healthy kinds of faith, as opposed to cult forms? I think we can each do these things, but I suspect that I would not draw the lines where you would.

Jacob: Nice question. I would love to explore that sometime and see where others draw the line between healthy and unhealthy media socialization. I imagine answers that would look not too dissimilar to a related classification of religions and perhaps even businesses—e.g., when does a company's product create healthy vs. unhealthy patterns and dependency? Based on my study of anti-depressant drugs, I think those judgments would vary as much by people's experiences as their ideology. In any case, the point here is simply that this conversation deserves to happen.

Phil: If media content is a problem—and I think it is—then what *exactly* is that problem? Let's take an example like sex. For many liberals, and certainly for me, the thing we should be concerned about in this regard is the intense commodification of the human body. Today's culture sends a strong message to young people that their worth and popularity hinge on successfully competing in a battle of sexual attraction based on how they look, and that upsets me deeply. I don't think, however, that young people have too much knowledge about sex, that society allows too much nudity, or anything of that sort. I also don't believe that teaching rules like "no sex before marriage" can possibly make a dent in the problem. What can that do in the face of the never-ceasing efforts of a vast marketing industry looking to find which buttons to push and how best to push them? Shouldn't we instead seek out better (more human, more loving, more realistic, more balanced) depictions of sex, bodies, and sexuality, and push the media to provide more programming of that kind?

Jacob: More loving and ennobling depictions of sex would be a good thing, Phil. And I agree that some appropriate scenes of intimacy can send a strong, uplifting message about love and commitment. A recent film, *The Painted Veil*, provides a good example. One can contrast that film with the aforementioned *No Strings Attached* or recent *Transformers* movies that target adolescent boys and include jokes about pornography, masturbation, and explicit images of the leading actress. So yes, media presentations send differing messages, depending on how sex is portrayed, and what purposes are linked to it.

Details aside, the fact that liberals and conservatives may have some common cause and concern in critiquing the media and holding it accountable is really interesting to me. Here's my best stab at identifying two commonalities:

- Many liberals and conservatives share a belief that *some kind* of discipline or set of guidelines ought to be in place in society when it comes to sexuality—especially for youth. By this, I mean something as basic as a stance on casual sex asserting that "anything goes" is not okay and sex without any real commitment is not a healthy norm.
- Many liberals and conservatives believe that youth should be protected in some way from destructive images of and exposure to sex and taught how to think more by parents and teachers than by media outlets.

Phil: I agree that there's a great deal of shared territory on this issue, Jacob. There might even be enough to support joint political action of some kind, and there's certainly enough to make it a no-brainer that liberals and conservatives should at least talk to each other about it.

Jacob: That would be nice! We both know, of course, that those conversations would not be easy. But they could be worth it—especially if liberal and conservative citizens could be mobilized in effective, nonpartisan efforts. One small example models itself after the effective "Truth campaign," which aims to remove allure from cigarettes and reframe them in ways that encourage youth to rebel against the profitable tobacco industry.[11] Fight the New Drug was formed in 2011 and similarly attempts to reframe the pornography issue in a way that invites youth to rebel against an industry that disseminates objectifying images and messages. The successful organization is not religiously affiliated nor does it use conservative, moral language in its campaigns.[12]

If new collaborations along these lines are to expand, however, more discussion is definitely needed. In our faith community, once again, we regularly talk about helping families avoid harm that can come from pornography. When I was in graduate school, however, I raised pornography as an issue in a class discussion about families in communities. My classmates and professor looked at me like I was crazy: why would that be a problem? Likewise, I rarely hear media commentators or government leaders (whether left or right) speaking about the issue. They're eager to talk about race, civil rights, and climate change, but pay little or no attention to another kind of "climate change" happening: the systematic shifting of the social and cultural atmosphere around relationship norms over time—largely via the media. Where are the public examinations of how to forestall this kind of atmospheric shift? Anyway, I suggested to my classmates that a father who gets into erotica will likely come to relate to his spouse in different—and not more positive—ways. I realize that some people believe that consuming porn together can be healthy for relationships. My observations of families have, however, suggested the opposite—that husbands sometimes leave their wives or neglect their kids because they have become consumed in an endless array of airbrushed images. In short, Phil, I believe that pornography invites a particular (objectifying) way of thinking, feeling, and relating to others that is, in my belief, antithetical to lasting relationships.

Phil: Jacob, I agree with you about the power of images and the damaging effect on relationships of pornographic images. But what exactly makes an image "pornographic"? Is all sex, when seen, pornography? Is the sight of other people's naked but otherwise unsexualized bodies enough to undermine monogamous relationships? I can't adequately delve into these questions here, but I can say that I think to answer them we would need to make distinctions between natural nudity, sex, and pornography. I don't think that calling for "modesty" is the right response to media objectifications of sex and the body. Such calls could even be counterproductive because it's possible that the practice of modesty in its own way sexualizes the body and thereby tends to create its opposite.

Jacob: Thank you, Phil. We can disagree about whether modesty fuels or combats sexualization. But your agreement that this is an issue worth talking about hints at a broader conversation that can perhaps emerge in this nation.

If you will pardon the elaboration, let me add something more to underscore the urgency of having broader media discussions together. Recent neuroscientific research shows that daily activities as simple as learning something new or meditating can change the pathways of the brain. As Gary Marcus states, "The brain is capable of . . . *impressive feats of experience-driven reorganization. . . .* The structure of the brain is exquisitely sensitive to experience . . . so supple that it can *refine and retune itself every day of our lives.*"[13] If this is true, what are the effects of about four hours of daily media messages on a child's (or adult's) brain? Have you ever wondered how someone gets to a point where he forces sex on a child? I work in an agency that helps child victims of these crimes—and have been compelled to wonder myself. I've heard some argue that rape reflects an inherent, evolutionarily based impulse of men to "propagate." I think that is an absurd notion. Something must happen between the time boys start out as innocent children and the time they are willing to treat women and/or children as objects to be used at their discretion. Without doubt, sometimes this attitude emerges from their own unhappy homes of childhood. But something else happens to almost all children, whether or not their home is happy, and that is incessant exposure to ubiquitous mass media. And those media are, once again, not just entertaining—but teaching specific lessons again and again about how men should treat women (and vice versa): what counts as a valuable man or woman, what relationships are like, how to think about sexuality, what beauty is, etc. I believe these messages can over time literally change the brains, and therefore the dispositions and appetites, of growing boys, in some cases to the point where men may ultimately develop an almost animalistic inclination toward others that are then reflected in rape and child molestation.

Phil: Thanks, Jacob, for educating me about brain science. I feel my brain changing as a result, right this minute (I hope for the better). Seriously, in my view, your words underscore the need for more dialogue between liberals and conservatives about these issues, as it seems there is common ground to be uncovered. After all, we all oppose rape and child molestation. And there are many leftist scholars who share with conservatives an outrage at how people are shaped by the presentations of sexuality and gender in the media. Perhaps, then, liberals and conservative could work together to educate the public away from thinking that "mere entertainment" doesn't affect us profoundly.

Jacob: Thank you for hearing me out, Phil! I admit your response is a bit surprising and more than a little refreshing.

Phil: One qualification for you, "pardner": It's interesting to me how, in these sorts of conversations, we (myself included) easily fall into ways of talking that make the media seem to be united in a single system that one can blame or praise, and which does this or that to us (or for us). This seems to me both right and wrong. On the wrong side, the thing people call "the media" is really made up of many avenues of culture and cultural presentation added up together. Moreover, this plurality of things isn't entirely separate from and other to the people who consume media presentations. Instead it is part of us. On the right side, there is something singular about media: many of the organizations and systems that specialize in serving up culture are alike in being deeply guided and shaped by the profit motive. How, then, should we frame the problem? Maybe like this: we humans have put ourselves in the grip of reproduced images, and we need to recognize the dangers that come with that, and take steps in response.

Jacob: I like that, Phil; it helps me see the media in more nuanced ways.

Phil: To conclude our media discussion, let me return to my first point about those who claim a "liberal elite" is in control of this all. I think many people find reassurance in what Bennett, Reese, Limbaugh, and their colleagues have to say on this subject, and I can see why. It would be welcome news indeed if good character and responsibility were determinative in the end, despite the fact that day-to-day living entwines each of us in the workings of large, impersonal organizations, so much so that at times it seems like the human species is in the grip of rapid change controlled by no one, and unpleasant dilemmas lurk around every corner. How nice it might be if the only obstacle to morality and virtue was the excessive influence of a set of bad guys who are fundamentally different from the rest of us. Granted, it would not be good to be under siege at the hands of a villainous "they," but we would at least have virtue on our side, and we would also have the option of turning away the evil without paying any cost ourselves (except perhaps for the expenditure of energy we would need to summon the gumption to get the job done).

Jacob: You speak with a fair dose of sarcasm, Phil. This aside, as one holding some of the views you refer to, it *is* pretty nice to know there is good and evil and that our choices largely dictate the direction of our lives (and our society). But don't get me wrong. This is not a cartoon for us. Overcoming destructive forces is not something that happens easily or without a precious cost. In its fullness, the conservative Christian narrative calls for the deepest of changes in ourselves and "who we are"—rotations of heart and mind toward all that is good and away from anything that corrodes the soul and society: a change that invokes both gumption and grace, and that will not come simply or without all we can give.

I do resonate with your dismay at the conservative "preachers of righteousness" whose words of accusation and resentment are evidence of their own hypocrisy, and who have more to say about "evil liberals" and their need for virtue than they do about systematic evils around them or their own need for virtue. I'm saddened at the degree to which the Bill O'Reillys and Rush Limbaughs (not to mention their counterparts on your side) systematically stir up the populace into accepting false narratives of each other rather than moving the populace in the direction of less blame, fewer simplistic explanations, more mindfulness of complexity, and more dialogue.

Phil: Me? Sarcastic? No way. Now, about pundits (everyone's favorite punching bag): my main peeve is that they, in their focus on condemnation, often fail to acknowledge that many of the pleasing and moral aspects of our lives are connected to a reliance on systems and large organizations that don't always serve us well. And conservative pundits are perhaps especially prone to deny the degree to which that dependence has reduced the power of personal responsibility.

To be clear, I don't mean to suggest that individual humans have ever been fully responsible for their fate; human notions of morality have always leaned toward exaggerations in that regard; that's one way we encourage one another to do the best we can. But the modern reliance on large-scale impersonal systems of partially interconnected organizations has changed the equation, to the point where humanity is pushed around in a new way. And a common response is to insist on the adequacy of very old rules and ideas: e.g., all we need is for men to be warriors and women to be nurturers, live by the Ten Commandments, or (as Reese insists) elect legislators with the guts to outlaw social and economic problems.

Jacob: Very old and very simple rules—but not enough to "save us" for sure. I hope it is clear that, beyond those self-proclaimed spokespersons you will find a sizable majority of conservatives who do *not* believe character is enough—and who, almost categorically, acknowledge the need for a divine hand interceding precisely because we are embedded in a fallen world that impinges on us, and literally enslaves us—even with many good intentions.

Phil: While I can't go along with the "divine hand" idea, I think we agree that many people are woefully unaware of the role played by systems and institutions in shaping, or at least influencing, thought and action. Also, how about this: maybe one reason our culture is now so unfriendly to dialogue is the way our large institutions work (and fail to work). The mass media and the economy, for example, tend to situate people as consumers, whether of products, services, information, entertainment, or political parties and candidates, rather than as doers and talkers. Might we agree, Jacob, in seeing that as a problem?

Jacob: Right on, Phil. This is fun. And overall, we've identified some powerful answers to the issue kicking this institution discussion off in the first place: Namely, can we say *anything* nice about each other's ideologies at all? And why would we ever care to, anyway?

And once again, my first answer is because it's fun! So much more enjoyable than trashing our opponents all the time! Every once in awhile, I'm surprised by a political leader who bucks the trend and demonstrates memory of what his or her mother undoubtedly taught long ago about how to treat other people. In Governor Mitch Daniels's response to President Obama's 2012 State of the Union address, for instance, he began by saying:

> The status of 'loyal opposition' imposes on those out of power some serious responsibilities: to show respect for the Presidency and its occupant, to express agreement where it exists. Republicans tonight salute our president, for instance, for his aggressive pursuit of the murderers of 9/11, and for bravely backing long overdue changes in public education.

He then added, "I personally would add to that list, admiration for the strong family commitment that he and the First Lady have displayed to a nation sorely needing such examples."[14]

Although Daniels went on to outline a voluminous list of disagreements with the president, that opening paragraph was a unique and refreshing acknowledgment that Obama, however much even Daniels himself disagreed with him, was not a demon (and yes, that *is* news to some conservatives).

Phil: Daniels did well to speak as he did (and, as you know, I don't believe in demons).

3

WHAT TO MAKE OF VALUES
AND MORALITY

Upward of 90 percent of the residents of Farmington, Utah, consider themselves Mormon. Thus, it was not surprising that when the city decided to build a community pool in the early 1990s, the city council planned for its closure every Sunday. That was consistent with the faith-inspired commitment to Sabbath observance held by Mormons and other religious residents in the city. There were, however, many non-Mormon residents who believed that everyone should have access to the pool throughout the weekend. An ugly showdown ensued, complete with town hall discussions that featured acrimonious comments from both sides, ranging from "Stop imposing your moral/religious views on us!" to "We refuse to abandon our values and standards!"

How should the residents of Farmington have responded to this impasse? How should other communities respond when they find themselves divided by issues that seem to allow for little or no compromise, such as the opening of a clinic where abortions are performed, or a display of the Ten Commandments in a public building? As you know by now, we believe the best response is often for each of those concerned to make an effort to better understand the viewpoint of the other, if only to clear away misunderstanding and get to the heart of the matter. We also believe that what frequently lies at the heart of the matter are differing takes on values and morality. Thus this chapter.

In order to get the discussion under way, we reached some agreement on basic definitions. We define "values" as the commitments, customs, principles, institutions, and behaviors held to be intrinsically desirable by individuals and communities, and we understand the word "moral" to hold a similar meaning, with an added claim of rightness. One might value free time, for example, but also believe in a moral duty to give up some free time to help someone else.

Definitions only go so far, of course. What is morality *really*? What is the source of legitimate moral standards and values? How exactly have liberal and conservative communities come to diverge so widely in their respective value positions? And what do these differences mean when it comes to the potential for those two groups to work together?

To be moral or not to be moral: is that the question?

Jacob: The swimming pool episode happened in my hometown when I was a teenager, and left a lasting impression on me. While the animosity of local residents was itself troubling, it was the strange way the community discussion was *framed* that was especially discomfiting. Specifically, only the Mormon residents were seen as approaching the issue from a moral standpoint. This buttressed a narrative of religious people either trying to "defend their values" or "impose their values"—depending on one's position. The ensuing acrimony and resentment were attributed to a cultural divide prompting conflict that was sadly inevitable—however painful both sides had experienced it.

What is most remarkable, in retrospect, is how avoidable some of the more intense resentment may have been. As I came to eventually realize, rather than one side alone "having morals," each side had a contrasting view of what was moral, right, and good. While the pro-Sabbath-observance view was more obviously a value commitment, a value position was also evident in the minority view: "It is *good and right* to be able to bring our families to the pool on Sunday and thereby have that time to build our relationships, exercise, and get needed rest."

Once the conversation had been framed as a battle against moral imposition, however, the competitive tone was set. If, alternatively, everyone involved had seen that two different moral/value positions were in play, they might have understood the primary problem as *each* side (not just one) attempting to impose its own view of the good. And that kind of awareness might, in turn, foster a greater willingness to compromise and accommodate community-wide needs on many issues, not just pool hours on Sunday.

Phil: I think part of the problem is that people from many different points of view see no purpose in talking about why something is right or wrong. For some, what's right is too obvious to talk about, as in "God says so." For others what's right is personal, as in "it's right for me, so butt out." Still, different ideas of right are bound to collide. And in the face of that, many people yearn for a public world that's value-neutral, as in "keep your values to yourself."

Jacob: Good point, Phil. One of my college mentors, Brent Slife, taught that early philosophical attempts to move toward value neutrality were an understandable reaction to the genuinely abusive imposition of values by kings and popes in the Middle Ages. That push-back against narrow bias was healthy but set in motion an expectation that it is possible and desirable to be value-neutral and free of any personal bias. Thus some professional therapists presume to speak from a value-free position, as in "My only commitment is to find what is best for you." Scientists also present their data as if personal bias had been irrelevant to analysis. In each case we see what continental philosophers call a "bias against bias,"[1] a way of thinking that makes it all too easy to accuse any individual or organization one doesn't agree with as "biased" and not worth listening to.

Phil: That's a big-time conversation stopper, meaning there's no way to productively converse across a disagreement if the discussion becomes "You're biased" vs. "No, I'm not" and "You're the one who's biased." From then on, there's no way to talk about the actual content of anyone's moral or value claim.

Jacob: You're right, Phil. And the reality is that moral claims—including ideas about what is best for all—are not optional. A sense of what is valuable and good is an ongoing and *inevitable* backdrop for all that humans do. Charles Taylor, for instance, writes of humans dwelling inextricably within a "moral space" in which judgments about the good are required all the time and everywhere.[2] The implication is that no one—not Christians, not atheists, not researchers, and not counselors—can escape taking *some kind* of moral position about the complex situations and circumstances that we each face as humans beings.

If this is true, then perhaps we might all more openly and honestly acknowledge the standpoints from which we speak and work—and accept others doing the same. It was this kind of deliberation on the nature of the good, Aristotle once said, that was a defining feature of citizenship itself.[3]

Phil: Yes, we all make value judgments, and we citizens should regularly talk about, and explore, those judgments. But isn't it true, Jacob, that many of your religious compatriots are not as inclined toward dialogue as you are, because they see the content of morality as obvious, something they have direct access to, and something that shouldn't be compromised by giving credibility to the views of those who have not seen the light?

Jacob: Yes—you're right. Just the act of talking openly to someone who seems fundamentally wrong can feel like a potentially dangerous cop-out or compromise. However, even a religious believer-in-absolutes such as myself has found it exciting to explore in this way—sharing and hearing different views on what is good. But I wonder, why is that threatening? Nothing about that arrangement would mean we conservatives need abandon or compromise any of our values or moral positions. Engaging in such dialogue might even provide a *wider audience* for our religious values, just as it would for the views of anyone else involved.

And what about learning from each other? On that note, I feel sad for those who are fearful of talking with someone like you, Phil!

Phil: And it seems to me that you're a somewhat unusual religious conservative in your ability to separate listening to someone else's point of view from condoning or supporting it. Maybe that's in part because Mormon teachings, compared to other versions of Christianity, emphasize that every human has an inborn sense of moral truth at some level and that humans possess inherent goodness. Certainly there are many Christian religious conservatives who are more in agreement with Islamic fundamentalists in understanding sinful desire as too powerful to allow for any debate whatsoever with the "devil." What humans need instead, according to that point of view, is strict tradition, firm teaching of the one true way, and penalties (and/or confession) for straying.

Jacob: As an aside, Phil, especially since Mitt Romney's campaign, Americans are raising some concern as to whether "those Mormons are really Christian"—with Latter-day Saints equally interested in persuading others in the affirmative. I sometimes wish I could stop this predictable, ping-pong exchange, and say: "If by Christian you mean a belief in the fourth-century Nicene creed, the three-in-one Trinity, and the inborn depravity of man, then no, we Mormons are not Christian—not in that sense." Given meaningful differences in how the nature of God and man are understood, I wonder why these (and other) faith communities can't talk together more openly about the different ways Christ and His message can be understood and interpreted—rather than exhausting our time and attention debating where exactly to draw boundary lines and cut-off points for defining a true Christian.

But again, this conversation—like that between liberal and conservative citizens—can feel quite scary, I'm sure. When I was a kid, my friends and I played a game where we drew a line down the middle and if you got close enough to the line, someone on the other side could pull you across. The fun was flirting with the line . . . tempting others to pull you over. This seems to be how others tend to see open conversation and dialogue—as if it's a decoy meant to distract you long enough so someone can drag you over to the dark side! Granted, there might be legitimate reasons to fear dialogue in certain situations, for example when the participants include impressionable youth or the conversation includes ultra-destructive ideas. There is less reason to fear, though, if you believe every human possesses a degree of truth and is a literal child of God. From that perspective, you are not to be feared, Phil, even if you happen to believe some of the devil's ideas (smile).

Phil: Thanks Jacob; I'll try to keep the devil in check.

How are morals and values related to rights?

Phil: A "rights" claim is a special moral claim, in that it asserts that someone deserves a certain kind of treatment no matter what (or unless that treatment conflicts with another right). In the United States, rights claims are very popular: people claim a right to health care, a right not to be taxed, and so on. Do rights make sense? In my view they do, but only to a point. They make sense in that morality requires us to put some moral rules ahead of others, and also because some moral rules are of the kind that, were we to authorize following them "most of the time" rather than all the time we might find that we're not following them much at all. Consider speech rights. If speech is only protected most of the time, then it *won't* be protected when what's being said is highly unpopular or displeasing to those in power. So it's best to declare a right to speech and stick to it. On the other hand, the idea that people have a right to something can never serve as the last word on the subject, because the notion leaves too many questions unanswered. What counts as speech? What counts as "private property"? What limits, if any, are appropriate when it comes to the right to gun ownership or health care? And what should be done when rights conflict? Because the answers to these questions are by no means obvious, morality is still in the picture.

I hope you're noticing, Jacob, that I'm not one of those liberals who leans on rights claims in order to avoid discussing the merits of something. When it comes to pornography, for example, the right to free speech doesn't settle the matter. Even if the publication of certain erotic material ought to be allowed as a matter of right, we nonetheless can—and often should—have a public discussion about whether or not it is moral or wise to publish that material. It's important, then, to make a distinction between the legal and the moral. We might agree, for example, that you should possess the legal right to be rude to me, but also that you shouldn't be rude to me.

Jacob: That's helpful, Phil. I have often heard conservatives complain about how often rights are discussed, with little discussion of responsibility. It's refreshing to realize that we can have a thoughtful conversation about rights and moral responsibilities—and their meaningful linkages.

Where do various moral convictions and value positions originate?

Jacob: Another assumption often made about values and morality might be contributing to how frequently the two are minimized or vilified. That is, morality and values are spoken of as inherently *subjective*—as the opposite of hard, objective realities—and thus in the same realm as whim, opinion, and fancy.

Phil: Yes. Often one of my students will claim that their view of what's moral is merely that, their view, and not about what anyone else should believe. That, however, is a contradiction. Granted, people sometimes act morally merely because they prefer to act that way for other reasons (like to avoid going to jail). But if and when they call those actions "moral" they're by definition claiming something beyond preference. They're claiming that what they prefer is *also* "right," meaning right for others who are in the same situation. That's the basic meaning of "moral," a concept I'm confident appears in every language.

Jacob: Along the same lines, Charles Taylor writes that to value honesty is to *demonstrate* honesty, rather than simply to hold a subjective commitment to honesty.[4]

Phil: I don't mean to suggest that the people of the world are in agreement about what counts as morality. Far from it. You and I, Jacob, disagree about what's good and what's right, where morality comes from, and more. On the other hand, humans everywhere speak of the goodness or rightness of actions and ways of living.

Here's my view of the moral: I believe that humans have a best nature. Best nature is what humans are when at their best, meaning healthy and in balance. And the achievement of best nature includes living in certain ways and in accordance with certain principles. Those ways and principles are, then, "good" for humans and so we humans should do our best to live in accordance with them.

Other people, of course, have other ideas: Morality is what God says it is or "reason" says it is. Morality is whatever pleases the gods, is natural, or has "always been done that way." Morality is whatever fits with the almighty right of the individual to be free from interference, or fits with the "laws of history." Do these differences of opinion mean that morality has no basis? No. It means that what humans are able to know of morality leaves room for uncertainty. Granted, some ideas of what is moral appear in every culture and historical setting, but there's nonetheless room for plausible disagreement about moral rules, not to mention where they come from.

Jacob: That reminds me, Phil, of several recent studies. Social psychologists Jonathan Haidt and Jesse Graham argue that people use five psychological "foundations . . . for detecting and reacting emotionally to issues," and that these foundations (also called "systems" and "orientations") are combined by different people in differing ways to constitute "the world's many moralities." These orientations are (1) caring for others; (2) fairness, justice, treating others equally; (3) being loyal to one's group, family, and nation; (4) respecting tradition and legitimate authority; and (5) purity/sanctity: avoiding disgusting things, foods, and actions, and otherwise seeking virtue by "controlling what you put into your body."[5] The liberals and conservatives studied by Haidt and Graham were alike in emphasizing "care" the most, but differed with regard to the remaining foundations. Those identifying as liberal tended to emphasize care and fairness more highly than loyalty, respect, and purity; while the self-identified conservatives tended to emphasize loyalty, respect, and purity at the same level as care and fairness. Liberals and conservatives also differed when it came to the *kind* of purity emphasized: "While the political right may moralize [about] sex much more, the political left is really doing a lot of . . . [moralizing] with food. . . . A lot of it is ideas about purity, about what you're willing to touch or put into your body."[6] Thus these two researchers offer a possible explanation of many of today's disagreements. What do you think?

Phil: Hmm . . . I like their idea that people have different ways of arranging and prioritizing the things they deeply value, but I can't go along with the idea that liberals fail to "emphasize" loyalty, respect, or purity. I don't believe, moreover, that the priorities people have are best thought of as "psychological systems." There is only one human "psychological system." How about this: all people, in every culture, weave each of the five "foundations" together, but in different ways. And, those differences occur because people disagree about what each of the foundations really are or mean (e.g., what *counts* as "caring" in a given situation) and how those foundations interact and depend on one another (e.g., whether or not proper care requires being pure, and how). In fact, I would call the foundations "competing moral goods," and simply say that different people prioritize those moral goods in differing ways. Perhaps, for example, liberals often decide who has authority and who should be respected by making an evaluation of who harms whom and who cares for whom. Whereas maybe conservatives believe that the best way to care for one another and minimize harm is to be obedient to a system of authority and respect. And if that's the case, then it stands to reason that it might be beneficial for liberals and conservatives to engage in dialogue about these different understandings.

Jacob: I like this, Phil—rather than operating out of different psychological machinery, we're all working with similar dispositions, but in different ways. In my liberal/conservative interviewing study of 2006, a progressive colleague and I asked diverse citizens to share their detailed and candid thoughts on a variety of social issues. We found some interesting nuances, similar to what was reported by Haidt. For instance, conservatives and liberals *both* spoke of ideals for personal behavior, with the former emphasizing standards of purity and the latter emphasizing openness and respect for diversity. Similarly, both spoke of the need for societal action, with conservatives stressing the importance of preaching the gospel and holding the media accountable and liberals stressing the importance of confronting oppression and eliminating social disparities.[7]

The pattern holds; while conservative and liberal citizens *both* embrace certain lifestyle standards and guidelines, they differ in the details: Is "right conduct" a matter of working for social justice or preaching the gospel? Is the work of greatest urgency improving the physical environment or purifying one's own soul? Should we focus more on becoming "green" or becoming "clean"?

These are considerable differences, buttressing competing definitions of "the moral and noble life" along distinct axes. On one hand, goodness comes to be defined by a certain set of behaviors—from reducing one's carbon footprint, recycling, and not driving drunk, to tolerating differences, wearing condoms, and not going to war. On the other hand, the centerpiece of goodness includes moral purity, worship activities such as prayer and scripture study, faithfulness to God, loyalty to family, charity towards others, etc.

Phil: If we're on the right track, Jacob, the differences between you and me are more philosophical than psychological. In other words, it's not that we each emphasize different "psychological systems"; we just disagree.

Why should one person's morality matter to anyone else?

Jacob: We have been exploring different ideas of what the moral yardstick for everyone, independent of preference, ought to be. Some readers might, however, want us to address a more basic question: Why would there be any independent yardstick at all? Isn't that idea just an illusion? Are not moral preferences, in the end, just preferences?

Phil: Interestingly, even when people call morality a matter of preference they tend to offer a moral justification for that idea, as in: the right moral rule to follow is to let each person follow their own moral rules, as long as they let others do the same. Or, as my students often say, "I won't tell you what's right for you, and you shouldn't tell me what's right for me." But, as I said, that idea is itself a moral rule. If what rule to follow really were a matter of individual opinion, then there would be no way to defend the rule that everyone should honor everyone else's individual opinion, because that would be just another opinion. In other words, if someone tells me not to tell them what to do, then they are telling me what to do. And the relativist who says that other people should be relativist is thereby not a relativist.

Jacob: So relativism reflects an implicit moral position as well, along the lines of "it is *good* to not take firm stances or to not have absolute views." This may appear to work well individually, but on a community level, once that making-my-own-rules individual starts living with others, the "ideal" of relativism must necessarily break down and show itself unworkable, perhaps even painful.

Phil: It seems we understand each other thus far, Jacob. And that's interesting, given that liberals and conservatives more generally seem often to misunderstand each other on precisely this issue. Indeed, those misunderstandings seem at this point to be woven into the very definitions of "liberal" and "conservative." It seems to me, for example, that many conservatives consider themselves conservative largely because of what they imagine to be true of liberals (as in "they have no moral thinking at all, but we do"). And some liberals consider themselves liberal because they don't agree with what they imagine conservatives to be (e.g., moralizers, greedy oil executives, or ignorant rednecks). Let us hope, then, that through dialogue such misunderstandings can be reduced, and that people can thereby more often find themselves arguing about the issues that truly divide them.

Jacob: Amen to that, Brother Phil!

Why are religious conservatives so confident in their moral views?

Jacob: What you just said, Phil, makes me think of the way some people react to conservative people and positions: with a mixture of amusement and criticism along the lines of "What are they thinking!?" and "How can they possibly think the way they do about that issue!?" Media outlets in particular seem to enjoy painting many kinds of religious conservatives with the same fanatical brush—as fundamentalist, prudish, straight-laced, oppressive, and even deluded. Underneath that rhetoric, however, lies a legitimate and understandable question for conservatives, along the lines of: "How do you people feel justified in being so strict and uncompromising in your beliefs—in seeing things in such an absolute way?"

The answer when it comes to religious conservatives is that the certainty they have about their view of the good derives from their belief in God, and in particular from two specific aspects of His relationship to us. The first conviction, beyond God's mere existence, is that He has the legitimate authority to counsel, direct, and lead us—and sometimes even to simply "tell us what to do." Why? Because, according to most world religions, monotheistic or otherwise, He created or organized all things. And, as Creator, God has legitimate authority to decree and dictate certain conditions across His creations, including in the realm of "the good."

Phil: Why is it given that one who creates thereby has authority over his or her creation?

Jacob: Our own explanation is based on a conviction that humans are *literal* children of God: "And God said, Let us make man in our image, after our likeness."[8] Essentially, then, it's parental authority.

Less than a year ago, my sweetheart and I were blessed with a pudgy baby boy. Like most parents, we sense a compelling responsibility to care for, protect, and guide him—and not to control him (unless it's nap time).

We see God's prerogative to parent similarly, as the literal father of our spirits. Rather than being created *ex nihilo*—out of nothing—Mormons join other faith traditions in asserting a meaningful existence prior to this one. We believe that, before our arrival in this earthly life, we grew and developed under the care of our spiritual parents and were at that time given lessons, instruction, and even particular callings in anticipation of our mortal experience.

And that teaching, instruction, and guidance continues here. In other words, God is not a permissive parent! He has things to teach, insights to share, and warnings to lay out. Rather than winding up the universe like a watch and letting it run, we believe that God prepared a detailed plan for our well-being—a "plan of happiness" centered round our continued progression as His children. Like kids who grow up once they are away from parents, central to this plan was an opportunity to leave home, so our minds and hearts could be tested.

Phil: Of course I accept your explanation of why you are so confident, and what else can I say? I can't really contribute much to a discussion of the nature of God, since as far as I'm concerned people made him up.

Jacob: That's okay, Phil. One day you and God can make up and be friends again. In the meanwhile, like we discussed earlier, you don't have to believe the same as us to continue offering excellent questions and insights that teach and press people like me in good ways.

How do we understand evil differently?

Jacob: "And there was war in heaven: Michael and his angels fought against the dragon."[9] These words from the *Book of Revelation* are understood by

Mormons to be a description of events that took place in the premortal world. The same story of the "dragon"—also known as Satan—is told as follows by Lehi in the *Book of Mormon*: "An angel of God . . . [fell] from heaven; wherefore, he became a devil, having sought that which was evil before God. And because he had fallen from heaven, and had become miserable forever, he sought also the misery of all mankind."[10] Thus for my community, the battle between good and evil began as an ancient war, a war that was centered around many of the same basic issues now being contested here on earth: freedom, agency, rights, and the best plan to help people grow and succeed. Satan's evil was in rebelling against God's plan and persuading many of God's spirit children of an alternative plan, which he claimed would save and exalt all humans, without fail. A primary difference between the competing plans was the degree to which humans were allowed agency to make their own choices and mistakes.

Phil: As myths go, the one you offer seems in some ways a good one. One might, for example, say that democracy is encouraged, because humans are said to have, and to deserve, freedom to make their own choices and mistakes. An undemocratic element, on the other hand, might be that humans don't get to decide what truly counts as a good choice. God decides. And if one's plan is the "wrong" plan, then one is on the side of the devil—a being not only in the wrong but also opposed to good itself.

Jacob: Yes, you're right, the agency I speak of is not the freedom to "do anything." As with our country's democracy, individuals under God's plan have the freedom to make choices. But they do not—with some exceptions—have the freedom to make the laws.

And by the way. . . one reason you're able to believe God is a myth, according to our understanding, is the world was set up to give you and all of us that choice. In order to not be unduly influenced by a perfect memory of the past, we believe our minds have passed through a "veil" of forgetfulness that renders most of the events of that distant past inaccessible to us. And on earth, we are then allowed to be exposed to all kinds of different ideas so we can choose for ourselves where we stand. Since "choosing for ourselves" requires having other options, God allows the adversary and his followers to influence and tempt his children yet again. For us, then, evil and its draw are very real, not some fiction conjured up to keep people scared.

Phil: What you call evil I call wrongdoing, harm, or injustice. And wrongdoing is any serious harm that's both avoidable and morally wrong. And for me there are multiple types of wrongdoing in the world, as opposed to one single force of badness. Also, in my view, each act of wrongdoing or injustice has an element of error to it, or an element of tragedy—as when good things conflict, or someone makes a terrible choice because they don't know better or are emotionally damaged. For you, however, evil is a singular pseudo-human force that works totally for bad, desires the bad as such, and leads people toward bad. In my view, that idea is likely to encourage humans to seek to smite those with whom they disagree rather than try to understand them, learn from them, and respond with generosity and moral principle.

I do realize that your idea of evil can be read as saying that no one should be smitten, that instead those who are evil should be converted, meaning pulled away from temptation and toward "the Word." And I realize as well that the idea that we're all God's children can be interpreted to mean that all people are worthy of care. But those good notions are in my view trumped by the way the devil notion encourages people to define some other people as not-really-human, as lost to evil and best opposed by war. You believe, after all, that "there was war in heaven"; why not, then, wage war on earth, so as to smite the devil and his minions?

Jacob: To clarify, the war to which that verse refers is largely a spiritual battle, Phil—a contest of ideas that, yes, we believe has continued unabated throughout human history. You are right, though, that attention to evil can be misused to label and vilify. For us, however, the acknowledgment of evil is a tangible safety and protection—something Satan would love to have us ignore, or see as mere myth.

Is the world fallen, deluded, oppressed, or none of the above?

Jacob: Although Islam, Judaism, and Christianity all agree in seeing Adam and Eve as the first mortal man and woman created with physical bodies, evaluations of this event vary widely. For many, it was an unfortunate and sad rejection of a "golden opportunity" to dwell in the paradisiacal Garden of Eden—a tragedy that some are very ready to blame on Eve as the first to partake of the fruit. Others, however, do not believe that the event was a major mistake or a surprise to God, or that Eve was foolhardy in partaking. In the same sermon mentioned earlier, for example, the ancient American prophet Lehi teaches:

> If Adam had not transgressed he would not have fallen, but he would have remained in the garden of Eden. And all things which were created must have remained in the same state in which they were after they were created. . . . And they would have had no children, wherefore they would have remained in a state of innocence; having no joy, for they knew no misery; doing no good, for they knew no sin. . . . For it must needs be, that there is an opposition in all things. . . . Adam fell that men might be; and men are, that they might have joy.[11]

Rather than remain in a neutral state of zero spiritual friction, the idea is that there is wisdom in being allowed to experience intense opposition. Without such turbulence, there would be no growth and no learning, no testing and no progression. The challenges of life thus become a necessary platform from which we learn what we need to learn. We learn more of our identity—who we really are—for instance, by being constantly invited and provoked in this world to be what *we are not*.

Phil: I agree with much of what you just said, but of course I don't buy the idea that a "test" has been assigned to humanity. Instead, I see us as complicated animals capable of thriving and as being out of balance, even at the same time.

I do agree, though, that we humans are indeed often provoked away from our best selves. And yet to that reality you apply the idea of having "fallen." Why? Why project ideas about what human life ought to be into an imagined past that you then hold up as a standard?

Jacob: Implicit in the idea of a "best self" is the understanding you can deviate and depart from that, right? Is the idea of a "fallen world" really that different than what many others believe, Phil? For instance, Buddha taught that all humans dwell in the midst of constant, pervasive delusion—from which the individual and collective goal is to *awake*. I also see parallels to the attention progressives pay to the constraints of surrounding societal structures and how best to resist their oppression on a personal level.

Phil: It's true that Buddhism understands humans to be deluded by ego and mere appearance, and claims as well that each person has the capability to achieve full balance and awareness by gradually letting go of ego and coming to experience the connectedness of all things. Buddhism makes no claim, however, that human delusion is caused by a fall or by sin, much less that some sort of evil will is at work in the universe, and must be fought. Delusion is instead understood as a natural condition.

Jacob: Fair enough—although, once again, the idea of delusion does seem to presume an implicit (if not explicit) distinction between something good and something less so.

Phil: The idea that there's evil in the world is not at all the same as the idea that some things are better and some worse. Humans have a nature such that some things are better for us and some are worse. That which is harmful, in other words, can be understood as that which throws us away from our best selves and our natural balance. And perhaps, Jacob, we can agree about that, if not on the idea of a fall.

Jacob: That's helpful, Phil. There's a reason why I think this discussion of shared terms and language for moral discussion is especially significant. A popular notion exists that all natural impulses should be embraced as inherent to the self and therefore good. On the other extreme are those who insist that all natural impulses are inherently corrupt or depraved.

It seems to me we're exploring language that acknowledges these two impulses, while avoiding their excesses. Instead of asking if natural inclinations are always good or always bad, what if we spent more time considering where, how, and in what ways natural human impulses, inclinations, and dispositions are being exercised in a good, healthy way and in what ways are they not.

My natural inclination to eat food, for instance, has been exercised in both good and bad ways over the course of my life. Rather than condemn that appetite as categorically good or bad, I could instead report where it has been engaged well and where it has not.

Phil: Interesting point, Jacob. One cause of imbalance these days is that our technologies are changing faster than our cultures and our evolved nature. For example, humans evolved to enjoy things they could only have occasionally (e.g., meat, and sugars as they appear in plants and honey) but have since figured out ways to make some of those things available all the time (even inventing concentrated sweeteners that lead to cravings and at times to self-perpetuating cycles of imbalance). And that process has now proceeded to the point where each person must work toward balance in the face of powerful forces that push against it. Call those forces "Satan" if you will; to me they cannot be thus personified because they are not outside of us and they are not part of any campaign of evil intention.

Jacob: You must not have watched the documentary, *Food Inc.*, yet, Phil! How interesting, though, that we see similar broad brushstroke patterns, despite the fact that we understand their sources so differently. There's something about that which feels pretty exciting.

Should general moral standards be promoted?

Jacob: Let's leave the negative stuff now (however it is labeled), and explore a little more how to respond to it. Take any appetite, Phil—for food, for sex, whatever. If you let yourself follow it, without any restraint, what would you say it will do to you?

Phil: Me personally? I would drink way too much espresso, and would deeply regret it. So yes, I do indeed believe in self-restraint as one of the human virtues. Simply giving in to all of one's impulses as they come along has to add up to something destructive. Moderation is perhaps an especially demanding virtue in modern times, given how much temptation the commercial world throws in everyone's face, not to mention the widespread availability of powerful drugs (legal and illegal, chemical and cultural, for the mind and for the body).

On the other hand, many conservatives mistakenly believe that the philosophy of no restraint comes from liberals who, starting in the 1960s, changed America from a nation of virtue and faith into a nation of hedonism and atheism. Never mind that the Catholic Church, fundamentalist Islam, and other religions have for centuries been cultivating the intensity of people's desire, in part by making excessive demands for self-restraint (e.g., hijabs), and in part by declaring even our most balanced desires to be the stuff of sin. Never mind also that a consumer mentality has been encouraged by the invention of credit accounts and mass marketing, and that that process began well before the 1960s. Never mind that living within capitalism means that the only way to avoid economic downturn is to maintain continual economic growth, which requires more and more sales of goods and services, year after year, in perpetuity. Never mind all that. Instead, let's pretend that people's lack of restraint is solely the result of one group of people and their bad ideas, and thereby also pretend that many of the things we love (economic growth, freedom of choice, modern gadgets) are not implicated in the things that hurt us (lack of balance, addiction, obesity, pornography, sexual trafficking, etc.).

Jacob: So that's not all the liberals' fault?! You're elaborating an important point, Phil, and I'm starting to see how much easier it is to live in that cartoon world of perfect villains we can all love to hate. It's also interesting what you say about moderation. There is a perception, among some conservatives at least, that liberals do not accept any kind of standard or line around personal behavior. I myself held this essential view for many years—literally believing, for instance, that the liberal stance on sex was "anything goes—if you feel like it, go for it." I'm a little embarrassed to say it was not until I actually listened carefully to progressive friends on the subject that I discovered this was not the case.

Phil: That's just because we eventually get too old to have sex all the time. Ok, I'll be serious: yes, progressives believe in moderation and self-restraint. But let's first make sure not to confuse law and morality. The idea that there should be legal freedom to choose (that people possess a "right") is not the same as the idea that no messages should be sent—via culture and teaching—to individuals about how best to behave. And I realize that liberals sometimes confuse the two. Or, to say it better, some liberals have a tendency (shared with economic conservatives, but not with religious conservatives) to frame every issue in terms of "rights" and leave it at that. And you and I, Jacob, agree that we should *not* leave it at that. On the other hand, when it comes to exactly *which* moral messages should be promulgated and how, I expect we disagree. Let's take a specific issue we've been exploring already: when to have sex, and with whom. The way I see it, young people are best off if they take having sex as a serious step, fraught with emotional challenges, and not to be undertaken lightly. Sex is potentially harmful both emotionally and physically, but also potentially fulfilling and connecting, as well as something that can deepen and solidify a committed relationship. People should therefore not have sex with each other unless they're willing to follow through and look after each other. Also, generally speaking, it's a terrible idea to have sex with multiple partners, or with people one doesn't care about, or with anyone who's not a very close friend. So when conservatives say "young people need to be taught that they should wait until marriage to have sex" I see their point. On the other hand, to me the issue is love and a commitment to taking care of each other, not marriage. Indeed, the marriage-is-the-rule message may sometimes be harmful as it can downplay the idea that we need to take good care of each other in favor of merely following rules.

Jacob: You're right, we disagree here—although you're also right to say that marriage devoid of love and commitment is nothing to celebrate. Even so, we see marriage as the most likely place for that kind of love and commitment to flower. In broader terms of general sexuality, it is cool to hear you draw a line. I'm amazed at how long I've personally taken for granted what "people like you" believe on the matter, Phil. Among other things, your comments hint that people as different as you and I can do more than arm wrestle about appropriate sex education, and can instead agree that some basic and sensible standards need to exist. And I would bet that when liberal/conservative conversations are framed in that way, the discovered commonalities might actually emerge as more important than the differences. Good parents everywhere, for instance, might realize that *none* of them really want their kids to be anything-goes-promiscuous!

The reason this feels exciting, Phil, is that we conservatives often feel alone in advocating for some kind of basic collective, societal standards. From the gradual "coursening" of our culture, to the sexualization of all forms of entertainment, we often feel like the only ones who see these things as issues: "Oh, here goes those prudish conservatives again. . . . " How cool would it be for us to find common cause with nonreligious communities on general standards around some of these issues?

Phil: Okay, Jacob. But is a loss of God's guidance the problem, or is the problem instead a reliance on an economy that takes away personal space and teaches the value of the immediate and of that which can be bought? I believe that what's needed are ways to live according to the demands of compassion and equal worth, even in the face of our dependence on the political economy of mega-businesses that are half-merged with one another and with the world's large, interconnected governments. We have to somehow get that colossus off our backs, and yet throwing it away is not an option.

On the one hand, I would say that the problem just described is a central moral issue of our time because it lies behind so many other problems, from global warming to human trafficking and sexual slavery. On the other hand, I don't think that the problem has much to do with a lack of "morality," as that word is usually understood. Moral people are just as implicated in the system as immoral people. Instead of trying to become more moral, what we-the-people need to do is spend more time and energy working on public problems. And that means we need to face the music about the dilemmas that confront us and then work cooperatively and imaginatively with others to do something about them.

Jacob: Hmm. Economic forces instead of God . . . Couldn't both be at play? We'll have to talk more about that later, but I do like your push in the direction of movements instead of monasteries alone as the site of the most truly moral work. In the Bible, James called feeding the hungry and serving the orphan a central part of "pure religion."[12]

Should personal changes in a particular direction be encouraged?

Phil: While we might agree that society needs "movements instead of monasteries," toward what should we move? For most social conservatives, the answer is faith, family, responsibility, tradition, moral certainty, and patriotism. And for most, the problem to be addressed is moral decline. That decline is, moreover, largely attributed to a rise in selfishness, hedonism, and relativism. And that crisis, once again, is understood as the work of an immoral group, "liberals" (activist gays and lesbians, socialists, artists, journalists, and college professors like me) who have no scruples and who share an "agenda" to gain power, fulfill their immediate desires, spread the worship of nothing ("nihilism"), get government to do everything, and so on.

In my view, however, the villains just described only exist in a cartoon. The liberals so many people love to hate are merely an invention that serves to provide a clear enemy, a righteous war to fight, and the (impossible-to-fulfill) promise of a once-and-for-all, no-issues-need-be-debated, fully moral world.

Jacob: As I've said before, Phil, I place more of the blame for our societal moral crisis on the powerful mass media, than on leftist professors like you (although I've never sat in the back of one of your political science classes, so who knows!). I am sympathetic to your critique, at least in its reference to the many self-proclaimed conservative leaders who make the accusatory statements to which you allude. But for every pundit, there are many conservative folks like me who are tired of the cartoonish debates and who honestly enjoy our progressive neighbors, even if we think they are wrong about a lot of things.

Then again, the idea that society is facing a moral crisis is something we conservatives do indeed agree on, including the many conservatives out there who frame and describe that crisis much differently than Glenn Beck. As I see it, the crisis is one of society back-stepping and walking away from time-honored principles of living: everything from honesty and integrity to self-discipline and temperance. And perhaps if we are careful in the language we use, people like you and me might actually agree there is something of concern happening.

Phil: You're right that society is in crisis of a sort. But the problem is not moral decline, nihilism, or bad art exhibits so much as a loss of moral bearings centuries in the making, and that has come as part of shifts in moral thinking that are in some ways wonderful. One might summarize that change this way: we have yet to fully figure out how to do individualism right. Individualism is on the mark in asserting that autonomy should be honored more than it was in the precapitalist period, but how much autonomy is healthy? How much is even possible? Does capitalism steal autonomy in some ways while also creating new forms of bondage that look on the surface much like autonomy? If rigid rules, tyranny, and public opinion shouldn't tell us each what to do, what ought to guide us in their stead? Surely we each need limits of some kind. And yet, it's not easy to set limits in the face of the pressures to consume and compete that stem from our reliance on capitalist markets. Thus we face dilemmas, rather than a "moral crisis."

Jacob: I'm still not sure why you struggle so much with a language of morality itself. But in terms of commonality, I keep hearing you say that otherwise well-meaning humans are caught up in something bigger than themselves . . . something that inclines them in certain directions and shapes their choices in sometimes harmful directions. Even though you, Phil, depict and characterize these surrounding forces differently than do I, it seems that we both see a need for individuals to rise above or resist them—so as to thereby preserve their well-being and health.

I make a point of that to reiterate how much this desire to resist cultural forces stands at odds with the popular notion that whoever and however we are—and whatever direction we feel like going—is okay. From that perspective, the individual's central need is more self-acceptance and self-esteem ("If we only loved ourselves!"). But if the world (however we label it) impinges upon us in the ways we've discussed, then something more than self-acceptance seems in order. Like most of my brothers and sisters of the various Abrahamic faiths, I believe that one core need of any human being is to undergo some kind of repentance or change process in response to the residual effects of living in this society. Like a kind of spiritual detox program, this involves turning away from corrosive actions and behaviors, whatever those might be in each individual case. And for Christians, more than the shaping of behavior alone, the ultimate goal is a deeper, more expansive change: a "rebirth" of our spirits through Christ and a "restoration" of our true identity.

Phil: Hmm . . . You say that individuals need to repent or change. That's pretty vague. Could each of us somehow change for the better? Sure. Should we each move away from destructive behaviors? Of course. But do you and I agree about which behaviors are in fact destructive? No. On the other hand, maybe there's some overlap. And maybe the ideas we share about destructive actions are more important than whether or not we think of change in terms of "repentance before God" (that being lights years away from my way of thinking).

Jacob: You may be right, Phil. I could see us agreeing a good deal about what experiences count as uplifting or degrading and it's cool to think those commonalities may extend across boundaries of faith/nonfaith. You're not exactly the kind of guy that most conservative Christians would see as an ally. But you've convinced me that on some level, we've been wrong.

We don't want to overstate agreements, of course. And even among people of faith, the details of what personal change is needed and how to approach it vary widely. From Muslim friends, I have learned of their belief that God can forgive and release someone from the consequences of harmful actions simply through His goodwill. Implicit in Christian belief, by comparison, is a presumption that resolving the implications of harmful actions is not that simple. There is a sense that anytime we betray His will and law, negative consequences are set in motion—a kind of bad karma that follows from our self-betrayal or sin. Specifically, sin permits Satan to achieve a degree of authority over individuals, in proportion to their betrayal. And rather than the effects of bad choices being swept away out of sheer goodwill, God is required by the justice of the universe to do something that exerts an equal and opposite force in order to undo the destruction caused.

That provides a little more backdrop, Phil, for why we place so much emphasis on one person and one event foretold by many ancient prophets: "the time is not far distant that the Redeemer liveth and cometh among his people. . . . He shall go forth, suffering pains and afflictions and temptations of every kind. . . . And he will take upon him death, that he may loose the bands of death which bind his people; and he will take upon him their infirmities . . . that he may know according to the flesh how to succor his people . . . [and] blot out their transgressions according to the power of his deliverance."[13]

Those in my faith community believe that it was precisely because He experienced and endured this atoning burden that Jesus was literally "given authority" to act as the Redeemer: the point person for the salvation of the human family. As we repent, Christ can release us from the effects of sin, because He has borne the consequences Himself and knows how to free us. In short, we believe change is possible, because of Him.

Is a belief in God necessary for moral belief and practice?

Phil: Clearly, Jacob, morality is for you grounded in the idea of God and His plan for the human race. And in that regard you're like many people, including many liberals. But other people, myself included, don't see why "God's plan" (if such a thing exists) should be at all determinative. Supposing God were to descend from the heavens in a chariot and tell me what's right; why should I go along with what he says? At the least I ought to demand a good argument. And nothing God or anyone else could say can change the fact that reason supports more than one plausible answer to many moral questions. Therefore God should, like the rest of us, be humble about his beliefs.

Of course, many people have faith in God's omniscience, meaning that he knows all, including what's right. And some believe as well that faith overcomes the doubt inherent in reason, and that what I and other heathens need to do is to make a leap of faith whereby we come to accept God's word as true simply because it comes from him. My view, however, is that the only way humans ever know truth is by means of the merely human enterprise of considering ideas that are in principle falsifiable and seeing if they hold up in the face of available evidence.

Jacob: First of all, my friend Phil, I believe in a God of dialogue and deliberation[14] . . . a God who loves to field our questions, helps us solve problems, and sometimes even comes up with some pretty good arguments. I look forward to your first conversation with God (and not because I think it will go poorly!) My experience with you tells me you are a truth seeker, some-one who is sincerely looking for and glomming on to further goodness and insight, in spite of your views of God. That someone can relish truth and follow it even without accepting the reality of God (and that they can find some real happiness too) is something I think religious conservatives could acknowledge more.

Second, Phil, the "faith" conception you speak of is not mine. Simply put, I *do* believe in the falsifiability of faith claims. It's true that faith has tra-ditionally been seen as a placeholder for knowledge, as something we turn to when we do not know. But, as the philosopher Richard Williams points out, the Bible's teaching of faith as the "substance of things not seen" suggests another idea.[15] Instead of seeing faith as the opposite of knowledge, faith can be understood as a kind of first-person knowledge gained from our own lived experiences and personal assurances. One teacher compares the process to planting a seed—an act that, admittedly, takes faith that something will come of it, an assurance that you're not just crazy putting that little thing in the ground. Then, as the tree grows, that growth itself offers a natural confir-mation of your assurance. According to this view, legitimate faith thus yields tangible, observable evidence of its authenticity.[16]

Phil: Interesting. I myself believe that we all make leaps of faith of one kind or another. Faith, moreover, often brings benefits, for example by cementing communities and powerfully grounding people's lives, even to the point of bringing very direct health benefits. Probably religiosity and religious myth were crucial survival mechanisms at one time in human history, and that's one reason why humans are now so prone to use them. But at most what these observations tell us is that faith can be helpful, not that it tells us the truth. So, again, I don't see why it matters whether God exists or not when it comes to the validity of moral claims. In other words, even if God exists and is right about everything, God is not right *because* he says so. Nothing is right or wrong because of who said so. And I will not use the idea of God to escape my own responsibility to make moral decisions amid the possibility of conflicting answers.

Jacob: Your "just because someone (God/prophets/Oprah) said so" concern is justified, Phil. While we do believe that God can give direction without a full explanation, like any good father, most often God wants us to have (a) enough explanation for what He asks of us and (b) enough space to explore His teaching freely . . . even to the point of disagreeing when we have concerns.

By contrast, God is often portrayed as some kind of authoritarian, even arrogant figure who lives just to tell us what to do and offer more commandments, all the while just waiting for us to slight Him ("Sinner!"). Like the abused child who struggles to relate to anyone in authority without fear and dread, so also, it seems, the oppressed masses cannot seem to escape a view of God as oppressive. I, once again, believe in a God who loves His children enough to provide direction, but not without also listening intently to their questions and concerns.

Phil: Well then, if I ever do come to believe in God, it'll be your guy (though he and I would need to sit down and have a serious talk about gender and sexual orientation).

Should moral standards be open to debate and discussion?

Phil: While I believe in the existence of right and wrong, for some people there are beliefs and institutions that are to them not only right but also not to be critiqued. For some it's capitalism. For some it's Islam. For some it's Christ our Savior. And for some it's heterosexual marriage. In my view, however, all claims can be questioned. We are, after all, merely human beings living in history, and our knowledge is necessarily incomplete and imperfect.

Jacob: When talking about critique, Phil, can we differentiate more clearly between kinds? On one hand is criticism that has an agenda to tear down, contradict, and refute. Openness to learn and explore are not present, only criticism. Not surprisingly, conservatives (like most any group) are not likely to welcome that sort of critique, even when it comes clothed in the language of open conversation or "dialogue." If, on the other hand, critique refers to open, civil discussion of differences and the exploration of questions, bring it on! Anyone who claims to love knowledge and truth should welcome participation in such an exploration. If you are raising concern with a lack of this latter kind of openness, Phil—a not-to-be contested, wrong-to-question attitude—then we are in agreement. I believe that having space to explore and question any claim—from a testimony of Christ's divinity to the defense of heterosexual marriage—is supremely important, so much so that, as I said earlier, I think God Himself would agree on this point.

Phil: I'm not just saying that people should be "open" to questioning; I'm saying that every idea is *itself* open to question, in other words that humans have no access to moral rules that can't be legitimately questioned. Granted, people can be confident. Some have confidence thanks to their faith in the existence of an infinitely wise supreme being. Some "know" a course of action is right because they have a strong and powerful feeling they cannot deny. Some decide (as I have) that humans have a nature and a connectedness to others such that certain ways of living are best. Each of these reasons goes beyond mere preference, but each can nonetheless be plausibly challenged.

Jacob: Okay, Phil, in that case I challenge your idea that every idea can be challenged! Just kidding. As I said, I have no problem with your insistence on the contestability-of-all. That does not threaten, for me, the possibility of (eventual) firm knowledge nor even attaining certainty about something; instead, it calls on me to stay open to learning more and never assume I "know enough." I used to remind our foster girls, when giving them feedback or trying to teach something: "Remember, you don't have to agree with me. I want you to disagree sometimes. Just work on sharing it in a way that allows others to really listen."

Phil: Perhaps it's worth remembering at this juncture that every time humans ruminate on the subject of morality they come to many of the same conclusions: be honest, take care of others, serve a larger whole, honor those who taught and cared for you, honor the dead, honor commitments, don't steal, and so on.

Jacob: Yes—and still we manage to find so many less important things to fight about! After a lone gunman in Tucson shot Representative Gabby Giffords in early 2011, and killed many others, there were widespread calls for more civility in public discourse. And yet even that issue got sucked into acrimony. In the words of one commentator, "The debate over which political side is most uncivil has dwarfed our nation's crucial discussion."[17] Some people do seem as crazy as we thought!

Phil, I've agreed with your insistence on the contestability of moral claims. Now I need to explain more of why, in spite of this agreement, some of my own conclusions have become so settled. Once again, I believe in the existence of a God who wants to guide and help us, and show us lots of cool things on our life journey. In speaking about this with different progressive friends who are very religious, their responses surprised me. To paraphrase: "Isn't it kind of arrogant to think we can know God's will about something? After all, God is a paradox and mystery—a being so different from us in form and nature that we simply cannot comprehend Him. That is part of what makes God . . . God."

The basis of my faith community's contrasting view of God comes from an experience we accept as legitimate history. As a young boy, Joseph Smith grew up during the second Great Awakening, a time when preachers traveled the American countryside attempting to win people for God. In his memoirs he describes the great animosities existing between different religions and his struggle with how to respond and what conclusion to reach.[18]

Amid the confusion of these religious debates, Joseph recounts reading in the Bible a passage in James that encourages those who "lack wisdom" to "ask of God who giveth to all men liberally . . . and it shall be given him."[19] (No, Phil, this doesn't mean God is a liberal!)

Joseph describes retiring to a quiet place in the woods near his home where he knelt and offered up the desires of his heart. He recounted, "I had scarcely done so, when immediately I was seized upon by some power which entirely overcame me, and had such an astonishing influence over me as to bind my tongue so that I could not speak. Thick darkness gathered around me, and it seemed to me for a time as if I were doomed to sudden destruction."[20] He continued:

> But, exerting all my powers to call upon God to deliver me out of the
> power of this enemy that had seized upon me, and at the very moment

when I was ready to sink into despair . . . I saw a pillar of light exactly over my head . . . above the brightness of the sun, which descended gradually until it fell upon me. It no sooner appeared than I found myself delivered from the enemy which held me bound. When the light rested upon me I saw two Personages, whose brightness and glory defy all description, standing above me in the air. One of them spake unto me, calling me by name and said, pointing to the other—*This is My Beloved Son. Hear Him!*[21]

This account illustrates why we see God as more than a mysterious essence or force that defies explanation—but rather, a being that can speak and interact with us clearly, "as a man speaks to his friend."[22]

Why share so much of this story? Am I surreptitiously trying to convert you through our dialogue, Phil?! Since dialogue welcomes both strong conviction and a desire to share things you love, there is always hope in dialogue of having the other person appreciate and even accept some new possibilities. The primary aim of this kind of conversation, of course, is not to persuade—but instead, to cultivate better understanding.

In an age where revelatory experiences are often placed in the same category as schizophrenic delusions and the experiences of madmen, we are defending two-way communication with God as a reality. No, I have not seen God or angels, Phil—at least not yet. But I will tell you that I know Joseph's account is true. I know it in the same way I know other things, such as that my mother loves me or that you are my friend: from feelings of peace and assurance felt in quiet moments. The Apostle Paul writes that the way someone can identify something as true and coming from God is "love, joy, peace . . . , gentleness, goodness, etc."[23] Or simply put, truth "tastes good,"[24] as Joseph once said.

Phil: You, Jacob, have made it clear that your certainty about right and wrong comes from your certainty about God and his teaching. I get it and I appreciate it. As for the story of Joseph Smith, I do not presume to fully understand what he experienced. But my reading of it is that what he saw and heard somehow came from inside of him and was a response to what he was dealing with in his life and had witnessed around him. I do accept that revelations are sometimes true, but that doesn't to my mind mean that they came from God. And doesn't it stand to reason that the ideas offered by one's "witness" are also sometimes untrue? After all, cultures often pass on falsehoods, and individuals are sometimes out of balance emotionally, psychically, or physically. So I can't say that I trust the results achieved by everyone who consults their witness.

Let me ask this: is a given moral claim true—or more likely to be true—because it came to someone in a vision? It seems to me that, when it comes to assessing moral claims, it doesn't matter where they came from. When I was little my mom and dad had great authority in my eyes, and for good reason, but they were nonetheless not always right. In short, I consider rightness to be intrinsic to a claim, not dependent on who said it. In other words, I'm sticking to what I said earlier: humans have no surefire way to know which claims are right.

Jacob: Yes, we would say that seeing something in a vision is a pretty surefire way of knowing something is true! But you are again suggesting that uncertainty and contestability are inherent and inescapable aspects of life, Phil. In that case let *me* ask: If this was always the case, what would be the point of discussing anything, as you and I are doing now? Is not one purpose of dialogue to seek greater insight and clarity, and invite the same in others? No, we are not promising to "resolve" things for each other, or for our readers, but neither would I see us holding out indefinite arguing and uncertainty as the ideal of our work together. My point is this: like overdone certainty, an insistence on inherent uncertainty could also shut down conversation and prevent individuals from recognizing assurances of truth. What about a place to pursue greater understanding and insight with both epistemological humility *and hope* in regards to the truth that might be revealed to both parties (from whatever source it comes)?

Phil: It seems to me that you want it both ways; you want to accept contestability *and* believe that absolute truth can be had.

Jacob: Yes, contestability of claims during the open exploration process, and eventually (by that authentic, searching process), clear assurances as to the reality of things as they are.

Phil: The truth I hope to possess is of a provisional, merely human variety. Let me give you an example: Thousands and thousands of fossils have been found in the earth, and every single one of them confirms the theory of evolution (by virtue of which layer of the earth's crust it was found in, the kind of rock it was found in, how it dates using carbon dating, etc.). Likewise, every measured feature of every plant and animal ever studied fits with that same theory. Thus I am convinced that the theory is true. But at the same time, I know that the theory can't be proven in a final sense any more than can any other scientific theory. Does that mean that the scientific investigation of biological origins is useless? Not at all.

Jacob: For a merely provisional theory, Phil, you speak with quite a bit of absolute certainty ("every plant and animal ever studied . . ."). You're right, the evidence does clearly confirm intra-species evolution (finches growing longer or shorter beaks, moths changing color). But the fossil record for inter-species evolution (one species changing to another) has sizeable holes.[25] Yet the evidence for the former is often leveraged to support the latter and "evolution" generally. When I've asked these questions in biology classes, professors have looked at me like I was silly. One teacher asserted, "Oh, evolution has already been proven; really, it's only the details that are left to explore." Discussion over. Where's the open exploration and dialogue with this question, Phil?

Phil: Well, what you call "holes" are not what I would call pieces of disconfirming evidence; they are things we do not know (e.g., fossils we have not found, and might not ever find). To challenge a theory, however, one needs evidence that suggests it's wrong; it's not enough to point to evidence undiscovered. If the latter were enough, then every theory in the world would be wrong.

Jacob: Yet the burden of proof lies with those coming up with these theories, I would think. Who's right and who's wrong, however, is less of my main concern here; rather, I'm wondering whether we can have space to talk openly about it. Ben Stein's 2008 documentary, *Expelled*, does a pretty good job of showing how academic and scientific exploration can be stifled on contested issues such as evolution. The same can be said, by the way, of climate change findings, where those posing questions about the theory are now regularly labeled "climate change deniers"—a rhetoric hinting in not so subtle ways that their questions are about as sensible as those who question the Holocaust. Whatever the issue, rather than engaging in intellectual "power plays" that silence dissent, why not open up the conversation?

Phil: I only brought up evolution to make a point about how provisional human knowledge is. Let me add this: I agree that no view should be excluded from the discussion (e.g., intelligent design), but I also think that people *do* sometimes engage in denial, as opposed to scientific disagreement. And when someone pulls out a conspiracy story about liberal scientists acting as a group to "promote" the theory of global warming (and people are making that argument), it smells like denial to me. Moreover, in my view "intelligent design" is more of a religious narrative than a scientific theory—at least thus far—just as the big bang theory is merely the way most scientists make sense of the available empirical evidence. To me it's apples and oranges. Anyway, I think the important thing to argue about here is the idea that human knowledge is just that, *human* knowledge, based on merely human experience.

Jacob: You're right to say that conspiracy theories don't help anything, Phil. And thank you for hearing me out on this, by the way. The reason I've pressed you a bit, is that your illustration of provisional knowledge minimized my own version of provisional knowledge in a remarkably absolute way. This made me want to push back and ensure "equal opportunity" for Christian knowledge claims as well. And on that note, depending on one's view of science and the nature of valid evidence, strong arguments can be made for intelligent design as a viable scientific theory.

How much do we really share in the area of morality?

Jacob: Phew! Laying aside questions about competing grounds for knowledge, what can our communities agree is concretely, thoroughly good, Phil? When I participated in an interfaith service effort in Illinois that brought together Jain, Hindu, Muslim, Baha'i, and Christian believers, as well as those without religious faith, what stood out was how surprising it was for participants to realize, simply put, that each of our communities believe in the value of love and service.

But why was that a surprise? And similarly, why was it a surprise for me to learn in graduate school—really learn—the degree to which my progressive/liberal professors were genuinely motivated by desires to help the nation: that my main advisor at the University of Illinois, Nicole Allen, for example, was a passionate and inspired leader in the fight against domestic violence?

Phil: Thanks for inviting nonbelievers to your gathering. Allow me to likewise share some thoughts about what we might hold in common. I'll bet you that we both believe that all life has value. Therefore we might agree as well that we each have a moral obligation not only to treat each person as intrinsically valuable but also to live in such a way that we honor all living creatures. Maybe we agree that the balanced and healthy human feels compassion. Maybe we agree that humans are quite capable of suppressing or rationalizing away that natural compassion. (By "compassion" I don't, by the way, mean pity. I mean an aversion to see or to contemplate the suffering of others in exactly the same way as one is averse to one's own suffering. At least one experimental study reports that the witnessing of an injury to another causes the same "pain center" brain activity as one's own experience of injury.[26])

Jacob: Some beautiful thoughts, Phil! The value of love is a wonderful commonality to explore. And in general, it seems to me that there might be a good deal of common cause between liberals and conservatives when it comes to jointly promoting some of the more fundamental moral standards—from love and service, to hard work, patience, and civility.

Coming full circle, then, the common debate between "standards" vs. "no standards" surely reflects a false dichotomy in that literally everyone I know—regardless of their particular beliefs—holds to *some* kind of standard. And certainly most everyone—including my hometown residents—would (if pressed) agree that everyone has moral views of some kind, even if many people would add, "But their moral views are wrong, so why should we listen?" The question, then, is really about *which kind* of morality we want, or what standards exactly we want—rather than whether to have standards at all.

On an interpersonal level such a shift would mean we move from asking *whether* someone is moral to exploring *in what ways* they are moral. And that in turn could cultivate a willingness to welcome diverse participants into conversations that openly explore competing views of the public good. Admittedly, the shift we speak of could make some people uncomfortable—since it seems to smack of relativism and a denial of deep convictions. My own experiences with dialogue have, however, led me to lose my fears on that score. I now believe that dialogue and conviction are compatible as long as the people who are exchanging ideas are each given room to retain their convictions. If I can personally make that shift and find thrilling experiences in dialogue on diverging moral views, I believe many in my camp can do the same . . . at least under the right conditions.

Phil: I agree 100 percent. Even with competing moral issues at play, it's not at all pointless for opposing groups to talk and to listen across the gap that divides them. True, such talk might do nothing to generate compromise on the particular issues at hand, as there might not be a law or policy both sides can live with. But common ground would be discovered, and mutual respect and compassion for the other would be cultivated.

PART II
HOT TOPICS

4

TRADITIONAL GENDER ROLES: BLESSING, OPPRESSING, OR WHAT?

In 1972, a constitutional amendment was proposed as a way to guarantee equal rights for women under the law. Although the law passed both houses of Congress, a contentious battled ensued. Groups like the Concerned Women of America, a conservative Christian public policy group, joined forces with traditional religious associations in opposing the amendment, while the National Organization of Women and other liberal advocacy groups defended it. In the end, it failed to gain state ratification.

How could a proposal centered on something so seemingly simple as equalizing rights be the subject of such controversy? And why would large numbers of women in some communities stand against the decision? One reason was surely that what counts as "equal rights" is, in fact, far from simple: What are the rights in question? What exactly does "equal" mean in this context: identical, or fair? And if the latter, what counts as fair or equitable? To complicate things further, does the goal of equal rights need to be balanced against the duties men and women have, both as members of families and members of society? For example, does good parenting require gender roles? And if so, what should these roles look like?

People around the world continue to disagree strongly about these issues. Thus it's not surprising that our conversation on the subject raised considerable differences. We did not, however, differ in the ways we had anticipated, and we also discovered surprising areas of commonality.

Some readers might object that, because we are both men, a dialogue between us on the subject of gender must necessarily be inadequately informed. We respectfully ask those readers for a fair hearing, before they judge the chapter and book by its gendered cover.

Different roles for men and women: A good or bad idea?

Jacob: So how could something as nice as "gender equality" be questioned by religious conservatives across the nation, Phil? Because of the many levels of this question, my own answer to that question will take a little bit of time to unpack. The short response is that we are in favor of many kinds of equality. But when an argument for equality minimizes unique capacities or complementary roles specific to each gender, a line is drawn for us, since such a view conflicts with core beliefs about who we see ourselves to be.

As you know, religious conservatives generally believe that some aspects of traditional gender roles are part of God's plan for His children. In my own faith community, for instance, one prophetic text on families states: "The family is central to the Creator's plan for the eternal destiny of His children," adding that gender is an "essential characteristic" of an individual's "eternal identity and purpose." The document later continues:

> By divine design, fathers are to preside over their families in love and righteousness and are responsible to provide the necessities of life and protection for their families. Mothers are primarily responsible for the nurture of their children. In these sacred responsibilities, fathers and mothers are obligated to help one another as equal partners. Disability, death, or other circumstances may necessitate individual adaptation.[1]

Phil: Interesting. I think that the first thing I need to say is that I accept nothing as "prophetic" if that means somehow tuned into or expressing the views of a divine being, nor would I accept any idea as compelling *simply* by virtue of who offers it to me—even if it's "God" Himself. From earlier discussions, however, I've learned how much you *do* believe those things— reflecting what might be our most fundamental difference. While you're helping me better understand the source of your convictions on this issue, it leaves me wondering if you have a nonreligious justification to offer for the gender role divisions you've described. Perhaps, for example, you think that it's the best way to meet the needs of children.

My view is that it is not the best way, at least not for every family, or as a rule. I instead see the division of labor you describe as just one of many ways that families organize so as to meet the needs of children. In my view the stakes here are high, for the simple reason that what you call for is (at this time in human history and for the foreseeable future) not compatible with equal opportunity for men and women.

To be clear, I have no problem with the idea that there are biological differences between men and women. The average female athlete of a given age seems, for example, to have more endurance than the average male athlete of the same age, while the latter appears to have an edge when it comes to upper body strength. Also, no one can reasonably deny that it *could* be the case that nurturance and selfless caring come more naturally or automatically to women (again on average) than to men, but so what? I fail to see how that would call upon us to support gender roles.

Jacob: You ask for more justification than "God says so," Phil, and you are right to do so. Even God has reasons for what He does, after all. The average biological differences you refer to as fairly arbitrary and inconsequential, we would see as a natural imprint of the very roles described above—a kind of physiological predisposition toward the kind of lives that will fulfill us most deeply.

On that note, I've noticed how uncomfortable many of my liberal-leaning friends seem to be with the notion of *any* role distinction between men and women, Phil. In the context of parenting, allow me to ask you an honest question: Why do you feel so sure that these distinct roles for mother and father are not needed by children? In my own community, we would point to ongoing experiences in our own families and the function of these gender roles throughout human history as evidence that complementary roles often make a meaningful difference (for the better). Also, please say a little more to help me understand why you see distinct roles as intrinsically "incompatible" with equal opportunity: couldn't such partners still be *equal* partners in the most important sense of the word?

Phil: I'll start with the latter question. To be in favor of the roles you outline is to say that women should live one way while men should live another—that each should live different lives, and in fact be different sorts of people: girls and women piling their choices and self-socialization on top of their (supposed) nature so as to make themselves into "feminine" persons, and boys and men crafting themselves into "masculine" persons. It seems to me that that's asking a lot. To my view, that's restricting their freedom in fundamental and irreversible ways. Nor do I believe the stated roles actually allow for equality; given the world we live in, they would give most "providers" much more feasibility-of-exit from the intimate relationship than they would give their nonproviding partners, and that would often create a power differential.

Jacob: You're right that gender roles can create a difference in power in some ways. Is this necessarily a bad thing, however? Certainly, power can be abused. But as we discussed in chapter one, power can also be used for good things, as in Christ's teaching that "he that is greatest among you shall be your servant."[2] If power differences exist in a family, couldn't they be used to serve and "bless" the other individuals in the home?

Phil: But Jacob, we're talking about the *primary* adult relationship in a person's life; we're talking about their attempt at love partnership. If there's a serious, consistent inequality in power between someone and his/her partner, won't that be harmful, even if that power is exercised wisely? Also, the power often will not be exercised wisely, and what then?

Jacob: Good points, Phil—each helping me understand your concerns better. I think I'm also starting to understand one of our deeper differences that we need to clarify. We keep talking about inequality and power differences as if we're all on the same page about what these look like and mean.

Yet there are multiple ways power can differ between two people, and additional variation in how these differences may be interpreted. As you and I launched into this conversation, Phil, I asked my wife, who works as a full-time mother, to honestly share whether she thinks a power difference exists between us. She responded that neither of us had more or less actual power than the other. My observation is that if any power difference exists between me and my wife, it is more of a qualitative one (a difference in kind) than quantitative (a difference in amount). In other words, though we each apply our energies in different (complementary) realms, the *sheer amount* of power she exercises is the same as (and sometimes more than) the amount that I do. The only difference is that we are applying our power in different realms—full-time nurturing of children for her (with meaningful contributions to providing), and full-time providing for me (with meaningful contributions to nurturing).

So would *that* kind of power difference be threatening too, Phil? Although our roles differ, her energies and efforts are as important and meaningful as mine. Neither of us see my research job as any more important than her work at home with children. In fact, if we had to rate them, hers would come out on top for both of us.

Phil: I hear you, Jacob. Let me offer a few thoughts in response. First, as far as I'm concerned the issue isn't my feelings. (In other words, it's not about whether I feel "threatened.") Instead, the issue is what power dynamics are created by the promulgation of the gender roles you speak of, and whether those dynamics are good or bad, morally acceptable or morally unacceptable. Second, I see nothing wrong with the way you and your wife have worked things out; it sounds wonderful. What I oppose is the promulgation of that arrangement as a general standard.

Let me explain the last idea further by asking you this: Are the standardized role directives you call for in fact needed? If men and women are each inclined by nature toward the duties called for, why socialize them into those very same duties? Nature, after all, must win out, right? In other words, if men are truly inclined in a certain direction then, given freedom and with no roles assigned, won't they move in that direction? And doesn't the same go for women? Why, then, can't we let it be?

Jacob: "Let it be, oh let it be . . ." Now I understand what John Lennon was singing about! In response to your question, I would say that individuals will just "move in that direction" as much as any child grows up moving in some direction . . . without direction. To let children decide independently what and how to be in relation to life is, I believe, to let *someone else* socialize them. And there are plenty of other willing parties.

But that doesn't answer your question about the harm of leaving out gender roles in the teaching of children. That will require some more groundwork to be able to answer fully. For now, let me reiterate this general point: Absent the active teaching of what to be and how to live, Phil, I believe that individuals can lapse into ways of being that are *not* true to themselves. In this way, they can fail to reach their full potential as men or women.

Phil: So your thought, Jacob, is that our natures need to be supplemented by role prescription, that nature is not strong enough on its own? I have no problem with that as a general idea. But why do people (children and adults) need to be taught the specific things you speak of? Why do they need to be taught *gender* roles, not to mention the *particular* gender roles that you call for, whereby the man "presides," while the woman is the primary nurturer and allows her husband to preside over her? You make it sound like we have only two choices: either parents don't socialize their children *at all* or they socialize them into the gender roles prescribed by your faith community. Why not instead teach boys and girls alike to be, for example, good citizens, thoughtful friends, hard workers, and contributing community members?

Jacob: Another good question. . . and of course, we want these same things, Phil. Any of these are great lessons to be teaching anyone. I don't think they are contradictory to a plan that specifies a few distinctions as well.

But I'm noticing that you hint that this socialization in traditional gender roles is an unusual pattern and perhaps contrary to what is natural and sensible. To appreciate our position, please understand that we believe these roles reflect something quite inherent and natural about our identity.

And to your first question, yes, even though the tendencies are "built-in," we do believe they can be overridden by other socialization. This would not be unlike other common tendencies: to nourish our bodies, to get physical activity, or to sleep soundly—each of which are good for us, but can be thwarted by the rapid-fire, fast-food socialization around us. Just as we benefit from having certain guidelines and standards to shoot for in this realm (e.g., "get some exercise; taper off the Twinkies!"), so also relationship guidelines and standards can be helpful in either cultivating or discouraging certain tendencies.

Before turning it back over to you, let me just give one concrete example from my own family of the practical benefit of these complementary roles. Several years ago, three different members of my immediate family were diagnosed with cancer within a short period of time. Looking back on this experience, I often think about my dad. Even when all hell seemed to be breaking loose, he stayed calm and solid; he held it together—and frankly, he held us together too. He still got up and went to work every day. He kept his emotions in check and didn't cry (at least not in front of us). If Dad had crumbled, Phil—if he had broken down—I think our family could have broken up. What I would call his, yes, inherent masculine qualities were a part of that (less emotionality, more physical/emotional hardiness, etc.). And let me be clear about my mother. Was she also strong? Absolutely. But her most striking quality and contribution were the remarkable nurturing and care she provided during that time of need. While my father was protecting us from the storm, my mother was making sure there was enough warmth and love to go around. By my father's side, her own unique qualities (and role) had an equally important impact on our family.

Phil: Jacob, my condolences to you and yours, and my kudos for how you all handled the situation. But I must ask: do the different virtues exemplified by your mother and father provide an argument in support of gender roles? I don't see that they do. To be clear, I'm all for giving men the space to be the person your father was when the going got tough. I have no problem with men being strong, just as I have no problem with women being strong. Also, is it okay if dad is the one who offers the steadiness and unflappability, while mom offers warmth and love? Certainly it's okay! Parents don't need to be identical and shouldn't try, and I have no agenda to erase gender differences. What I *do* call for is letting each individual bring their unique combination of strengths to the table when they make the effort to be there for others in this or that unique situation. The gender *roles* idea, on other hand, says that the strength of your father, Jacob, is (as you say) an "inherent masculine" quality (not just something about him in particular) and that such strength should or will come from fathers in general. The gender roles idea also says that what your mother had to offer was not unique to her so much as what women in general have to offer and should aspire to. Why not leave it instead that loving is a virtue, and then let individual variations shine? I see no reason, in other words, to push each mom and dad toward a standardized specialization of virtue. I say that instead we should, as a society, give men and women alike the space to be strong in many, and in overlapping, ways. And I say also that you, Jacob, may be shrinking that space somewhat when you call the strength your dad mustered a set of "inherent masculine qualities."

Let me add this: even if women more often take to nurturance easily, isn't it good if men nurture? I think it's great. Men in history often have, and now often do, nurture well. Clearly they're capable of doing so, taken as a group. On the flip side, there are plenty of women in the world whose nurturing and parenting aptitudes and skills are minimal or wanting. So let's leave it that nurturance is generally speaking a good thing, whoever is doing it. And let's say also that those who are unable to offer the support of unconditional love may nonetheless possess other virtues, such as moral strength and steadfastness. Above all, let's not discourage men from caring for others by "assigning" them a different role, and let's not push women into roles of caring just because they are women. After all, don't children *benefit* when they have two caretakers who share parental duties in an overlapping and democratic, fashion?

Jacob: For heaven's sake, yes! Let's embrace individual variation and also encourage nurturing everywhere and with everyone. Of course, we would see nurturing as something men can and should do as well, Phil. Do men aspiring to be "protectors and providers" minimize their own nurturing capacity sometimes? Yes, I think you're right—some men do. If a man understands the spirit of these different roles, however, he won't. He will instead try to be an "equal partner" in sustaining and contributing to the nurture of his children, just as his wife sustains and supports him in providing for and protecting the same children.

Phil: Okay, so now help me to understand: What am I to make of the text you cite about it being the job of fathers to "protect" their families? Protect how? As far as I'm concerned, nurturance, which is said to be the role of the mother, is a form of protection. And can't a woman install a security alarm, or call the police, or argue with the elementary school principal as well as a man? Are those actions "nurturance" or "protection"? They seem to be both. I conclude that the passage cited as God's will is rooted in a prior form of society where "protection" was more about the possession of physical strength and personal prowess in battle. That concept seems to me to be irrelevant to most of today's families.

Jacob: Once again, without denying that women have the capacity to protect themselves well, this is simply a call for men to stand up in defense of their families. And yes, this certainly goes beyond the rifle-under-the-bed kind of protection to an even more important emotional and spiritual protection in the current world barraging us at every turn with another consumer materialist message (a kind of protection that, you bet, mothers do as well). Consider rates of eating disorders among women and the vast majority of women who dislike their bodies. Did you know that one of the major things that can prevent those problems is parents who counter those body image messages at home? That means a father and mother who, instead of just letting the television do all the teaching, reinforce a clear message in the home—for example by insisting to their daughters that, as one song puts it, "there will never be a more beautiful you."[3] That is a very practical example of a father and mother protecting their families as coequals.

Phil: Okay. I'm with that. But Jacob, aren't you changing your tune? Your first claim seemed to be that men should specialize as caretakers who provide the strength of hardiness and women should specialize in the provision of unconditional love. Yet your last statement defines the father's role so broadly that it's hard to distinguish from the provision of unconditional love, or for that matter from any other mode of being a loving parent. In other words, it seems to me that you're calling upon fathers *and* mothers to send the *same* message of love to their daughters. Are you, or are you not, calling for fathers to do one thing and mothers another? If not, then what do you mean by "gender roles"?

Jacob: There is still a distinction, Phil—but it is not as rigid as it looks from the outside. When we talk of an "equal partnership" between a mother and father, we really mean it—e.g., Dad doesn't leave dinner and bedtime stories just to Mom, and she contributes to providing where she can. Remember there is within these roles the flexibility and freedom to honor individual variation. But I think you're making a helpful point that perhaps we sometimes overstate the differences in these roles and do not emphasize the overlap and the importance of mutual support enough.

Having said this, there is something unique and crucial about a father's role in a family—a point that is growing increasingly clear to society, I think, as we observe the disheartening results of a long, national trend toward more homes where single mothers raise children. Can single mothers do amazing work and often raise competent, healthy children? Obviously, yes. But equally obvious is the fact that in many cases they simply can't or don't, due, in part, to physical exhaustion and human limits. The lack of complementary partnership surely adds to single mothers' difficulties as well. In some sense a mother and a father's teaching and socialization are unique and nonreducible to each other. A mother's assurances and counsel, for instance, provide socialization that is distinct in helping a child feel emotionally secure and "worth" something. And a father's direction and counsel have similarly distinct effects. I recently sat next to my two-year-old niece as she read a book about all of the Disney princesses. After finishing, she told me, "I know all their names—Jasmine, Ariel, Belle, Cinderella, and Sleeping Beauty." I then asked her, "What about you?" She smiled broadly before saying shyly, "Our daddy says we are real princesses."

Can my sister—her mother—send the same message? Yes, of course—and she does. Would it have the same effect, standing alone—to stabilize her daughter when a boy at school tells her she's fat or ugly? I think maybe not. In any case, when she comes home from school upset about a situation like this, both Mom and Dad can reinforce in their own unique and complementary ways the truth about who she is.

Phil: Jacob, if you're saying that fathers need to be deeply, regularly, and reliably involved in their children's lives, and also work closely with their children's mother so as to together send the children consistent messages of worth, then I couldn't agree more. But if you're saying that a return to traditional gender roles is the right way to respond to today's crisis of fatherly disinvolvement, then I strongly disagree. I suspect, in fact, that traditional gender ideals are part of the problem. How could that be, you ask? Well, what if fathers who *can't* preside or provide (e.g., because they lack adequate income or don't live with their children) respond by running away from their family responsibilities entirely, so as to avoid feelings of failure? In that case, don't we need a new model of fatherly responsibility, one that's compatible with today's economy, independence and equality for women, and families that live across multiple households?

By the way (and on another note), I agree with the claim—emphasized by some conservatives—that all previously existing societies have imposed gender roles to one degree or another. And there's no denying that ideas about "real" masculinity and "real" femininity are still expressed everywhere and also considerably internalized, to the point where men and women often freely choose to live up to them. Thus, it's reasonable for people—including those in your community—to read those facts as evidence in support of differential gender nature and gender roles. But I read them differently. As I suggested earlier, it could be that the gender roles we observe are the legacy of a distant time in human history, when the survival of the human species was more precarious and more dependent on the use of force against other animals. More specifically: humans were, in the distant past, very vulnerable to attack by other animals. And, once humankind became dependent on cooked food, the individuals who did the cooking for the group were presumably more vulnerable than those who did not. This may have led to a division of labor between "cooks" and "protectors." If so, it stands to reason that it was the men, on average bigger and more muscular than the women and with their hands free from holding nursing babies, who became the protectors. And, if that's how gender roles developed, isn't it reasonable to believe that there's no longer any good reason to maintain gender roles at this time? After all, humans have for centuries needed the protection provided by systems, groups, and ideas (e.g., money, police, high-tech agriculture, teachers, schools) more than they have needed the protection that physical prowess might provide. A person's security, in other words, now comes mostly from the strength of their national or regional economy, their class position, the quality and number of the weapons they possess, the degree to which the police or local warlords provide defense, the quality of the locks on their doors, and how much trust and mutual support (social capital) circulates in their community. So why do we need ancient gender roles?

Jacob: You're right that the world is much different now, Phil. And the level of physical danger faced (by most of us) is not the same as in the past. If the purpose of gender roles was primarily physical protection, I think I might harbor the same questions myself. As mentioned earlier, however, it is the mental, emotional, and social realms that currently call for nurturing and protection as much as anything physical—at least in this society. Indeed, as we discussed in chapter two, the media-saturated world has become even more dangerous, more emotionally and socially toxic, than it has ever been before. If so, the protection that these specialized functions provide any family is that much more crucial and necessary today.

And what about the past? To your depiction of human history, Phil, I can only highlight, again from an earlier conversation, the consequences of different "creation stories," if you will. Laying aside arguments for the practical value of traditional gender roles, a primary part of my assurance in this regard is a belief in an ancient precedent dating back to our first parents created by God. If I believed what you did about how humanity began (and as you know, I do not believe science has settled the question), then I could see myself coming to similar conclusions. It's interesting that one divergence in belief can be so linked to divergence in another set.

You also spoke about the crisis of absent fathers and whether or not traditional gender roles help or hurt. First, let's not exaggerate our differences here, Phil. Consider, for example, statements made by President Obama in his Father's Day talk in June of 2010. He began by speaking of the "vital role fathers play in the lives of our children" and went on to say: "Fathers are our first teachers and coaches—or in my house, assistant teachers and assistant coaches—to mom. . . . They're our mentors, our role models. They show us by the example they set the kind of people they want us to become." The president next outlined the problem: "We also know what too many fathers being absent means—too many fathers missing from too many homes, missing from too many lives." He then emphasized, "it's hard to live up to the lifelong responsibilities that come with fatherhood . . . it's a challenge even in good times, when our families are doing well." And, to your point about shouldering the burden, Phil, Obama then asked, "How can we as a nation—not just the government, but businesses and community groups and concerned citizens—how can we all come together to help fathers meet their responsibilities to our families and communities?"[4]

What surprised me and other conservatives, as well as many progressives, is that Obama didn't stop with calls for more external support. He went on to call on fathers themselves to stand up:

> Our children don't need us to be superheroes. They don't need us to be perfect. They do need us to be present. They need us to show up and give it our best shot, no matter what else is going on in our lives. They need us to show them—not just with words, but with deeds—that they . . . are always our first priority. Those family meals, afternoons in the park, bedtime stories; the encouragement we give, the questions we answer, the limits we set, the example we set of persistence in the face of difficulty and hardship—those things add up over time, and they shape a child's character, build their core, teach them to trust in life and to enter into it with confidence and with hope and with determination.[5]

I wanted to share this at length, Phil, because it sounds much like the sermons we regularly hear in a conservative religious congregation. While some conservatives were surprised by the tone of Obama's remarks, some progressives were also upset. The fact remains, however, that he is a full-fledged progressive and also cares about fatherhood. In short, his Father's Day talk illustrates nicely that liberal/conservative communities might not be that far apart on much of this. He pointed this out himself, in closing:

> Now, unfortunately, the way we talk about fatherhood in this country doesn't always reinforce these truths. When we talk about issues like child care and work-family balance, we call them "women's issues" and "mothers' issues." Too often when we talk about fatherhood and personal responsibility, we talk about it in political terms, in terms of left and right, conservative/liberal, instead of what's right and what's

wrong. And when we do that, we've gotten off track. So I think it's time for a new conversation around fatherhood in this country. We can all agree that we've got too many mothers out there forced to do everything all by themselves. They're doing a heroic job, often under trying circumstances. They deserve a lot of credit for that. But they shouldn't have to do it alone. The work of raising our children is the most important job in this country, and it's all of our responsibilities—mothers and fathers.[6]

Make no mistake, I disagree with plenty on President Obama's larger agenda. But as a conservative guy, it is pretty cool to hear our president talking like this!

Phil: Well said, Jacob. Well said, pastors in your sermons. And well said, President Obama. I am all for the message you send, that fathers should be there for their children. I did not, however, find in Obama's words any hint that the duties he calls upon fathers to perform are uniquely those of fathers, as opposed to mothers. Did I miss something?

Jacob: Right; Obama is obviously not saying mothers cannot do any of this. But he is pointing out an absence of fathers fulfilling *their roles*. Thus where you, Phil, see insufficient support for gender roles, I see confirmation that they are meaningful distinctions, but necessarily flexible.

Phil: Again, all I hear Obama saying is that each father should be a good *parent*. It's difficult to pin down exactly what it is you're asserting, Jacob. On the one hand you call for distinct roles, and on the other hand when I push back you define those roles very vaguely, to the point where they become indistinguishable. I'm sure you're not doing that as part of a conscious strategy to avoid criticism, but it does make it hard for me to agree or disagree with you.

Maybe it will help if I take a moment to summarize what I have tried to say thus far. I oppose gender roles but do not oppose gender itself, at least if the latter means simply that being "male" or "female" has a natural component, and that people will always make distinctions between the two. In other words, I favor more gender freedom, but do not hope for (or expect) the end of "men" and "women." Instead, what more gender freedom would provide is more playfulness about what counts as male and what counts as female, more equality of personal possibility, and more social room for hermaphrodites and people who are otherwise androgynous. In my book, all of those outcomes are desirable.

Jacob: You're right that I'm unwilling to go beyond general distinctions here, Phil. Other conservatives may be different. But for me, a gender role is not like other roles—like a job description, with specific guidelines of when to do this, and not to do this, etc. What you call vague, I will call flexible, general, and adaptable.

For example, when it comes to the details of the different responsibilities specified in gender roles for us (see chapter beginning), there's nothing about a woman's role being "shopping, cooking, cleaning, and mopping the floor." The standard is general and the key word is *nurturing*. The emphases for men being protectors and providers are similarly general.

And to your comments on androgyny, within certain boundaries, I would embrace the same spaciousness for difference, Phil. But when we question the value of promoting seemingly *any* norm around masculinity or femininity, this "playfulness" has gone too far—even to the point of making a standard out of no standard.

How can anyone be against "equal gender rights"?

Jacob: Whenever I start talking about different or unique roles, no matter my insistence on complementariness, the first image that comes to mind for many of my progressive friends is Jim Crow. Since "separate and equal" was indeed used to justify the oppression of African Americans, it is easy to conclude that *any* distinction between groups that does not preserve identical rights is automatically harmful or unfair. My question here has simply been: is it theoretically *possible* to have real differences in roles between two persons who love each other and for those differences to complement and bolster each other? As rudimentary as that sounds, I honestly don't sense that many people even believe that, Phil. They seem instead to assume that all observable differences are actually 1950s-style "hidden oppression" in action.

Phil: Who have you been hanging out with? None of my liberal or left-wing friends decry difference. On the contrary, they usually celebrate difference (a few of them in excess, in fact). More to the point, no one I know, or whose writing I have read, says that two parents who live together should each do 50 percent of a given family duty. And virtually no one on the left now assumes that someone is "oppressed" because they're a housewife, stay-at-home mom, or breadwinner man. Those assumptions are way out of date, having long ago been ripped apart by difference feminists, ecofeminists, and many others. There might be a few half-fossilized professors here and there around the nation who, along with a few ex-1960s activists, believe "all difference is oppression." Also, I'm not surprised to learn that a handful of wonderfully zealous graduate students have, thanks to courses taught by those out-of-date professors, cut their intellectual teeth on left-wing books that are over forty years old. Nonetheless, I stand firm: the idea of the "feminazi" who denounces all difference between men and women is a myth created by a well-funded right-wing political machine.

Jacob: If no liberal decries difference, Phil, with all due respect, what have you been doing through the first half of this chapter? You seem flatly uncomfortable with my suggestion there are complementary roles that befit men and women. In doing so, however, you've been helpful to point out exaggerated images that still have a life of their own. I hope you'll show the same willingness to puncture distortions about wealthy right-wingers.

Phil: Before I go there, Jacob, I first need to say that I don't understand how the issue of equal rights fits into your argument. "Rights" are claims about what treatment (and what zone of freedom) the law owes to individuals, not claims about what individuals should do with their legal freedom, or how much people will differ from one another if and when they enjoy those rights. And therefore, I can, without contradiction, champion equal rights for men and women *and* champion the appearance of differences when it comes to what the members of each gender actually do with their lives. Indeed, most people who call for equal rights expect the exercise of those rights to lead to different (and therefore unequal) results for different people.

I hope I'm beginning to make it clear that I do not decry difference. Instead, I merely call for equal rights and freedom from pressure to play this role or that. Whereas you, Jacob, seem to call for a distinction between men and women that "does not preserve identical rights" (your words earlier in the chapter). And that sounds to me like talk about what the law should be, not just what people's roles should be. So . . . what exactly do you mean? Do you think that society should maintain (or intensify) obstacles to women holding full-time jobs, as compared to men? Do you think that divorces should be made even more expensive, harder to get, and more enforcing of traditional gender roles? Do you think that people should get tax credits for living in what you call "traditional" families? Do you think that we should teach girls and women that they are born to be helpmeets and emotional servants to men? Do you think that single-parent, female-headed households and parents living as gay and lesbian couples should be cast as immoral and that that label should be reflected in law? You seem to think that society should somehow tell *individual* men and women what roles they should play in their relationships based on a particular theory of the differences between the *groups* they belong to. And that does seem to go beyond merely opposing sameness and into the territory of opposing equal rights. Perhaps, then, you could explain more exactly what it is that you favor.

And, before I let you speak to that, I need to voice a question that seems to be lurking here: are we, or are we not, now in a state of gender freedom, where expressions of gender reveal true underlying differences and/or preferences? You seem to think we are in such a state, whereas as in my view we're not. In my view, each one of us is subject to powerful gender expectations that function much like an old-fashioned system of explicitly mandated roles. These gender scripts are all the more powerful when they're not reflected on, or when the associated behaviors feel as if freely chosen. Boys are, for example, under more pressure than girls to be winners and wielders of power, while girls are under more pressure than boys to be beautiful and ornamental. There's steroid use in the gym by guys trying to look buff, Botox use by women trying to look younger and thus more "feminine," female politicians who get votes if they say they're in favor of traditional motherhood, and so on. These pressures and practices do real damage: some boys are tuned out at school, some girls never feel free in their own bodies, domestic violence becomes a way some men avoid feeling out of control and like a loser, and more.

Granted, the exact content of today's gender scripts is shifting and contested, and that increases the level of gender freedom, but by no means are those who consider gender roles oppressive in the political or cultural driver's seat.

Jacob: Good question! You're right about cultural constraints on gender, but wrong that conservatives don't see them as well. The real difference, perhaps, lies in what socialization you and I find concerning and what precisely we should seek "freedom" from in terms of gender. That part of gender socialization that tells a woman (and the men around her) she is merely an object for the use and pleasure of those around her is something that I think many, if not most, would condemn—from varied political backgrounds.

However, you seem to connect that aspect of gender socialization seamlessly to traditional gender roles, whereas I see them as coming from different sources entirely. In other words, the message taken by a man to serve his family as a provider and to protect and cherish his wife is *not* cut from the same cloth as the message to objectify, demean, hurt, or control a woman.

But your questions deserve even more than that, Phil. You've asked for clarification of what we mean by defending, as a community, a system of socializing men and women into roles that are admittedly nonidentical and qualitatively different.

Do we believe that society should present obstacles to women holding full-time jobs, as compared to men? No. But do we celebrate equally women and men with children holding full-time jobs outside of the home? No.

Do we believe that divorces should be harder to get for those who really need them (abused women, etc.)? No. Does that mean we should make sure that anyone tired of supporting his/her spouse and children should be able to get a no-fault, quick divorce? I wish not.

Do we believe that society should provide some kind of reinforcements like tax credits for traditional families? You bet. Does that mean any other families (e.g., single-parent or LGBT families) are evil and deserving of no help? Certainly not.

Do we think that girls and women should be taught they are born to be emotional servants to men? Absolutely not. As for the word, "helpmeet," commentators point out that the word as used in Genesis is better translated as two words, as in God providing a "help" who was "meet" for Adam—that is, a "good match" or an "appropriate fit." One scholar defined the term to mean "one equal in power." That is how I see my sweetheart, and I imagine it's similar to how you see yours.

Although there are plenty of intense issues to discuss, Phil, it seems to me that the most incendiary differences on this and other issues often survive on stereotypes and blanket statements, while real people live in nuance and complexity. While differences in our interpretations will continue to be real and numerous, I'm not convinced you are on Mars and I on Venus, or Jupiter, for that matter.

Phil: Well said. Perhaps we should for a moment return to a point that we seem to agree on, which is that it makes no sense to call for total freedom or oppose the presence of gender in any way, shape, or form. For one thing, humans are by definition always (and necessarily) less than totally free. All humans need, inherit, create, and recreate institutional structures and ideas that enable them to live but that constrain as well, and all human preferences are shaped by culture, rather than spontaneous inventions or purely individual phenomena. On the other hand, the fact that we can't be totally free doesn't mean that the limitations we now experience are necessary or just. Instead, there's plenty of imposition of gender difference that we would be better off without.

Are traditional gender roles oppressive?

Jacob: As we're finding out, you and I are in agreement that the culture around us is limiting on this issue, even as we interpret the nature and source of these constraints quite differently. While resonating with your focus on socialization and culture, I see that socialization as perhaps less monolithic and linear—and as moving in two opposing directions. Although I support expectations of traditional gender roles being consistently reinforced, I see another, quite destructive message being disseminated within the larger culture around us—one inviting men to live promiscuously, and women to fashion themselves into accommodating sex toys. Would you say a little more, Phil, about how you understand the relationship of these two streams of socialization?

Phil: Hmm . . . You ask a good question. I understand the two sets of messages you speak of as more or less two sides of the same coin. What I mean is that the sexualized gender we see around us is connected to the old gender ideal of male and female virtue and duty. Each of those gender worlds contains and expresses the same basic idea: that men are by nature promiscuous culture-makers in need of being directed toward morality by heading a family, whereas women are fulfilled by being objects of desire and are less capable of agency and societal leadership. These ideas, while very old, came to the fore in a new way when the industrial revolution required someone in almost every family to leave home in order to work for cash. The notion that formed was that the promiscuous energy of men could be channeled and made more moral if each man was in charge of and provided for a woman and their children. The woman would be the man's legal property and without sexual freedom, whereas the man would have access to prostitutes and mistresses. Women would be idealized as sexually desirable objects who contain their dangerous sexuality so as to be mothers and serve their husbands, and men would be idealized as promiscuous at heart but strong enough to make commitments and provide for and protect family members.

What you call two streams of socialization, then, can each be said to flow from a nineteenth-century idea of men and women, an idea that leads to a false choice between oppressing women as sex objects or "protecting" them by holding them up on a pedestal or making them property. In my view, sticking to that idea can only mean the failure of attempts to counter today's rampant sexualization. Sure, we can try returning to traditional gender roles and duties, but that will just re-present us with the same false choice. It will further feed the notion that men are promiscuous and women are sex objects.

Jacob: So to make sure I understand, are you arguing that traditional gender roles make assumptions similar to sexualized gender roles (e.g., that men are naturally promiscuous)? And that, by the same token, a return to traditional gender roles will likely only provide additional reinforcement to these tendencies?

Phil: Yes. But I can say this: a renewed emphasis on the idea that women are essentially mothers might reduce the pressure on women, or on some women, to be winner sex toys. But my thought in response is that it wouldn't thereby *challenge* the sex-toy idea as the basis of womanhood *in relation to* men. More to the point, it would at best give women only two boxes to choose from (mom or slut), and why settle for that? Of course women are often mothers, and as far as I'm concerned that's fine. Many women find great fulfillment in motherhood. I'm not against motherhood! But there are other women who find fulfillment without being married or being mothers, and isn't that great as well?

Please note, Jacob, that I'm *not* using the loaded word "oppressive" to characterize roles. All roles limit freedom, but only some roles are oppressive. Gender roles certainly *can* be oppressive, but aren't necessarily so. What I believe is that, given the incredible power of the call of gender, we don't need to pile role socialization on top of nature. And I also believe that existing, traditional gender roles are by no means the best ideals we can imagine and offer to the world's boys and girls. We can do better.

When it comes to the socialization of men and women, why not, once again, encourage all of them to be nurturing, caring, and protective of others, and leave it at that? Why not teach everyone that fulfillment in life fundamentally includes taking on obligations to significant others, to specific children, and to future generations. Isn't that what's really needed?

Jacob: As I think you know, I like the idea of teaching everyone the value of such nurturing and caring. Your suggestion that traditional gender roles are on the "other side of the coin" of sexualized gender roles, however, lays bare some of our deeper disagreements. Rather than the same coin, I see traditional gender roles as reflecting a whole different currency, with a different ruler, in a different kingdom—when compared to the hypersexualized, objectifying gender roles being preached by that little black box residing in all of our homes.

One of the factors continuing to fuel our disagreement, Phil, might be meaningful variants of "traditional gender roles": qualitative distinctions in *how* different men enact authority, only some of which have been broached to this point. When you hear me speaking highly of traditional gender roles, you might be tempted to think I'm defending anyone who has ever claimed to a patriarchal right to "rule" in his home. This would be, of course, to defend innumerable abusive fathers and battering husbands who happen to justify their oppression through lame references to some biblical mandate. To cluster all applications of traditional gender roles in the same basket will understandably lead to throwing them all out.

Even so, Joseph Smith once acknowledged, with some regret, "We have learned by sad experience that it is the nature and disposition of almost all men, as soon as they get a little authority, as they suppose, they will immediately begin to exercise unrighteous dominion" (i.e., abuse their power). He goes on, then, to assert this: "No power or influence can or ought to be maintained by virtue of [sheer authority], only by persuasion, by long-suffering, by gentleness and meekness, and by love unfeigned; by kindness, and pure knowledge."[7] The point is this: in spite of many bad examples of poor patriarchs and abusive husbands or fathers, this role can be enacted in beautiful and profoundly helpful ways, Phil! Discussions of internalized oppression and subtle dominance aside, we believe in the real possibility of loving and uplifting power exercised by both men and women acting out their unique, individualized roles, with complementary, ultimately synergizing effects.

What kind of gender roles are we talking about?

Jacob: I hope you'll indulge me on a few more crucial aspects of this issue. I find it curious that we often talk about traditional gender roles as if it were a unified concept that we all understood. My advisor, Nicole Allen, recently finished a paper entitled "Gender as Ecology: One Understanding of Men's Use of Violence against Women"—an excellent essay that examines the nuanced role of gender in violence. Prior to publication, she requested my feedback, and one thing that caught my eye was a paragraph where she described a recent study that examined boys' use of violence against girlfriends: "Violence was used as a means of compensation when there was a threat to masculinity, and it was clear that the expression and maintenance of masculinity was tied to violence and domination. This does not necessarily imply that being boys *makes* boys more violent, but that such displays of violence may be a venue by which masculinity is expressed."[8]

My response was to make two small edits to her words as follows (with my additions in bold): "Overall, the author concluded that for these boys, violence was used as a means of compensation when there was a threat to masculinity, and it was clear that the expression and maintenance of **a particular vision of** masculinity was tied to violence and domination. This does not necessarily imply that being boys *makes* boys more violent, but that such displays of violence may be a venue by which **a certain brand of** masculinity is expressed."

My point, Phil, was that the "ideal man" being characterized in this paragraph is based on one version of masculinity, rather than masculinity itself. Whether we call it "hypermasculinity" or "distorted masculinity," this reflects a substantial, qualitative departure from what I believe it means to "be a man." One could just as easily articulate another version of masculinity that is violated by expressions of violence—i.e., a man who controls his own behavior, one who genuinely respects and values women, etc. In the absence of these distinctions, Phil, masculinity may be framed as some kind of a uniform monolith that deserves to be categorically held in suspicion or contempt.

Phil: Bravo, Jacob. I couldn't agree more. When I say that we don't need gender roles, I mean that we should minimize the degree to which we socialize boys and girls into a gendered division of labor and identity and we should emphasize that there are many valid ways to be a gendered and moral person. I don't mean that we need to abolish (or that we ever could abolish) masculinity and femininity. And yes, there are many versions of masculinity (and thank you, early Christianity, for challenging the Roman idea of the warrior man with the Jesus idea of a peaceful family man who is good to women).

Jacob: Thank you again, Phil. I would make similar arguments about patriarchy, which is now commonly defined as a belief system that supports the victimization of women. The reality is that, as with masculinity, patriarchy varies meaningfully in its manifestations across cultures. And as I said,

I know many families where a man and woman stand as genuinely equal partners, but with unique and complementary roles that reflect some patriarchal distinctions.

I would advocate, in short, for acknowledging meaningful distinctions that can exist in how masculinity and patriarchy are both practiced and framed. Yes, in a world where men are still far too likely to be abusing any power given to them, let's not be naïve and close our eyes to reality. And yet, as illustrated by my family's story earlier, religious conservatives still want to preserve some of the meaning that is carried by each of those terms (and the associated gender roles), as not only defensible, but—when approached in the right heart and spirit—complementary and healthy.

Phil: I hear what you're saying and, as I said, I do at least agree that some ideas of masculinity are better than others.

If oppression is often linked to traditional gender roles, why not "upgrade" them?

Phil: You emphasize, Jacob, that conservatives won't abandon traditional gender roles because there's a possibility of them being positive. Could you still be denying the larger reality of how they now play out so negatively?

Jacob: Perhaps in isolation, my comments may sound like a defense of ideas that have been used to justify much harm. In light of so many instances of men abusing their position to hurt their wife and children, you're right that an adequate defense of gender roles needs to go beyond the mere *possibility* of abuse not happening—to more positive reasons for this model. And doing so adequately requires me to share something that our community considers sacred—a conviction we discuss only with great care and reverance.

You heard me say in an earlier chapter that we believe God did not create man and woman out of nothing. Instead, we believe that our existence is a continuation of a previous existence where we lived in the presence of Heavenly Parents. Although we are asked to pray to "our Father in Heaven," from the early days of my faith community there has existed a treasured awareness that He does not work alone:

In the heavens are parents single?
No; the thought makes reason stare!
Truth is reason; truth eternal
Tells me I've a Mother there.[9]

Notice that this idea is quite different from the more common idea that God has a "feminine side." In addition to having these gender roles modeled for us before coming to earth, we believe we also have them in our "spiritual DNA" as it were, as children of our Heavenly Parents. Perhaps this is why the role of a mother seems to make sense intuitively for many, if not most women.

In short, it is through these family relationships that we ultimately become more like our Heavenly Father (and Mother). For my faith community, this is the whole point of our experience here on earth.

Phil: Isn't there anything you would want to change about traditional gender roles, Jacob?

Jacob: You bet. As mentioned in my comment about cleaning, cooking, and mopping, I think many marriages could benefit from openly talking about the nature of their expectations of each other—thereby helping to balance out the weight of responsibilities and finding ways to support each other more powerfully.

In previous generations, I do think families interpreted traditional gender roles as "Mom does the cooking and cleaning," which left a sizeable, and yes, sometimes oppressive burden on her. I know of some families where that still happenes, and would hope they someday realize that mothers are not household slaves whose purpose is to do everything that no one else wants to do! As I mentioned earlier, we see this as an unfortunate and unhealthy overstatement of the essence of the distinction, which should instead center on nurturing as a unique role for women.

Let me ask you the parallel question, Phil. Do you see anything *worthwhile* in traditional gender roles that you think is worth preserving?

Phil: Well . . . I don't want men like your father to stop being good dads in the best way they can, or to cease doing whatever is in keeping with the needs of their family at a given time. But what has that got to do with whether or not we should teach, or otherwise enforce, different *roles* for men and women? I say let's discard the latter, while also permitting each man and woman to draw on their unique and personal strengths in their various family situations.

Jacob: So your primary concern is with the general, blanket insistence on these roles ("for everyone")—rather than saying they are "bad" for anyone?

Phil: Right. Notwithstanding your explanations, that's still what I see a "role" is—a blanket insistence (or at least a set of social pressures). Let me say it this way: my understanding is that in your family the acting out of traditional gender roles worked in a powerfully good way, so I don't want a society where that doesn't happen anymore. What I want is a society that doesn't tell people that the way *your* family divided the emotional labor is the best way for families *in general*.

Jacob: What if that means fewer and fewer families attempt a model like my childhood family, Phil? Isn't that what is happening in our country right now—and will continue to happen, as long as the main gender role socialization for American families is one hour of *Family Guy*, et al. every evening? Having said this, it seems to me that neither of us is calling for the *Family Guy* standard, nor oversexualized or abusive standards. Instead, our disagreement seems to be primarily how intensely or absolutely to promote one particular standard.

On the other end of it, our gender expectations may not be that far apart either. I mean, come on . . . compared to abusive men or oversexualized women, we are talking about nurturing parents with some degree of standards and mutual support of each other in supporting the family, right? Is not the difference between our different gender role standards much less than that between either of ours and the media norms?

Phil: Putting aside the *Family Guy* for a moment, yes, we agree in some ways, and I'm glad for it. But big differences remain. For sure we both favor "nurturing parents" and oppose a culture of instant gratification, but who doesn't? Also: while I sincerely believe that you don't see yourself as asking for anything "extreme," I disagree. I think that what you and other conservatives ask for would roll back rights for women in a big way, penalize millions of men and women who want to live in relationships of equality that don't happen to fit your particular vision of being equal, lead people to stay in relationships they ought to get out of, and encourage the stigmatization of single parents, breadwinner moms, and gay couples who are good parents, loving partners, and good citizens.

Just to give one example, the vision you celebrate is linked to the notion that what truly fulfills women is to live vicariously through the success of others, in short to be sacrificial. More specifically, the nurturance idea is linked to women working fewer hours (for pay) than their partners and/or interrupting their careers for long enough to irreparably reduce their income-earning potential. This means, as I said earlier, that adherence to the nurturance idea would place many women in relationships from which they would have less "feasibility of exit" than their partner. In other words, many women would lack the income potential needed to leave a bad marriage, or at least be less able to leave than their partner, and that would put them at a distinct power disadvantage. Many women would, moreover, *believe* that they should stay with their partner no matter what. After all, their "job" is to love, serve, and sacrifice.

Some might answer that your ideal includes virtuous husbands as well as virtuous wives. Well . . . that's all well and good, but it's not always reality. And in any case, equality within a relationship is hard to maintain unless each partner has approximately the same ability to leave—even if neither one of them ever leaves.

Also: it needs to be said that what you call for is, for better or worse, nothing less than a serious revision of the individualism that's a central part of modernity. That's because what you call for defines individual fulfillment in terms of one's role in a collective and (hopefully) virtuous community (by which I here mean both the family and the wider community). Modernity, on other hand, has been built around the idea that each individual deserves—and benefits from—having some room to move (both literally and when it comes to self-definition and expression) relative to the communities they depend on. Is that aspect of modernity all bad? I don't think so.

Jacob: We're certainly not championing family at the expense of individualism, Phil. If anything, we see healthy, loving family atmospheres as the best place for individuals to grow, be happy, and reach their highest potential, when compared with other environments. These gender roles, understood as part of that picture, are intuitive and natural, rather than false, synthetic impositions. The problem is perhaps that we're not teaching (or being taught) well enough how to fulfill these roles virtuously. But to be clear, individuals remain free to adopt these roles in their own way, or not at all. So don't be too aggressive in your characterization of our presumed extremism.

That industrialization was hard on families and led to many negative sequelae is clear—just as clear as the sad realities you point to, wherein many men use these traditional role distinctions to systematically oppress women. I just finished a research project where we interviewed citizens about attitudes toward domestic violence. Consistent with the national and international survey literature, we found ten different ways that individuals were minimizing and discounting violence, including references to family relationships being sacred and "not something I should interfere with."[10] I agree that a clear message needs to be sent to all women, that divorce in an abusive marriage is not merely what they *can* do—it is what they *should* do.

Phil: Let me ask, then, is what you call for possible in the way you imagine it? In my view, the individualism I just described (I don't mean total license) is something people are deeply committed to and aren't about to give up. Also, that individualism is now built both into our capitalist economic structures and the ideas expressed by those structures, with their celebration of each individual making voluntary exchanges that benefit him or her. So, while we might modify the version of individualism that prevails, and in fact ought to do so, individualism itself is not going to go away. And so one could ask: what will happen, in that context, if women are again defined as the primary nurturers, as the ones whose job it is to temper individualism with love? I think that what will happen would not be good for women. And it would not be good for men and women who want to live together in relationships of equality.

Now, about *Family Guy*: a good friend of mine likes the show, so I tried to like it. Well . . . I just can't do it; I find the jokes not at all funny and I get bored fast, and there's lot of campy pseudo-violence that I find objectionable. But what's so terrible about its depiction of gender roles? Granted, there's much about the dad/hero that's less than admirable—e.g., his bouts of stupid selfishness, akin to those of Homer Simpson. But his moral dumbness is supposed to be funny precisely because it's dumb; what's supposed to be likable is how sweet and harmless he is when he's dumb. Thus, the way I see it, selfishness on the part of men is not being praised. And the mom on the show seems to be loving and forgiving, all in all. I would, in fact, go so far as to say that, if *Family Guy* deserves any gender critique at all, it deserves it for reinforcing traditional gender roles, in that the mom is more of the civilizing force in the family (improving her husband with love) and dad is the agent, meaning the one who acts in public and "gets things done," even if those things are often dumb. So what exactly is the gender problem you see, Jacob?

Jacob: Mocking fathers, Phil. Making them out to be imbeciles who are "civilized" by their wives, and otherwise act like animals. That may sound strong . . . but consider any of the contemporary sitcoms—any of them. Compare them with *The Cosby Show*—where Mr. Huxtable was still funny, but also sat down and counseled his kids wisely and kindly. On a media website, one consumer writes, "Does anyone else notice how American men are depicted as stupid and lazy in an extreme amount of movies and sitcoms these days? It's everywhere in commercials now too . . . dads depicted as slacking off and procrastinating, and it's so pervasive in television that nobody even notices it anymore."[11]

I would like to conclude here with a suggestion of what is perhaps our most important agreement on this issue, Phil. At a minimum, you and I might agree that society would benefit if liberals and conservatives were to talk and listen to each other on the subject of how best to understand, and perhaps improve, gender roles. But if this is true and such discussion needs to be had, it's worth asking, why aren't we-the-people having it? Why did it take till now—after years of school and research—to finally talk in depth with someone like you, Phil? My own feeling is that it relates to problems in the way our discourse is typically framed and "served up" to each of us. In a paper on this topic that I wrote with Nathan Todd, a progressive colleague at DePaul University, we suggest a needed "shift in public conversation from *whether* to change or not (the amount or quantity of change), to *what kind* of change is needed (the quality of this change)." We illustrated our point with gender roles:

> Rather than perpetually debating, for instance, *whether* to change or preserve traditional gender norms (a framing which effectively permits only two viable options: "change traditional gender roles" vs. "keep traditional gender roles the same"), conversation might be resituated to consider *how* or *what* aspects of particular norms or standards ought to be preserved, as well as what aspects could be modified. . . . From such a place, conservative citizens might consider more seriously aspects of traditional gender roles needing revision and liberal citizens, those perhaps deserving of some preservation.[12]

In other words, Phil, if we simply ask the right questions our communities will be more likely to unearth agreements on at least some important issues. You and I, for example, each find fault with the strong cultural message that the worth and role of women derives largely from their appearance—what one writer called "lookism."[13] And thus opposing that message might be something progressives and conservatives could do together.

Phil: I see your point about changing the questions we ask and seeing how that opens up our discussions to new possibilities. And you're right: we agree that people should be prized for their minds and hearts, not for their status as ornaments or instrumental utility to others. Maybe, then, we should conclude this discussion right here, so we can savor this piece of common ground.

5

SEXUAL ORIENTATION BATTLES: CAN WE DISAGREE AND NOT HATE EACH OTHER?

November 4, 2008, California: Proposition 8, a state referendum defining marriage as "one man and one woman" passed by a narrow margin, thereby becoming law. Many citizens, upon reading the news online, posted feelings in response:

"It's a sad day for the Constitution of the United States and the principles of individual liberty upon which this nation was founded. Who would have guessed that religious bigotry and fascism would prevail over the principles of liberty in America? I am saddened and sickened."

"This is a great triumphant day for morality and decency . . . in spite of the hatred, lies, and anti-religious bigotry. Family values have prevailed. . . . The line has been drawn and the voice of the people heard!"

"Shame on Proposition 8 supporters! . . . Stop placing empty principles ahead of people. This is intolerance, plain and simple! . . . Two consenting adults should be able to choose who they want to marry. Down with proposition 8!"

"With respect to Prop 8 passing . . . Hallelujah, Hallelujah!"

"It makes me sad that discrimination of a person's sexual orientation is considered acceptable . . . a sad day for California. Stop obsessing about what other people do and don't do in their bedrooms. . . . Leave people alone in their choices that do not affect you."

"Nice job California!! Passing Proposition 8 isn't a 'Mormon thing' or a 'Christian thing' but a 'right thing'! . . .Marriage is sacred, and we as humans need to get back to treating it as such."[1]

The depth of intensity and disagreement could hardly be more profound. Where one side declares a triumph of inspired virtue, the other side decries an instance of cruel oppression. Where one side sees bigotry, hatred, and shame reflected in the legislation, the other side defends its morality, decency, and sacred warrant. When someone comes to identify as lesbian, gay, bisexual, or transgendered (LGBT), internal rift and division within the person's family is common, and the personal and community heartache can be immense. What are we to make of such conflict? Is the intensity of disagreement and hard feeling inevitable and impossible to avoid? Are the differences unbridgeable? Do we have a cultural or sociocivil war on our hands?

Without equivocation, we answer . . . *yes and no*. On one hand, there is no denying that differences on this issue are intense, real, and often painful. It is not clear that a satisfying compromise resolution is possible, nor will dialogue on the subject likely ever be easy. On the other hand, people on both sides frequently use rhetoric that frames questions in stark, black-and-white terms that predispose animosity from the get-go. Could a move toward more genuine listening improve the situation, even if intense disagreement remains?

In 1994, after months of stark opposition and national tension over the abortion issue, a fatal shooting took place at a Boston clinic where abortions were performed. After that incident, leaders of pro-choice and pro-life movements in the area reluctantly accepted an invitation from the Public Conversations Project (PCP) to come together in a series of private dialogues. Although the resulting discussions did not change substantive views on either side, all participants spoke of surprise at discovering the humanity of others involved. This softening of relationships, in turn, led to a different tenor of activism in the Boston area, and to some concrete results as well. For instance, pro-life leaders, in an effort to defuse tension, decided to cancel a planned speech by a controversial right-wing speaker.[2] That changes such as these could happen, even when intense differences remained, surprised participants and observers alike. In the words of the PCP, "Shifts happen!"

President Obama, pointing toward this same abortion issue in a 2010 commencement speech at Notre Dame, called upon warring parties to recognize that, while their differences may be irreconcilable at some level, there was no need to "demonize" each other. He went on to suggest, moreover, that if they could move beyond "old ruts" in discussion, they might learn to coexist in new ways and discover surprising areas of common ground.[3] Based on our experiences discussing our differences about sexual orientation, we believe the same potential exists on that issue. Don't take our word for it, though—read on and see for yourself.

Isn't this just a matter of offering acceptance?

Jacob: I've often heard individuals claim that the questions posed by Proposition 8 and homosexuality are fairly clear and simple. For instance, members of conservative religious communities are sometimes challenged on this issue with queries such as "Shouldn't you love others for who they are?" or "Can't you truly accept others who are different?" Such language is understandable because the issue of sexual orientation is intimately linked with identity itself. When individuals first publicly state came out and that they identify as gay or lesbian, they typically make conclusive statements about their selfhood and identity, i.e., presenting being gay or lesbian as connected to the core of who they are. It makes sense, then, Phil, that any criticism of those self-understandings would be difficult to hear. At a minimum, religious conservatives could better recognize how painful certain kinds of language can be and speak out against tasteless jokes, epithets of disgust, and aggresive condemnations. Respecting an individual's choice to identify as gay or lesbian is something basic that conservatives can do.

Having said this, Phil, some activists would ask religious conservatives to do much more. For these, showing respect and love is not enough; until conservatives also accept an individuals' own views and beliefs about themselves they are somehow being intolerant.

Perhaps what those activists do not understand is that for us, doing what they ask is no small thing. I was once asked to explain why the Church of Jesus Christ believed what it did about sexual orientation during a weekly "diversity seminar" in graduate school. I said in response, "The first thing you need to understand is that our focus on the traditional family is not about hating or fearing those in the LGBT community or believing what we do just 'because the Bible says so.' Instead, our endorsement of the traditional family comes from a core belief that we are children of a God who we see as our literal parent—or, more precisely, our parents: two divine beings who were and are the actual Father and Mother of our spirits. For that reason, the traditional family is, for us, more than a 'social construct' developed at some point in history. The family institution is a reflection of our *own identity*—who we see ourselves to be on a fundamental level. Creating and cultivating this kind of family and home, then, is one of the most powerful ways that we can become more like our Heavenly Parents."

Social conservatives are sometimes asked why they can be so concerned with something like defining marriage, when society is faced with issues such as climate change, racism, or the economy. One answer, as reflected in earlier conversations as well, Phil, is that questions of gender, sexuality, and family are deeply connected to the purpose of life, as we see it. I would argue that our self-understandings and core identity as a people are as closely connected to these questions, as they are for the LGBT community.

Granted, the ideas I shared with my classmates are those of a particular faith, that of the Church of Jesus Christ of Latter-Day Saints. And while many other Christians and conservative religionists likewise embrace monogamous heterosexual marriage as the proper form of adult intimate relationships, they of course do so based on somewhat different ideas about God and human nature. From all these points of view, however, embracing an LGBT person's view of their own identity—however personally and passionately held it is—is no simple question of tolerance or acceptance, as in "If the conservatives would just be more accepting, everything would be resolved." Across different traditions providing the asked-for acceptance would essentially require conservatives to revise some of their core convictions about identity and purpose.

In my view, the deep identity disagreement just described is primarily what drives many of the larger societal disputes on legal and civil questions surrounding this issue. That is, for those who see the coming out of a person as LGBT as essential to embracing their true identity, campaigns to promote greater public acceptance are therefore seen as crucial and healthy, with dissenting efforts alternatively viewed as backward and intolerant. However, for those who see coming out as acting contrary to that individual's true, ultimate identity, campaigns to promote greater public acceptance of homosexuality are therefore seen as troubling and unhealthy for society, with efforts to oppose these initiatives likewise viewed as crucial.

Once again, the broader national conversation has taken for granted, at times, that the question to be asking when it comes to this issue is "Do you accept my identity as I understand it?" I would instead encourage attention to a more nuanced question: "What is the *nature* of identity?" or "*Which* view of identity do you embrace?" That approach would make room for further questions that lie at the heart of today's debate: e.g., "Is identity fixed?" "Is identity chosen?" and "Do humans possess an authentic God-given identity?" In other words, rather than insisting on only *one* legitimate way of thinking about identity in relation to same-sex attraction, the approach acknowledges that there are *competing* views of identity currently vying for acceptance.

Phil: Well . . . Based on what you have said thus far, Jacob (and you have said a lot) my guess is that we're not going to agree on much in this chapter. I strongly believe in equally including LGBT individuals and homosexuality itself into our society and our culture. Also, as far as I'm concerned, the evidence is overwhelming: homosexuality is a natural disposition; it's a harmless, healthy variation in human desire; it's a form of love just as good as any other; and it's something that appears in every human population in relatively fixed percentages. In other words, gays and lesbians really are gays and lesbians, all the way down.

Let me begin, then, with areas where we perhaps *do* agree. First: yes, the issue is not as simple as "just be more accepting." After all, no one will disagree that there are *some* human behaviors that should not be "accepted" regardless of whether or not they are a result of someone's "identity." For example, if it were part of my identity to kill randomly, that would not justify me doing so. If a given behavior is truly wrong then it's wrong. And therefore if you think that homosexual love is somehow wrong, then it doesn't make sense, nor would it be fair, for me to respond by simply saying "come on, Jacob, be more accepting." I also respect the fact that your position is rooted in your beliefs, not merely in your "attitude." Accordingly: I don't expect it to be easy for you, or for others, to overcome the centuries of tradition and culture that declare homosexuality to be unnatural, a sin, against God's wishes and design, and so on.

I also agree that there are competing views of identity in play in our society. You believe, for example, that there's an original, God-given and God-sanctioned pre-birth identity and lifestyle that humans need to recreate in order to achieve authentic self-fulfillment. Likewise, many defenders of gay and lesbian relationships make their claims using the language of identity, tolerance, and/or acceptance, just as you say.

On the other hand, we disagree about all-important details. I see being gay or lesbian as a disposition and physical fact, rather than something that can be done away with. And, I also see it as essentially just like heterosexuality when it comes to its value as a way of being and acting in the world. So as far as I'm concerned, it poses no threat.

Perhaps I should explain a little more about identity. I realize that some LGBT individuals speak about the issue of their acceptance using the language of identity, but in my view that should not be taken to mean that being gay or lesbian is an identity in the same way that some people "identify" with—say—a political party, an urban area, or a particular hobby. Those latter examples all imply an element of choice. But for millions of gays and lesbians from around the world and over the centuries, their homosexuality is something they discover, not something they choose. It's only after that discovery that the issue of identity comes in. Some who discover homosexuality within themselves deny it throughout their lives. Some muddle through with a combination of acceptance and denial, perhaps by leading a double life. And some kill themselves in the face of the travail they experience. Fortunately, more and more gays and lesbians instead come to fully identify as homosexual. And those who do that and also come out of the closet are surely the most likely of the entire bunch to be healthy and happy.

Jacob: That is indeed one place we disagree, Phil. This is the point at which people dig in their heels to debate the meaning of depression and suicide statistics within the LGBT community. I'm not interested in doing that, since the same thing happens among observers of the Mormon community, with mention of the numbers often functioning (in both cases) as verbal attacks. What I can say is that my friends who openly identify as gay and lesbian show plenty of real love and happiness reflected in their lives. As with anyone, of course, they sometimes face emotional sorrow as well. I am aware, for instance, of the heartache they can experience from scorn, disgust, and hostile condemnations from some individuals around them.

Having said all this, from both my theology and my personal reading of the data, I am not convinced there isn't even greater happiness to be found by these friends in following other directions. This brings me to a second point. All aspects of identity, from masculinity to religiosity to race, involve some meaningful degree of intentionality. This includes those who identify as gay or lesbian. I'm not talking about the silly contention that being gay is a simple choice: "Gee, I think I will be gay today." Instead, I'm referring to the implicit and ongoing contribution of one's own intentionality to an evolving persona and being. In other words, we cannot escape directing, to some degree, our own self-understanding and identity.

Phil: When I speak of an "identity," Jacob, I, like you, am speaking of something that is created, even if also something no one person has control over. More exactly: while every person has identities handed to them by the society around them, every person also has *some* say in how they deal with what's handed to them. All in all, I see identity as the result of an ongoing process of gathering up possibilities and using them to define oneself in relation to other people and other things. Thus every identity necessarily incorporates history and culture as reflected in language, symbols, institutions, rules, and the like. In other words, by my lights there's simply no such thing as *authentic* identity. And as a result, the language I use to talk about LGBT issues leans less on the idea of protecting authentic identities than on the idea that there's simply nothing wrong, harmful, or unnatural about homosexuality.

The idea of authentic identity is, moreover, dangerous. That's because it can be, and has been, used to justify oppressive attacks on existing identities, as in the missionary schools that were used to tear apart Native American families and Native American culture, the Cultural Revolution in Maoist China, reeducation camps in 1970s Vietnam, psychological prisons in the Soviet Union of the same time period, and so on. Granted, when that has happened it's been because people combined the idea of authenticity with other dangerous ideas such as "the laws of history," "revolutionary consciousness," "civilization," and "the white man's burden." Nonetheless, I find the idea of authenticity scary in and of itself; I think it's best to stay away from thinking that people have some sort of real or true self that lies hidden and that needs to be brought out by others.

This of course brings me, Jacob, to your creation story. To me, yours is just one of many stories invented by humans and as such it bears the marks of everything else human: point of view, culturally formed desire, political ideas, inherited visions of the good, and so on. For example, you call your preferred family form "traditional," when in fact many other family forms also have a long and venerable history, even in Mormon communities of the past.

Also—and I'm sure you have gleaned this already—to me your creation story has a dangerous side. To be clear, I have the utmost respect for you, for your intentions, and for the intentions of your faith community. But think about it from my point of view. You say that humans have an original identity and even an original pre-historical family and that this reality is available only to a few humans via revelation. Can you think of a more perfect mechanism by which some people might take their merely human ideas about how people ought to live and get others to believe in them?

Jacob: Let me interject to clarify a misunderstanding here. The experience of gaining assurance from God is an experience not reserved to a select group, but something available to everyone and anyone willing to be taught in God's subtle, no-drama way. In a culture where fewer and fewer individuals even care to read, let alone pray or ponder, this is no small condition. But even if you don't believe us, don't misunderstand us—as ecclesiastical epistemologies go, ours is radically egalitarian.

In the absence of such deep and abiding confirmations available to every individual, trusting in authorities who claim to speak for God, I would agree, can be dangerous. By contrast, when each individual relies on his or her own calm, enduring witness, there is protection from the kind of mindless following of authority often seen in religious communities. The very process of conversion itself, for us, cannot happen through unilateral manipulation. It requires authentically free and informed choice.

Phil: Fair enough, Jacob. What if I suppose, however, that humans do indeed have an original, divine family? Suppose even that it offers the model of family and sexual behavior you say it offers? In that case the question of authority arises that we discussed in chapter 1. Why should people shape their lives according to that divine model? Maybe they should improve on it? I know that my parents did the best they could and that in many respects they did well. And I'm grateful to them. But their power and position in my life don't tell me if their beliefs and practices were right. And that leads me to ask why God is any different. Perhaps, however, I said enough about that issue in our first chapter.

Jacob: You make me laugh sometimes, Phil: "Even if God exists, *who says he can tell me what to do?!*" You're right, of course, that just because someone lives a certain way—however venerable that person is—doesn't mean you or I "have to" do the same. Even if a certain choice will lead to a child's greatest happiness, we all know that parents who force or pressure their child in a certain direction are violating that child's basic freedom to choose.

How is biology involved in sexual orientation?

Jacob: While identity might be the most intense question at hand, the biological question seems the most often debated. Yet as with the issues of acceptance and choice, I think the way the discussion is typically framed predisposes confusion and debate. Let me explain.

In the current national discourse, it has become common to hear discussion about whether homosexuality is "biological" or not, setting up two distinct camps supposedly locked in inevitable conflict—i.e., "born this way" vs. "not born this way." In my dissertation research, this same dichotomy was observed differentiating people's narratives of depression: "it's biological" vs. "it's not biological." Not only does this popular nature-nurture dichotomy leave little room for meaningful distinctions *within* each position, it seems to overlook the clear evidence that rich biological processes are connected to many areas of our lives (as articulated beautifully in the writings of philosopher Maurice Merleau-Ponty). Simply put, anything we do we do in a body.

For this reason, Phil, I would argue that "to be or not to be biologically based" is *not*, in fact, the question to be explored—and that we might instead move to another question—one destined to make individuals on each side of the issue uncomfortable: *how and in what ways is homosexuality (and any other human experience) influenced by biology?*

For starters, conservatives should recognize that the particular state of a person's neural network/brain configuration is increasingly understood by researchers to play a role in what that person feels and desires at that time and whether or not he/she experiences inclinations in a particular direction. Therefore, rather than asserting that "homosexual feelings are entirely, freely chosen" or that "homosexual behavior is simple to avoid," Christians and other religious individuals can perhaps better acknowledge that current inclinations in many areas of life are often connected to particular, present states of the brain. And this recognition, to be clear, is not necessarily a threat to conservative religious theology.

Indeed these neuroscience discoveries over recent decades have revealed some interesting middle ground on the issue. As mentioned in an earlier chapter, neuroscientists now know that adult brains change over time, a phenomenon known as neuroplasticity (with "plastic" reflecting the notion of "malleability"). The brain changes, for example, when individuals learn a language, receive cognitive-behavioral therapy, or start a meditation practice.[4]

Other discoveries in genetics convey the same point—that the body is more changeable than had been thought. Granted, the precise extent of this malleability and the boundaries that surely exist are not known at this time. At a minimum, however, the latest knowledge unsettles prior ways of thinking about biology's influence on many issues: emotions, thoughts, dispositions, personality, gender, etc. In this way, these findings might open up the conversation on sexual orientation to some degree, with conservatives acknowledging a meaningful role for the body and liberals acknowledging a meaningful role for intentionality.

Why am I making such a point of this, Phil? Because openness to conflicting interpretations of sexual orientation has not always been a feature of professional circles. Some scientists have made statements claiming that there is "no evidence" for sexual orientation changing over time—hinting that those individuals who claim such changes do so in order to suppress or deny who they really are.[5] Like "climate change deniers" discussed previously, those scholars who have documented instances of individual change have not always felt comfortable sharing those findings.

Phil: Hmm . . . This is getting complicated. Maybe the most important thing I can say, Jacob, is that I do not find the position you consider "middle ground" to be at all near the middle. I do, however, appreciate your acknowledgment that being lesbian or gay is not a purely voluntary choice. That's a degree of common ground between us, and it stands in contrast to the persistent use, by many conservatives, of the misleading phrase "homosexual lifestyle." In other words, if being lesbian or gay is about brain configuration (or at least corresponds with a certain brain configuration or pattern) then for sure it's not merely a lifestyle, i.e., something willfully adopted by some people to imitate someone else, to annoy their parents, just for kicks, because liberals recommended it, and so on. And in that sense, the science you offer seems to support my position, in that it agrees with me that homosexuality is a physical fact more than an identity. So thank you for that.

On the other hand, I think perhaps you are now moving back and forth here between two different positions. First there's the idea that we each have an authentic heterosexual identity given to us or scripted by God in a previous existence. Then there's the idea that gayness is a result of brain wave patterns influenced by environment. How do they go together? Doesn't the new brain configuration research in fact *undermine* the idea of authentic heterosexual identity? Or is it that God is some sort of crafty wizard in that he grants us each an original heterosexual identity as our authentic identity and also makes it hard or impossible for some of us to access that identity by giving us brains patterns that get in the way? Or is the Devil instead at work in our brains? I'm not being flip here, I am seriously trying to understand how the different ideas go together. I don't think they do.

Maybe you're saying that what's important is that gayness, while a physical fact of sorts, is nonetheless malleable. If so, are you thereby suggesting that it would be good if science could "cure" people away from same-sex attraction? Is that what you're hoping for? Should we take advantage of that malleability by engaging in scientifically informed interventions? If so, my response can only be that that would be an abusive misuse of scientific knowledge. Or, to be gentler about it, it seems to me that the scientific discoveries you describe, while interesting, don't really do anything to alter the choices we face. They certainly don't give us any reason to think that people should not be lesbian, gay, or bisexual or refrain from changing their gender by means of surgery and hormones.

Jacob: I agree that biological malleability does not imply one particular evaluation or another about sexual orientation. That's the good news—at least if we care about open, loving dialogue in our culture. No one can or should leverage these findings as a "power play" to exert pressure or force their particular evaluation on others. This includes individuals who embrace an identity as gay or lesbian, as well as those who do not. One of my close personal friends, for example, has experienced sexual attraction to men for a number of years; he does *not*, however, see these attractions as a reflection of his core identity and he therefore does not want to embrace them. Should this man be pressed into thinking he is being "untrue" to who he is, Phil? That is precisely what some in the LGBT community have attempted with him. This is what I mean by opening up the conversation—reserving space for my friend to make the choice he wants, with others deserving the same. In short, individuals ought to be given the basic space and respect to be who they see and experience themselves to be—whether or not that fits your view of this issue, Phil, or mine (or neither of us).

Of course, if it were actually true that *no* evidence existed for the individual evolution of sexual orientation over time, then citizens—religious or otherwise—should accept the fact of differing sexual orientations as reality, even if that conflicts with their own previous views. But to deny the validity of stories from many men and women who claim to have experienced *just such* an evolution of feeling over time—to simply write off their experiences as categorically reflecting some kind of false consciousness or religious pressure—is both disheartening and anti-intellectual. Once again, just as conservative Christians should not deny basic space to those who experience and see themselves as gay or lesbian, others should not deny the same space to those who report wanting or having experienced significant changes in the orientation of their sexual feelings and behavior.

Phil: Putting it your way, Jacob, makes it sound like the people you refer to changed *on their own*, when they might have instead changed in response to (1) the pressure of a culture and set of institutions that celebrate and normalize heterosexuality, (2) the fact that most people are heterosexual, and (3) specific reeducation efforts that encouraged them to find inside themselves their (supposed) inner heterosexuality. And if people have changed in response to such pressures, how do we know that they really changed at all? Maybe they pushed themselves back into denial and self-repression. And maybe in ten years or so they will once again feel those gay or lesbian feelings, perhaps thereby profoundly devastating loving spouses who thought they were married to a heterosexual.

Jacob: Those same forces you refer to are clearly operating in the other direction as well: a community celebrating and normalizing homosexuality, specific education efforts to encourage people to find their true selves and come out of the closet, etc. Thus, which socializing forces are responsible for the devastation you refer to (for family, spouses, etc.) is an issue we will continue to disagree on.

To answer your question, no, I am not opposed to efforts to help those who experience LGBT tendencies to move in another direction—and even to "live in accordance with the teachings of their faith." I would say those who attempt to brand Christian therapeutic efforts as unethical are contributing to the same hostile atmosphere they claim to be opposed to in other ways. What I'm saying, once more, is simply that the *same* basic space LGBT activists ask for individuals who identify as gay or lesbian could and should be given to those individuals who do not embrace this identity and who desire professional or clerical help to move in another direction. Both are issues of freedom, and neither should be denied outright. Thus, while I feel strongly about this issue, on a personal level, I can and should respect my cousin's choice to participate in the LGBT community. And while she feels just as strongly, she can and should respect my friend's choice not to participate in the LGBT community. Does that make sense?

Phil: Yes, Jacob, that makes sense. I'm hearing you say that people deal in varying ways with feelings of same-sex attraction, unhappiness with their given bodies, and conflicts within themselves about who they are or how they should live. If that is the case, then let's respect people's choices to take different paths (yours or mine). That much I agree with.

What about same-sex marriage?

Phil: I would like to raise the issue of same-sex marriage by first bringing up a connected issue: that of the value, or merit, of same-sex relationships. What you've said thus far, Jacob, suggests that those relationships lack merit because they fail to actualize the participants' true and God-given nature. In other words, while you think it wrong to deny "basic space" to people who "experience themselves" as homosexual, you also don't believe that anyone is *actually* homosexual "deep down." Instead you believe that heterosexuality better reflects what humans really are. Is that your view? For sure it *is* the view of many who oppose same-sex marriage and other forms of more completely including LGBT individuals in society.

Jacob: Yes, Phil, that is essentially our view. Just as I may believe things about myself that you do not accept (e.g., that I am a child of God), we do not see homosexuality as reflecting an individual's inherent, eternal identity in the deepest sense—even if someone believes that about themselves.

Having said that, let me add this: I don't know any two persons who see their own identity in exactly the same way. And as I say later, disagreement between people—at the level of identity—is not that abnormal, nor perhaps, should it be that much of an obstacle and scary dealbreaker in relationships.

Phil: Good. That's clear. I hope I've likewise made it clear that in my view there's nothing to be gained in looking for a hidden essence. Let's instead just accept people's experience of themselves as providing valid information as to whom and what they are.

But, putting "real" identity aside, what about harm to society? Do homosexual relationships cause harm or don't they? That's what I meant by "merit" just now. And I think you know by now, Jacob, that I strongly believe that loving and committed same-sex relationships don't do harm. Or, rather, I believe that homosexual relationships of love and commitment add value to our society in exactly the same ways that heterosexual relationships of love and commitment add value. And, if I'm right about that, then why not support gay marriage? After all, a major reason why many people support heterosexual marriage is that it's thought to cement loving commitment between two people.

For many people, moreover, getting married is how they ask for, and receive, recognition from the wider world of the fact that they share love and commitment with another person. And of course that's a big reason why so many people want society to widen the institution of marriage to include same-sex couples. In their view, access to "civil unions" for all couples is not enough. They want same-sex couples to get the recognition that comes with the label "married."

Jacob: And that's precisely why religious conservatives resist the labeling of these unions as marriage, Phil; Moving in that direction is not something we would see as positive.

Phil: I understand. And maybe, since we understand each other, we also agree at least about the nature of the current political situation and why people take the positions they do. Why, for example, would a couple want other people to see their relationship as both committed and meritorious? Why isn't it enough if they alone see their relationship that way, regardless of what others think? One reason is obvious: most people like or need to be seen by others (or by others to whom they look up) as both good and meritorious. Surely another reason is that many people believe that a publicly recognized and legal commitment between lovers can and often does shore up love relationships, increase the level of commitment between them, and even deepen the mutual love that they share.

Granted, in theory the commitments entered into by couples could be publicly recognized without any involvement by the law. People could just say they're married in front of witnesses. They could even have a big party where they make the announcement. And people do in fact do that (e.g., in a "commitment ceremony"). But, were people to move en masse in that direction, many lawyers would be out of work. And (more seriously), society is not there yet. Right now, marriage is still the institution of recognition (even if most married couples don't in fact stay married until "death do them part").

And as you've hinted, Jacob, the idea that "marriage" is a special stamp of approval also explains why many people do *not* support the creation of a same-sex version. Instead, they want that level of approval given only to heterosexual unions. And for you and other religious conservatives (tell me if I'm wrong), to be "married" is not just to enjoy a given set of legal rights and obligations; it's also to be in a union with three aspects: (1) it's between a man and a woman; (2) it exists within a society that grants the status of "marriage" to those unions and no others; and (3) it's hallowed as sacred or especially deserving of honor. To say it another way, heterosexual marriage that's sanctioned by law is seen by you as the very *essence* of marriage. And from that point of view, it makes no sense to say that granting equal rights to gays and lesbians calls for giving gay and lesbian couples access to marriage or for doing away with legal marriage.

Jacob: Correct again, Phil. My only addition is that this isn't a conscious agenda to be exclusive per se, as in little kids fighting over toys ("No, marriage is *only for us!*") Instead, it's simply reflecting the social and theological definition of marriage as we see it. I have observed how easy it is for passionate individuals to create a pithy distortion, presented to others as an accurate label—a.k.a. "Proposition H8." Thank you for working hard to avoid that here—and instead, really trying to understand. I hope you see my efforts to do the same.

Phil: Allow me to try out a further example to make sure I understand the conservative position here. Does providing equal access to sports require changing each sport so that every single person is equally able to participate? If it did, then a problem would arise: there's no way to provide that degree of access to some sports without fundamentally altering the sports to the point where they are no longer what they were. In other words, many forms of sport would effectively disappear as such. Likewise many new sports would appear, each of which was based on mere imitation. Thus—or so your community's thinking goes—if society were to grant access to marriage to every sort of couple, then marriage as such would be fundamentally diluted, to the point where *no one* had access to "real" marriage anymore.

Jacob: Yes, Phil. This is a nice illustration of our concerns with "opening up marriage to everyone"—however nice that might seem.

Phil: A possible reply to this line of argument is of course that a new, same-sex-friendly version of marriage would not, in fact, be a dilution. And that brings us back to the central question of merit. If one believes that a committed relationship has to be heterosexual to be truly meritorious, then same-sex marriage *is* indeed a dilution. But that's an issue that rarely gets discussed head-on.

Jacob: I agree that a more open discussion of merit would be helpful. Liberals might be surprised to hear conservatives acknowledging powerful social contributions of individuals and couples identifying as LGBT. Conservatives might likewise be struck by the committed and loving relationships they find between so many individuals in the LGBT community. One of the most loving individuals I've ever known is a lesbian woman who supported my research in graduate school and welcomed me into her home multiple times, to spend time with her partner and daughter. I can't think about these issues without thinking of her and her sweet family.

Phil: You're a caring person, Jacob. As for the issue at hand, I hope I have made it clear that, to my mind, it's a mistake to frame the homosexuality issue as hinging on the "real" nature of marriage or whether or not being gay is natural. For me the bottom line is merit. I am convinced that homosexual relationships have just as much merit as heterosexual ones.

Another problematic framing one often encounters (and I now pick on my fellow liberals) is "it's about equal rights and nothing else." The problem with that thinking is that a "right" is merely a claim about what people deserve from the law and the state, either by way of omission ("leave me alone") or commission ("such-and-such category of persons is entitled to x form of protection or service"). In other words, the idea of right does not in and of itself say anything about the merits of whatever it is that one is said to have a right to. And, moreover, the idea of right carries with it the notion that "it's none of your business whether or not what I do has merit." Thus the claim "I have a right" tends to leave nothing more to be said; one is either for or against the claim, and that's that.

Don't get me wrong. I strongly believe in gay rights. But let's think about what that means and (to my liberal friends) let's figure out how to best defend gay rights. The way I see it, any belief in gay rights has to have at least two parts. First, there's the idea that people have a general right to personal freedom—that every competent adult ought to be granted the legal right to do as they wish unless what they wish to do violates the rights of others or significantly harms other people or society. Most Americans endorse this idea, and many LGBT advocates appeal to it. Second, there's the idea that same-sex relationships are not, in fact, harmful (or no more or less harmful than other consensual relationships). Clearly, if open homosexuality were significantly harmful, then there would be no grounds for the idea that any-one has a right to be publicly LGBT. Thus I repeat: merit is the key question. And I also repeat: I believe that same-sex relationships have merit—they add value to the world in the same way that heterosexual relationships do.

Jacob: I do not disagree, once again, that authentic good can come from a ho-mosexual union; from the aforementioned love and support I felt in graduate school from close friends within the LGBT community, I cannot conclude otherwise. My mentor and her partner mentioned above, love their daughter as much as any parents love their child.

Having said that, let me acknowledge that religious conservatives do be-lieve that unique benefits flow from the union of man and woman—merits that also deserve to be explored, both for children and for the individuals in the relationship. Once again, that obviously does not mean that (a) individu-als in homosexual relationships do not add good to society, or (b) individuals in heterosexual relationships add only good to society. It just means that, all other things being equal (partners treating each other with love and respect, socioeconomic parity, etc.), children raised by a man and woman in union as a married couple will, we believe, be better off on a number of levels.

But how and why this is, again requires understanding the backdrop narrative out of which my community operates—according to which individuals model their life after Heavenly Parents who created them with gender as an essential aspect of their identity.

Phil: It seems to me that we might best deal with the impasse between your side and mine by (a) having lots of public discussions, over time, about the merits of this and that kind of relationship, and (b) consider the no-law option I hinted at earlier. We could, that is, take the law out of the business of sanctifying this or that sort of relationship, period. Instead of widening access to legal marriage, then, society could convert marriage into a private status conferred by this or that community. That would give the law a smaller role in people's partner obligations. The law would merely provide civil unions and enforce parental obligations regardless of marital status. The law would otherwise leave it to civil society (to culture, community, religious institutions, and so on) to decide what makes for true partnership commitment between two consenting adults. Marriage would, then, be a non–legally binding public declaration rather than a piece of paper filed at the courthouse. And if that happened, the new version of marriage might have weight that a "commitment ceremony" does not have now.

Some might protest that one reason marital status has the effect of strengthening some relationships is that marriage is a *legal* contract rather than a mere community declaration. In the last half century, however, the sanction of law has in fact come to have less and less clout in shoring up commitment and strengthening relationships. So why not accept that trend and look for other ways to hallow commitment: people taking care of each other, taking care of children, lifetime friendships, and so on?

Jacob: True, Phil, both marriage and the law are being increasingly disregarded . . . but the solution to this, from our perspective, is seeking more, not less, respect for these things. Further, removing the legal status of marriage could also dilute the meaning of the institution—although we would see this as a better option than redefining marriage itself. Still, if neither side is willing to "cave," then what you propose may end up being a good practical solution to seriously consider—although neither side will likely see it as ideal.

Phil: I'm somewhat surprised by that response, Jacob. Thanks.

I want to make one more pitch in favor of the value offered by gay and lesbian relationships. In my view it's good when adults form nonviolent, voluntary, intimate relationships based on mutual commitment (and by commitment I mean just that, not necessarily being married or living together). Such relationships—be they homosexual, heterosexual, sanctioned by law, or not sanctioned by law—are good because they tend to create love, create community, and bring love into the community.[6] Love and community are, moreover, crucial bulwarks against savagery, depression, and despair in the face of the unknown, in part because they educate each person away from simple-minded, zero-sum conceptions of what's in their self-interest. So, to risk overstatement, committed relationships are everything. They are the kernel of truth in that overused, unhistorical cliché, "the family is the building block of society." For what is the family at heart, if not a group of individuals in a lifetime relationship of mutual commitment?

One could counter, I suppose, by saying that I have yet to talk about homosexual sex, as opposed to love and commitment. Isn't sex part of the issue? Well, yes and no. I think that all that needs to be said about sex is this: among heterosexuals intimate committed relationships are often supported by sexual desire and sexual intimacy, so why shouldn't that also be true for homosexual relationships? I think it's clear; it *is* true for those relationships. Granted, there are plenty of homosexual relationships in this world that are less-than-equal, less-than-voluntary, less-than-committed, not constitutive of love or community, and not educating anyone toward a more enlightened self-interest. But so what? There are also millions of heterosexual relationships of that kind. Indeed, history offers an appalling litany of heterosexual marital unions (not to mention divorces, bride burnings, abandonment, beheadings of unwanted wives, and so on) that were consummated for male convenience: to protect property, to provide men with servants or new land or heirs, to prop up political power, to maintain family name and reputation, etc. Despite all that, we rightly celebrate heterosexual relationships because they have the *potential* to be nonviolent, voluntary, intimate, and based on mutual commitment, and in my view we ought to do the same for gay and lesbian relationships.

Jacob: This helps me further understand where you are coming from, Phil. I agree that both heterosexual and homosexual relationships have the potential to be either degrading or loving and uplifting. While we disagree about the ideal family pattern, we shouldn't overlook our substantial common value of authentic commitment at the core of any happy home—a value evident in homes across the spectrum of difference.

Phil: Thanks again. To round out our discussion of family commitments, let's come back to the issue of children. I believe that evidence is overwhelmingly conclusive: there's nothing at all bad about children being around—or being raised by—openly homosexual adults. Likewise, there's not one shred of evidence to support the idea that gay parents (or gay camp counselors) make the children they care for more likely to become gay. So what's the issue when it comes to children? There is no issue except misguided fear.

Jacob: Can a child raised by gay and lesbian parents experience a loving, nurturing home that provides teaching and wonderful support? Absolutely. I have observed it myself. Even so, conservatives do have concerns with this trend. Yet I'm hearing you suggest that my community's concerns in this regard are based on fear and "not one shred" of evidence—in fact, in the face of "overwhelmingly conclusive" evidence to the contrary. Do you think our worries are really that baseless, Phil? What about the mountains of data confirming the power of modeling in shaping behavior? Of course, you would argue that there is nothing of concern being modeled.

Phil: Okay. Maybe we better agree to disagree on that one, and promise to stay open to the facts.

Is it really that wrong to disagree about identity?

Jacob: At this point, I wonder if we could return to the issue of identity to explore what I personally consider the most significant (and most underexplored) aspect of this discussion: namely, how unusual is it, Phil, in day-to-day relationships with friends, family, and neighbors, to disagree with others about identity? If I told my friends of other faiths about my belief in humankind's identity in relation to God, how many of these friends might disagree, even intensely? Would such disagreement mean that these friends do not love me, or that we should feel uncomfortable around one another?

My answer is no. I have seen remarkable friendships develop in the presence of these very disagreements. I've got dear evangelical friends who likely continue to see me as a candidate for hell if I don't change what I believe about my identity one day; and other incredible friends in the LGBT community who see themselves differently than I do . . . and that's okay! The larger point, once again, is that clashing views about identity may not necessarily be either unusual or bad. Indeed, as I said before, any two individuals selected randomly are likely to disagree in their personal views of identity and selfhood in a meaningful way. And why should that be such a problem?

Phil: I agree with you, Jacob; people disagree about identity. I identify with "humanity" first and foremost, even though I also consider myself an animal in general, a New Yorker, and, yes, an American. Others put national identity nearer to the top when it comes to "who they are." Another way people disagree about identity is by taking different positions on whether or not humans possess a basic, underlying, natural identity. Maybe human essence is more like a complex pile of natural needs, inclinations, and abilities, and thus humans have no choice but to use history and culture to take those materials and construct identities.

Let's suppose that you're right that humans have a basic identity they can realize in optimal conditions or by accepting God into their lives. It seems to me that even then there would be room for disagreement about the *content* of that basic identity. Even among religious conservatives, some (e.g., the late Ayatollah Khomeini, of Iranian fame) see humans as basically sinful and self-regarding and therefore in need of God's law and punishment to keep them in line, while others (e.g., you and Thomas Aquinas) think of humans as blessed by God with an underlying moral sense, so that (given the extra push of revelation and grace) they can construct a good world, and even be trusted to make some of their own rules.

So, yes, I agree that "there are competing views of identity in play" in our world. I agree that that's a good thing, not a problem to be fixed. And I believe as well that it's possible for a person (e.g., you, Jacob) to simultaneously believe that gayness is not a natural identity and also love and accept gay people as people. In other words, I can and do take you at your word when it comes to the love and acceptance you offer.

Jacob: Wow. Thank you, Phil. I've often hoped my progressive friends would believe that—but never had someone actually say what you just did. These kinds of simple acknowledgements we've made, although they may never satisfy activists on either side, feel considerable to me. I wonder what it would mean if such realizations (however modest) became more widespread between our communities?

For one, a greater awareness in our society of the okayness-of-disagreement (however deep) might enhance the ability of conservative and liberal communities alike to embrace diversity. In this case, for instance, it might help ease some of the "you have to change your views to love me" tension felt across the board. In place of that tension, we might remind ourselves that it is okay to disagree, even intensely, with people around us—and that doing so is quite independent of whether or not we respect and love one another.

Phil: Bravo.

Can we work to at least keep the discussion open?

Jacob: In the absence of accepting deep disagreement, citizens will likely continue to avoid discussion about serious differences and increasingly "cluster" together with those who think the same way as they do.[7] This is where I see your earlier book as crucial, Phil.[8] As you say, U.S. citizens seem to have lost some of their basic capacity to disagree in healthy ways, and we need to respond by proactively cultivating a greater willingness to talk openly about differences.

Talking in that way is, of course, a real challenge when it comes to the issue we are now discussing. For conservatives who have a close friend or family member identifying as gay or lesbian, and who want to maintain a loving relationship with that person, it can seem as if the easiest approach is to simply avoid the subject. On the other side, increasing numbers in the United States are concluding that the most beneficial way to respond to those situations is to completely accept each individual's own view of himself or herself, with no hard questions asked.

Phil: Yes, Jacob, as you said earlier, we needn't equate accepting one another as fellow human beings with accepting everything everyone believes as right. A person can be a fellow human being worthy of my respect and at the same time be wrong about all sorts of things.

Jacob: And once again, the basic issue remains: can we talk together openly and lovingly about deep differences in our communities? Conservatives in this country have sometimes found that the mere fact that they hold certain beliefs can automatically prompt being labeled as hateful or bigoted. Speaking more generally, it seems that a few people on each side of the issue insist that the other viewpoint does not deserve a legitimate hearing. For this reason, Phil, before a conversation on this issue begins, I ask something like, "Do I have space here to hold a different moral perspective on homosexuality and not be seen as hating or fearing you?" In graduate school, when liberal friends realized how silenced conservatives sometimes felt in academia, they worked hard to make sure to offer me space to participate in conversations without feeling automatically judged or labeled.

Phil: I, too, think it's important for everyone to grasp how difficult it can be for people to discuss the subject of sexual preference, to see that people's basic worldviews and personal identities are involved in those conversations, and to realize that people often feel silenced, misunderstood, or disrespected because of what others presume about them. And I specifically appreciate your willingness to give me—and others like me—a legitimate hearing with loving intention.

Jacob: I feel the same, Phil. Although I have found enriching relationships with friends in the gay and lesbian community, I've never had such a profound discussion of this issue.

What about learning to live together well?

Phil and Jacob: In spite of our shared optimism, we both know that there are no easy answers or political solutions. Particularly when it comes to policy decisions regarding marriage, adoption, and legal rights in general, hard decisions will need to be made. As liberal and conservative citizens come to talk more productively together, however, both communities will hopefully come to understand the need to make *some* accommodations politically. For conservatives, this includes measures to ensure that those who identify with the LGBT community feel safe and protected. And for liberals, this entails ensuring the space for religious conservatives to likewise be who they are as a people.

So is this simply mutual détente? If communities move in this direction, could we expect anything more than politely allowing one another to live how they want, and not interfere? We think there is reason for hope. To conclude the chapter, we share one story illustrating our optimism.

In 2009, the LDS church publicly announced their support of a proposed Salt Lake City ordinance aimed at protecting gay and transgender residents from discrimination in housing and employment. The church's influence was, moreover, helpful in the ordinance's eventual passage by a unanimous vote of the city council, something that came as a surprise to many residents—both Mormon and non-Mormon. On the occasion, church spokesman Michael Otterson issued the following statement:

> Our community in Salt Lake City is comprised of citizens of different faiths and values, different races and cultures, [and] different political views and divergent demographics. . . . The issue before you tonight is the right of people to have a roof over their heads and the right to work without being discriminated against. . . . In drafting this ordinance, the city has granted common-sense rights that should be available to everyone, while safeguarding the crucial rights of religious organizations, for example, in their hiring of people whose lives are in harmony with their tenets. . . . The church supports these ordinances because they are fair and reasonable and do not do violence to the institution of marriage. . . . I believe in a church that believes in human dignity, in treating people with respect even when we disagree—in fact especially when we disagree.[9]

Most important is what led to this surprising support by the church: two months of secret meetings between midlevel LDS officials and five of Utah's most prominent gay leaders. After LDS officials suggested meeting at the Church Office Building, gay rights leaders proposed the Equality Utah and the Utah Pride Center as an alternative location. A more neutral location was eventually selected in the LDS home of a close friend of Jim Dabakis, founder of the Utah Pride Center. According to a report in the *Salt Lake Tribune*, "Suspicion marred initial meetings. 'These were two communities living in the same town that just had no understanding of each other,' Dabakis said. 'It was quite uncomfortable in the beginning.'"[10] Over time, however, this small, contested group developed a growing sense of trust and a willingness to work together:

> They searched for common ground, understanding that the LDS Church wasn't about to back gay marriage and Utah's gay community would not stop pushing for what it considers civil rights. The meetings fizzled a few weeks [after], but then Dabakis got a call from an LDS official asking to reconvene the "gang of five." They met four times in the lead up to Tuesday's announcement. . . . Dabakis hopes it isn't the end of the discussion, but a high point in a burgeoning "friendship."[11]

More than orchestrating broad support for the city ordinance, it was the development of greater trust and good will that stood out to participants. Dabakis said, "The discussions we have had over the last several months have shown what a caring, loving, concerned institution [the LDS Church] is." The discussion, he said, "changed all of our lives." Former city council-woman Deeda Seed added, "What everyone found is that we really liked each other. There was a good rapport. . . . It reaffirmed for me the power of people talking to each other—even if you have incredible differences. You start to see the humanity."[12]

6

ONGOING RACIAL TENSION:
INEVITABLE OR ESCAPABLE?

On August 29, 2005, a hurricane hit landfall in southeast Louisiana. Beyond the estimated $81 billion in property damage, at least 1,836 people lost their lives, either as a result of the storm or the subsequent flooding, making Katrina the deadliest U.S. natural disaster in nearly one hundred years. Adding to the calamity, moreover, was the slow pace of the governmental relief effort, an effort that prompted a mountain of criticism.

Some of the critique went beyond accusations of incompetence and error to allege something worse: systematic ill will. In that first week after the storm, for example, an e-mail was sent out on the psychology listserv in Jacob's department, lambasting the federal government for the "obvious racism" reflected in its slow response to the destruction. Jacob posted a question in response, asking how we could make that kind of judgment so quickly without knowing more. The author of the letter responded that she was sorry he felt that way, but reiterated that the events of the past week had been an undeniable signal that racism and classism were alive and well in the country and to think otherwise was to do those suffering in New Orleans a great injustice. The emphasis, once again, was that the centrality of race relations to the devastation following the hurricane should be clear and evident to all involved.

As other participants in the listserv expressed satisfaction with this firm rebuttal of Jacob's question, he was left wondering: Why be so quick to conclude that racism was behind the slow pace of disaster relief? Where did the role of race end and that of other factors begin? And, most basically, shouldn't it be okay to ask critical and pointed questions about situations where race might be involved? Could those who think the truth is not blatantly-obvious also be given a full hearing?

Upon hearing of these events, Phil had some questions of his own: Has the word "racism" become so loaded with multiple meanings and so prone to create emotional reactions that it has become counterproductive as a way to explain anything? Also: to what degree are society's racial inequities largely the result of racist attitudes and intentions and to what degree are they primarily the result of structural forces that are both less tangible and more intractable?

In this chapter, we discuss and explore these questions against a backdrop of other related issues, including class and socioeconomic status.

When and how does race matter?

Phil: First, while my view is definitely left-of-center, I don't claim to speak for all liberals or leftists in this section; in fact I know some liberals will disagree with me. I hope everyone will hear me out.

In my view, there are several mistaken views afoot when it comes to exactly how race matters. Some people—more often liberals—assume that *any* observed racial disparities must be the result of the racist beliefs and actions of a majority or of people who are in power (e.g., "If Hispanics are not doing well in school we can assume that that is caused by racists who want it to happen"). And some people—more often conservatives—assume that racial disparities must be the result of defects in the culture and/or the behavior of members of the group on the short side of those disparities, those defects perhaps having arisen as a result of government handouts, special treatment, or victim thinking (e.g., "If more blacks would just sign on to family values, then the high unemployment rate among blacks would go away"). What these otherwise opposing views share is the myth that all of the world's problems are caused by present-day choices that could have been made otherwise, rather than being aspects of systems that rule over all of us to one degree or another and that were created by a host of choices made by thousands of different people over the course of centuries (see chapter four). More precisely, these common viewpoints on race keep people from seeing that today's racial disparities are closely connected with (a) the fact that society features a class structure that puts whoever is near the bottom at a big disadvantage, (b) the lack of adequate governmental investment in the public sector, and (c) the fact that the members of certain racial groups are more likely to be born into the lower rungs of the economy than are members of other racial groups. Add these factors together and it should be easy to see that contemporary racial inequities need not be the result of racist intention and attitude.

Jacob: And this is what some would call "institutional racism," right? What I hear you saying primarily is that these existing racial disparities are not necessarily the result of intentional, personal racism. You also see both conservative and liberal views on race as equally stuck on implicating someone (whether minorities or racists) as causing the problem—this, at the expense of adequate attention to historical and economic context. Am I understanding you?

Phil: Yes. Consider New Orleans as an example. When the hurricane hit, what mattered most was where people were on the economic ladder, not race per se. Those higher up had somewhere to go, a car that functioned, and money to travel and tide them over when they arrived somewhere else. They could therefore more easily decide to leave, and could perhaps leave sooner. Many of those with less, on the other hand, lacked those resources, and thus had good reason to stay and take their chances. Also the city (like many other cities) suffered from considerable residential segregation by class, meaning that the poor and near-poor are concentrated in certain neighborhoods, rather than spread out among other people. And that meant that those who were poor were likely to lack friends and neighbors with resources to offer them in an emergency. Additionally, many of the poor neighborhoods were in the flood-prone areas because housing was cheaper there. Also, being poor meant not being able to afford flood insurance and often also meant living in a house that couldn't withstand hurricane-force winds. Thus the poor of New Orleans bore the brunt of the storm. And blacks were overrepresented among the city's poor, something I will talk about shortly.

One reason private resources were so important when the disaster struck is that relevant public resources were mostly nonexistent—e.g., busses ready to go, special transportation for the elderly and disabled, readily available supplies of food and water, flood-resistant hospital designs, emergency power systems, shelters prepared in advance, proper funding and management for public relief agencies, emergency funds to assist those leaving town, and so on. Beyond such emergency-related resources are those that would have provided prevention: better dam construction, better dam inspection systems, more dam inspectors, etc. And then there were those forms of public spending that could have put more families in a position to "swim on their own" when the flood came: good schooling for all, so that more people have good jobs; a higher minimum wage so that more people have at least some savings; and a healthier population, thanks to better public health programs, more pollution abatement, enough primary care physicians, and universal health-care coverage.

Intentional racism and less-than-conscious racist attitudes surely exist in New Orleans, but they weren't and aren't the primary cause of the lack of government investment in the things listed here. The more important cause was and is the prevailing philosophy of economic conservatism. That's the American way: swim on your own or drown. Or get help from volunteers, friends, and neighbors, and hope they have something to offer. Need to get to work? Buy a car. Need health care? Get a job that gives you access to affordable private health insurance.

The "rely on the private sector" approach to taking care of people and preparing for the worst might work if life were agrarian and most groups of people that are woven together in interdependence were small enough for everyone to know everyone else. But that's not how it is. Like it or not, we need the government to serve as a mechanism for pooling resources across millions of people so as to pay for roads, bridges, trains, schools, hospitals, and economic stimulus. In the United States, however, those uses of government are subject to attack for being "socialist" and "violations of freedom."

Granted, there's no denying that it would be very expensive indeed to be truly ready to provide the enormous population of America's cities with safe exit, emergency medical care, a place to go, and a leg up to start a new life, should a major, city-wide calamity occur. But at the least the people of the

United States could have, by means of their government, more fully joined hands to pay for the preventative actions necessary to properly respond to the fact that New Orleans is below sea level, in a flood plain by the ocean, and vulnerable to hurricanes. Instead, many of the city's levees were not ready for a Katrina-sized emergency and hospitals had not been given the extra money needed to prepare properly for a massive flood and all it would entail. That would have made all the difference for many black, poor residents.

Jacob: Yet you seem to think conservatives don't mind if people "sink"— "Ahh, you wimp . . . just couldn't handle it, eh?" But that's not really fair nor accurate. I'm also not sure that simply investing more money in New Orleans would have prevented the problem. My understanding is that the city had received plenty of federal money that was poorly allocated.

Nonetheless, let me imagine myself a resident of the New Orleans you hope for. Like nearly every resident of the city, I've got a good job with a growing savings account, my kids have resource-rich schools, and local and federal government is watching out for families in the area both directly (health care, emergency food/water) and indirectly (maintenance of infrastructure like dams). Who could argue with the ideal of providing for the well-being of all residents? The problem I have, Phil, is not your desire to help others, but your idea about how that should happen. I'm noticing that your proposal says little about what individuals themselves can contribute. Surely their role goes beyond simply lobbying government leaders to do more? Would you agree that individuals also need to rise to make some kind of contribution to their own well-being—be that searching out and preparing for jobs, teaching their own children important lessons at home, preparing their own families for emergencies, etc.? Why is this left out of your equation, Phil? Generally speaking, if meaningful individual contributions are absent from societal expectations, why not just sit on the couch watching the tube? Oh, wait, that's what lots of people are already doing!

In short, why not directly encourage both individuals and government to "do their part" for the ideals you envision? Perhaps our differences here are less in the aspiration than in the method. And perhaps, frankly, both conservative and liberal methods could improve if we agreed to not discount the potential role of both individual and government contributions.

Phil: Fair enough. I am obviously not opposed to individuals getting off the couch and making a difference—only lamenting the fact that this sometimes remains an exclusive focus for conservatives—e.g., "Why can't those people just work harder?"

Jacob: And you have a point as well, Phil. As a psychologist, I'm reminded by your comment of attitudes often expressed to those who suffer from serious mental or emotional problems—"You're depressed/anxious? Just look outside at the sun . . . don't worry, be happy!" "Got anorexia/bulimia? Just take care of your body and eat right!" I suppose that's kind of the attitude you are highlighting as sometimes evident among my conservative peers.

Phil: Thanks, Jacob. Now let's directly bring race into the picture (though it has been lurking there all along). Why are so many of the poor neighborhoods I spoke of populated mostly by people of color? Why, for that matter, are blacks and Hispanics (along with a few other groups) more likely to be among the poor and near-poor in the first place? In brief, what happened is that centuries of market systems and their influence on politics and culture worked to situate many of today's blacks and Hispanics in relatively disadvantaged positions, and many whites reacted to that situation by going to great lengths to keep "those people" (the disadvantaged) out of their neighborhoods. Consider just a few parts of this story:

- Big Southern landowners were, after the Civil War, successful in taking away the right to vote, not to mention the promised "40 acres and a mule," from freed blacks.
- The sharecropping system that eventually took the place of slavery in the South was in many respects the same as slavery. This system pitted black laborers against poor white sharecroppers for the spots to work on rice and cotton plantations.
- Northern industrialists were mostly successful in keeping racial groups apart in the workplace and thereby sowing racial division.
- Changes in the South and jobs in the North led to migrations that in turn meant millions of blacks arrived in Northern cities, only to be kept out of most of the neighborhoods that offered decent, affordable housing.

■ Funding for public schools is largely based on local property taxes, and that makes for tremendous inequity in the access children have to a decent education.

I could go on. I advise those who want to explore the market/race relationship to check out Thomas Sugrue's *The Origins of the Urban Crisis*[1] or Carter Wilson's *Racism: From Slavery to Advanced Capitalism.*[2] For now I will sum things up by saying that when it comes to the Katrina aftermath, the underlying causes of the race differentials on display were not racism so much as they were class structure, inadequate investment by government, and the way history (including racism of the past) had already divvied up the neighborhoods, the stock of good housing, and access to transportation.

Why, one might ask, don't people see the power exercised by the class system and by history and give up the idea that race is in itself a cause of anyone's situation? One reason is simply that people, once labeled as members of a race, tend to remember that label and pass that identity on to their children as an important part of their heritage. Another reason that many people don't see the class barriers in society as that would be too discouraging; in other words they find race-based explanations preferable as a way to make sense of the inequities they observe. And yet another reason people tend to explain disparities by invoking racism is that there's still plenty of racism in our world. Look, for example, at the length of jail sentences for the same crime, or unemployment rates, or who gets a mortgage approved. In every case, one finds significant variation by race.[3] And yet—and to return to my point— in my view the primary causes of that injustice are economic in nature.

Jacob: So you see class discrepancies driving many of the patterns, but are also suggesting that it may be easier for citizens on a number of levels to make sense of what they are seeing by reference to race?

Phil: Yes, essentially. And I hope that tells you something, Jacob, about what I think about your classmate's response to your question. She seems to have assumed both that racism is ever-present and that race differences are necessarily a matter of some people having the wrong views (i.e., being "prejudiced") rather than—say—a result of impersonal systems that replicate historically established inequities. Also, keep this in mind: for many people, an important part of *being* anti-racist is making a *show* of anti-racism, sometimes to the point of reflexively jumping on any opportunity to put on such a show, as if declaring things racist will in itself do something to fight racism.

Another factor can be in play when people call out someone as being racist (as your classmate did): the existence of guilt, pain, and/or anger about our nation's sad race history. What I especially have in mind is when someone who feels the pain of racial history in one way or another (they have suffered under it, their parents suffered under it, they realize that they have somehow benefited from it, and so on) gets some relief by putting a white person "on the hook."[4] By this I mean that they take advantage of racial history and white guilt about that history by calling someone out as racist, without enough regard for the facts about that person. I suppose that, in the moment, such acts of accusation can feel good to the person making them. Certainly, when I've watched people making such accusations at academic conferences, and in other venues, it seemed to me that they loved doing it. And what can the other person possibly say in response? It's hard for a white person to say that "race has nothing to do with it" without seeming callous about racial history.

The difficulties do, of course, go in the reverse direction as well. Thus Dr. Mikhail Lyubansky, a scholar on race, writes: "Because their own experiences are rarely racialized, most white persons tend to underestimate the impact of race/racism in contemporary society. This, in turn, often creates a peculiar tug-of-war in which people of color feel as though they have to constantly defend their perceptions of reality against well-meaning (and less well-meaning) white colleagues and friends who tell them their experience had nothing to do with race."[5]

We should, then, generously keep in mind that performing one's anti-racism is not simply or necessarily about ego or guilt; it's also rooted in the insight that there are racial problems in this world and that people sometimes change society for the better by acting together to make a show of being for or against this or that. That happened in the civil rights movement, and many people still live by that model of how to improve society. On the other hand, we ought not be so desirous of putting on a show that we make unwarranted accusations or jump to conclusions in a knee-jerk way. Nor should we fall in love with any kind of analysis to the point where it becomes just a bunch of phrases we apply without thinking, or (worse) phrases that allow us to avoid thinking.

The crucial thing, I think, is that people want to believe in the American dream and thus don't want to believe that significant class barriers exist. Accordingly, they find race-based explanations of inequality preferable. And who can blame them? The idea of the American dream can serve as a major source of hope in the face of economic stress and uncertainty, periodic calamity, and persistent geographical pockets of major disinvestment and destitution. The realities of class structure, on the other hand, are downright depressing; indeed, political candidates who even suggest that class barriers exist are easily branded by their opponents as in favor of "class warfare," mean-spirited, or worse.

Jacob: So you think Americans perhaps can't handle the truth as you see it? What if we understand it, but simply don't agree with much of it? That's where I find myself. You seem to be speaking mostly to other progressives here, Phil, but it's an interesting way of thinking and helpful for me to hear as well. I now better understand that you are concerned about race in a complex way—one linked to many other aspects of a problem, including class. Your views certainly don't fit into the cable news stereotype.

Phil: My views also don't fit in every way with the views of other liberals, however, I'm still a liberal on this issue, for one because I think it would be wrong to dismiss your classmate's reaction as "PC" arrogance or as a mere symptom of "victim thinking" (much less as part of a plot by liberals to keep the race issue alive or to otherwise control people's thinking). Instead, your classmate was on to something in her inkling that the American class system differentially affects those who are black or brown, compared to those who are white. Nor was she wrong to want to do something about it. What she needed to see was that neither the exact nature of the problem nor the best way to fix it is beyond legitimate debate.

Granted, there are people on the left who do indeed fall into victim thinking, meaning that they take too much pleasure in the idea that they (or their allies) are being treated unfairly. But victim thinking is arguably even worse on the right these days, as when well-off people declare that their taxes are killing them, that public school teachers are stealing their money, and that the Obama administration is "taking their country away" by tweaking the health system to try to get more people health-care coverage, bring down costs a little, protect those with "pre-existing conditions," and so on. Victim thinking and the grievance industry is, in other words, present on all sides.

Jacob: You're right about that, Phil. Resentment and accusation happen all over. You and I still see the nature of surrounding oppressions quite differently, however. Where you see larger class/race structures as driving many of these challenges, I see a fallen world with painful conditions largely emanating from the collective choices of individuals, as we discussed earlier in the book.

So let me add a few words on the role of race and ethnicity in people's lives, as I see it. In one of our university diversity seminars, our assignment was to write down on a piece of paper all the "identities" that formed who we were. As we went around sharing them, I realized that I had either been misunderstanding instructions, or coming from a different perspective. Most people in the room listed among their top five identifier terms things such as ethnicity (Latino, African-American, Asian-American, etc.), class status, gender, and sexual orientation. When I shared my terms they were "brother, son, Latter-day Saint, Christian, and American."

Did it matter to me that I am also Caucasian? Honestly, not so much . . . unless you're asking me about family history. I do identify with Swiss and English ancestors and pilgrims who left the "old country" to come here and can understand, on that level, how all people identify with their roots and heritage. That's not, though, how most progressives I know experience and talk about race and ethnicity. In their feelings, there is something much bigger, and also more intimate and personal, than I am accustomed to. Laying aside your personal views expressed in this chapter, would you say race is a bigger deal to your community than mine, Phil?

Phil: Hmm . . . It's hard to answer your question because liberals and leftists come in many stripes, to the point where they by no means form a single community. Based on my experience, I would say that how a person sees their *own* ethnicity—as well as how "big a deal" it is to them—has little to do with where they're at politically and more to do with their racial and ethnic history. Those who are non-white, for instance, often experience their race/ethnicity keenly—i.e., they're very conscious of it as part of who they are. Most whites, on the other hand, experience their race/ethnicity less keenly, or even not at all. And that makes sense, given that over the past several centuries in the United States those who were white were marked by the general culture without reference to race, meaning that they were treated as the norm, as "just people," while those who were not white often found their race to be the first thing most people noticed about them. Of course, the reverse occurred in some situations, at least to a degree, for example when a white person walked through an all-black neighborhood and felt marked as different, but that was not really the same, since most whites could choose to avoid the all-black neighborhoods.

This same pattern can be observed in many contexts. Consider gays and lesbians, Muslims who live in the United States, and those who are obese, for example. They are constantly reminded of their status as non-normative and thus likely to internalize it as part of their identity, whereas those in the normative groups are not likewise reminded, and not likely to internalize. Thus some (but not all) diversity workshops aim to "educate" those in normative groups about how it feels to be non-normative, in other words to get them to stop "taking your privilege for granted." Perhaps, Jacob, you were supposed to learn that life is different for others, and thus become more sensitive. On the other hand, maybe you weren't. Diversity workshops and seminars aren't all the same.

I'm not a fan of diversity workshops if and when they seek to remind white people of their connection to oppression and chastise them somewhat for the privileges they experience without knowing it. And it really irks me when such goals are implicit and the up-front goal is merely to help participants "appreciate diversity." That said, it *is* important to realize that race is generally speaking indeed a "bigger deal" to non-whites than it is to whites, and for good reason, because non-whites "consistently have the lived experience of their race mattering . . . and then being told by white people (including those they trust and like) that it had nothing to do with race."[6] So maybe the workshop you attended had its point to make.

Jacob: Yes, so minority groups experience their racial identity more keenly. I get that. You're arguing that ethnicity is what is driving this differential valuing of race, rather than political ideology. I've still also seen a difference between how minorities who identify as either liberal or conservative talk about race. My progressive friends, whatever their race, seem to care more about the issue of race and racism than do my conservative friends, also regardless of race. Indeed, if one thinks about race as my progressive friends do, the issue seems all-covering and dominant. That mindset, moreover, makes racism much bigger and deeper than simple behavior. A professor whom I admire, Gregory A. Miller, wrote, as part of an e-mail exchange:

> I was raised with a very clear understanding of racism as a belief in inherent inferiority. . . . That clean definition [however] excludes all sorts of things (such as "separate but equal," institutional racism, stereotype threat, avoiding certain neighborhoods—or neighbors) that I gradually came to understand are just as racist but harder to combat. Honestly, it was quite a shock to discover those other paths to racism. Without that discovery, people can genuinely say things like 'I'm not a racist, but . . .' and end the sentence in a hundred ways that are very racist and very damaging, without any inkling of the damage.[7]

As reflected in Greg's comments, individuals can come to understand race and racism as vast and pervasive—something clearly beyond what individuals can see, be aware of, and dictate themselves. And that leads to another aspect of this issue I'd love to discuss, Phil: that of intention.

Does intention matter in understanding racism?

Jacob: Not long ago, a family began attending weekly services with my religious congregation. They were from another country but had been in the United States for a number of years, contributing to the community in wonderful ways and initially feeling like they belonged. In recent years, however, they became concerned about the changing tenor of the national conversation about immigration. Then, on a particular Sunday, they left a service distraught—one of them in tears—as a result of encounters with some of the other members of the congregation.

Afterward, since we were neighbors, I had a chance to talk privately with them about the situation and find out what had happened. They felt that members of the congregation had, in a variety of ways, been sending subtle messages that they were less than welcome. The man passing out programs, for instance, turned his face and looked away when distributing their program. A woman working with the children did not remember their daughter's name nor did she seem to call on her as often in class.

To help me understand their experience, I asked them, "Do you think the individuals doing this were intending to hurt you? Did they seem deliberate about sending that kind of message?" When I asked this question I was not ignorant that there are Americans who may indeed want to send that kind of message to an individual not originally from the United States. And like most Americans as a whole, I see any such behavior to be totally unacceptable.

I also knew the church members in question, however, and found it hard to imagine they would have intended such harm. Thus I asked, hoping to understand more of the details of what had actually happened. What surprised me was their response. One emphasized that intention "wasn't the issue," while the other said, "If they didn't realize it, then they are retarded."

I insisted that it might matter, and in an effort to get the point across I told them of the experience I had in graduate school after Hurricane Katrina, partially recounted at the beginning of this chapter. And I shared with them the rest of the story: After that e-mail exchange about "obvious racism," I could tell that my classmate was upset. We set a time to go out to lunch and talk about the issue. During that meeting, I explained that my intention was not to make her uncomfortable, and she in turn gave me a chance to talk openly. The result was that she came to realize I had not meant to assert that racism was unimportant or played no role in the storm's aftermath, but rather to better understand its role alongside many other factors. In other words, she saw my heart. And I in turn understood more how I had come across to her in ways she initially found offensive.

I shared this with my neighbors to suggest that the members of my congregation from whom they took offense might not have been fully aware of how their actions were coming across—and further, that if we raised their awareness it might do something to improve the situation. These friends, however, had no interest in having this kind of open conversation. They made it clear they didn't care whether the church members had intended offense or not. This leads me to two questions, Phil. Does intention matter when it comes to race and racism? If it does, why would people be so resistant to even discussing it as a potential player in the issue?

Phil: In my view, Jacob, intention is always important when it comes to judging someone's heart, and often is important in other ways as well. Sometimes, however, race differences *are* caused by hard-to-see factors that go beyond intention: e.g., by intelligence tests that accidentally favor middle and upper classes, by seniority preferences in a union contract that lead minorities to be among the first laid off, and by the internalization of negative self-images and negative ideas of schooling that affect the academic performance of minority youth. So it's understandable when people use the word "racism" to help explain it all. And it's understandable when some people say, "I don't want to talk about intention; it has nothing to do with it."

I think it's also important to say that intention and attitude can be very subtle; they can exist and do harm without being consciously thought out or based on any allegiance to a racist biological theory. Think, for example, of a teacher who without realizing it expects lesser performance from her black students than her white students. Perhaps she fails to check in with black students after they do poorly on a test, but always checks in with white students who likewise do poorly. In that case, we might want to call her actions racist, but also be generous with, and supportive of, the teacher. Maybe she simply has a less-than-conscious insecurity about speaking to (or e-mailing) black students, as in "Will I say things right?" or "Will the student take it the wrong way?" Maybe, in other words, that teacher needs some help to be a better teacher.

Jacob: So individuals can do or say things that reflect racial bias, but without being aware of it? In a situation like this, it seems better to withhold judgment until all the "data is gathered," wouldn't you think? Returning to my neighbor's story, I came to find that the man passing out programs (who had been accused of racist actions) actually has social anxiety disorder, and on any given Sunday can be seen turning away from lots of people as they walk by. This is not to say that the encounters were all figments that can be explained away. But since additional factors influenced the other encounters as well, it illustrates why my friends should perhaps have been less quick to label what happened to them as racist before understanding the hearts of those involved.

Phil: Using the standard I offered earlier, I would say that the man with so-cial anxiety disorder was not being racist when he handed out the programs. Granted, if he were especially anxious around black people then it might be fair to call his *actions* racist, but we might even then be better off using some other word to initially describe what happened, so as to avoid overtones of total accusation.

To speak more generally, there's no doubt that sometimes people think they're being mistreated because of who they are when actually it's for some other reason. But that sort of mistake is to be expected for many reasons, so we should not be too quick to attack people for "victim thinking." Imagine, for example, that you are a black American. One day all is going well when, for whatever reason, you're suddenly subjected to egregious mistreatment by a white police officer. Your initial reaction might well be to consider that mistreatment an example of racist policing. It's possible, of course, that that *particular* police officer happens to mistreat just about everyone. But how would you know? So you misunderstand and think the officer racist. Why wouldn't you? Maybe just last week your black friend was pulled over for nothing and his car searched for no good reason. Maybe years ago your father was pulled over unjustly and then beaten. I guess my point is that we should each (whatever our race) approach interracial encounters with generosity and with efforts to understand and build trust.

Jacob: I love that word "generosity," Phil. That's just what I'm talking about. Just as we are asking others to not make accusations of racism so quickly, the conservative community can be more understanding and accepting of the historical and present-day realities that sometimes lead individuals to make them. Generosity is needed on both sides.

Phil: So, does intention matter? Yes, it does. I believe, moreover, that most people, most of the time, have good intentions, or at least their fully conscious intentions are good. That's one reason why dialogue and mediation often help to resolve situations of conflict. There won't, however, be any dialogue or mediation if the parties involved don't participate, and sometimes they'll see no reason to do so. Consider what happened at your church, Jacob: The people who sent rude messages to your neighbor friends presumably didn't know it, so they had no reason to step forward and ask your friends if they were okay, much less begin that questioning with some sort of apologetic, friendly phrasing. And if your friends were sure that there was no good intention on the part of the rude members (which is my guess), then from their point of view there was likewise no reason to step forward. So it seems that the only way to improve the situation was for a third party to do what you did, Jacob: intervene.

That raises two points. First, what's the best way to intervene and bring about better communication in situations of conflict? That depends. In the case of your friends, pride might have been an issue to consider. Your friends probably felt soundly rejected, and thus it might be a matter of pride to them to refuse to step forward. To them, stepping forward might be the same as asking to be welcomed yet another time, after all they had done to serve the community already. Thus it might have helped, Jacob, if you had begun on the other side by pointing out to the relevant members that they did something that seems to have hurt your friends and also asking them to be the first ones to approach your friends and say something nice. But that's just a thought.

Jacob: I wish I had considered that at the time, Phil. That might have worked!

Phil: Here's another thought: it seems to me that people are more likely to intervene if they believe in advance that the people on both sides of the issue might have a degree of good intention (even when their actions were indeed racist, as some actions are). Just as you, Jacob, as a friend of all the parties involved in the incident you speak of, suspected that the cause was misunderstanding rather than ill will.

Let me take the issue of intention a step further. As I said earlier in this chapter (and in chapter three), I believe most people do in fact usually act with good will. Thus for me, what has been said here adds up to a general principle: those who believe in advance in the presence of good intentions and who therefore embark down the road of dialogue are likely to discover good intentions before their travels are over. And you and I might provide an example, Jacob. Before we met, we each believed it worthwhile to talk to our political opponents, and now, after lots of talking to each other, we have come to discover each other's good will and sincerity.

This discussion of what to do about events of prejudice or perceived prejudice leads me to hazard a second general principle. I believe that even those who have been mistreated—or feel mistreated—have an obligation to work (if they can) to end the mistreatment and thereby help reduce mistreatment in general. To say it another way, when it comes to making the world a better place, no one is off the hook. It's not good enough to say (as I have sometime heard), "You created the problem, so you fix it." After all, the person who has been mistreated might happen to be the one best situated to begin the process of ending that mistreatment, for example by holding out an olive branch of patience, generosity, and good will. Obviously an olive branch is not right for every situation, but when it's the best thing then it's what must be done, even if "they started it" (also, it's worth mentioning that the notion "you created the problem" is never literally true, in that those who mistreat others always to one degree or another are thereby passing on a problem they inherited, and there's nothing wrong—and everything right—with helping them to break that chain).

By the way, those who want to read more about how to best talk across races about issues of race and racism might want to read *Race Manners: Navigating the Minefield between Black and White Americans*, by Bruce A. Jacobs.[8] It's a great book.

Jacob: Cool, Phil. Thanks for the reference. This has all been really interesting. I wonder if we could summarize and elaborate a little, by discussing the relative importance of race alongside other issues.

How does racism compare with other problems?

Jacob: It seems that we both agree that racism matters, but in quite different ways. Clearly there are some people who are racist—individuals who consciously harbor resentment toward other people because of their race. We both agree that such attitudes are a problem—just as resentment across other categories of difference would be. From our discussion so far, however, you've confirmed that a progressive mindset often goes beyond overt behavior to explore subtle, even unconscious actions or surrounding societal structures (especially economic ones). We went on to discuss how, from this vantage point, racism (not to mention classism, sexism, and other -isms) can become a preeminent, cross-cutting philosophical framework used to explain modern societal ills. One day one of my progressive friends and I got to talking about the "major problems facing the world." His answer: "Racism and water." He believed those to be the two biggest issues facing our human society.

For those who think about race and racism on this level of intensity, Phil, it may be confusing why conservatives seem to not care as much about race. Of course, some may *not* be confused, immediately seeing in this inattention a sure sign of white privilege or racism itself. Because I think we're often misunderstood on this point, I'd like to briefly explore an alternative explanation for why conservatives don't seem to share the same "moral fervor" about the issue as liberals.

When my friend asked me the same question about the major problems of the world, I responded: "The widespread disregard and minimization of God's words and will." The resulting betrayal against God (sin) is what many members of my faith community see as the most crucial problem facing our society. Racism, of course, is one of these sins—but it's only one. Among the many ways to betray God's will and teachings are resentments and hatreds of multiple forms and across various differences. A husband may resent his wife for having a big nose, a wife may hold disdain for a neighbor for not inviting her and her husband to a party, and an employee may resent a coworker for getting a raise. And, of course, someone may resent another for his/her ethnic background or the color of their skin. They are all, to my view, hostile ways of being that displease God. And from this vantage point, racism is not necessarily preeminent in its seduction, danger, or destructiveness.

This position, to be clear, is different from the common "color-blind" perspective, which asserts that race doesn't matter anymore (as in "We're beyond that!"). I believe that racism still exists and is still a problem; it just isn't the "problem of problems"—the be-all, summative problem it is sometimes presented to be. Perhaps some would argue any minimizations of the issue reflect a kind of color-blindness. Still others might read my comments (and perhaps yours too, Phil), once again, as evidence of white privilege—of merely having the luxury to minimize our racial status, because we are white. I would object to those characterizations, however, in part for not attending carefully enough to the narratives out of which social conservatives operate. And I would encourage more determined efforts on all sides of this issue to try to understand the more nuanced realities beneath simple appearances.

Phil: I agree.

Jacob: So do conservatives care about race and racism? Of course, but in a different way than many in your community appear to. And for that we sometimes get criticized.

Phil: For the record, I have never thought "conservatives don't care." Of course you care.

Let me turn again to the issue of the "size" of the racism problem. While I agree with you that each act of resentment is a moral failing to one degree or another, I don't agree with the idea that the various resentments you listed are all of a piece. To my mind (and on this I would say that I line up with most progressives), they're apples and oranges. Someone who's disrespected by her neighbor can presumably find respect somewhere else, and more importantly the messages carried by culture would support her in thinking herself in the right. That's not the case for someone who faces a wall of cultural messages and practices that line up in unison to say that every member of her group is inferior, to blame, stupid, dangerous, deserving of lesser roles, and so on. And those, of course, are among the elements of the historical edifice we call racism. Thankfully, centuries of anti-racism struggle and economic change have undermined intentional racism of the traditional kind, meaning the racism of the bigot. I would not, however, say that we are all the way there even on that score. And as I said, I don't think all forms of resentment have equal power to injure or do equal amounts of harm. Do you, Jacob, believe they have equal power?

Jacob: Yes, in a way. But you've got a point, that there are meaningful differences between resentments which can't be denied. And surely we need to pay attention to the harmful impact of any kind of resentment; I don't see why it is helpful or necessary to single out any one kind. And if I had to single one out, it would likely be resentment between family members—spouses, parents, and children. If we could weigh and compare the sheer human cost of different resentments, wouldn't we find the intra-family kind more pervasive and destructive than racial resentment?

If we understand racism as one form of resentment among many, then discussions of that particular form won't overdominate. Other resentments will also be discussed—and other factors besides resentment. In the case of something like Katrina, then, we might more naturally see race as one set of factors in a complex array of variables.

Phil: As I said before, I very much believe that there was more involved than race and racism in Katrina. It sounds like you just want to make sure the discussion is open enough to consider the range of factors—not necessarily to deny that race and racism could be one of them?

Jacob: That's right.

Is it possible to "repent" of racism?

Jacob: In race-related experiences with both my church and graduate school friends, I sometimes felt like asking: Can people "repent" of racism? Is fundamental change allowed?

The couple who walked out of our church refused to talk or offer feedback that might help other people change for the better. To them, nothing could excuse the behaviors in question: these other members of our congregation were racist and that was unforgivable. Thus I ask in regards to perceived or actual racism: Can people change? Is that allowed? Folks in my community would be much more comfortable with a portrayal of racism, Phil, that allows people like me to apologize and learn greater sensitivity when another has taken offense.

Phil: In my view, yes, people can change. For those who don't agree, I recommend reading Studs Terkel's famous interview with ex–Ku Klux Klan leader C. P. Ellis, who eventually rejected the Klan and everything it stands for.[9] I also believe that each of us should treat others as if they can change, even if we're not sure, or have been convinced in a particular case that it's hopeless. After all, for every person who can't change or will not change, there's surely another person nearby who is not as sure or as hardened in their view, and is paying attention. And all in all, efforts to reach out to those who hate, fear, and distrust can only have a ripple effect of reducing hate, fear, and distrust (unless of course the effort to reach out is manipulative, or does not let a person labeled as a hater have any real input into a discussion intended to change them).

Jacob: Thank you, Phil. Your views of racism are more accessible to me than others I have heard.

How can we avoid a culture of fear?

Jacob: In this and other chapters we've been talking about meaningful differences and how to navigate them. In discussions of diversity, the focus is often on how people can be more sensitive so as to avoid hurting or offending others. This is a fine discussion to have, Phil—but sometimes, once again, this issue has been emphasized as a preeminent moral issue. If the world had a secular ten commandments, I think one of them would definitely be: "Thou shalt not offend."

In one diversity meeting where we were again discussing how to be more sensitive to others' differences so as to not offend them, I asked the group whether it would also be worth spending some time discussing how to not be too easily offended? An awkward silence followed. But I do think it's something to think about: It was the Apostle Paul who wrote encouragement to the people of Corinth to be not "easily provoked, think no evil . . . bear all things" and "endure all things."[10]

In my view, if we do not aim for such change towards greater generosity, to use your word, we risk descending into a rawness of discourse in which people are almost looking for a reason to cry foul. Just think of the last time any celebrity uttered a word that seemed even remotely racist—and the kind of reaction that evoked. My brother-in-law recently corrected a fellow employee after shoddy work and was in return criticized as racist. Upon hearing his story, my mother added: "We feel fearful as conservatives about this issue, like we can't say anything."

I recognize that this is tricky because it is important not to downplay anybody's real experiences, especially those of victims who have faced real harshness and mistreatment. But allowing others to have their own experiences does not mean that we must automatically accept all that they assert as true. In order to create a healthy discourse, as tough as it sounds, I think we need to ensure space to question people's experiences of racial victimization (question, not invalidate). Otherwise the catch-22 will remain, where any question posed about an experience of racism risks you being accused of being racist yourself.

Phil: I agree with all that you just said, Jacob. Not all accusations are true, even those made by people who have indeed suffered from racially motivated mistreatment. I agree, as well, that those on all sides of the issue have work to do, and that one type of work needed is for some people to learn to be less easily offended. Unfortunately, being offended has become popular in our culture, as if it were a way to solve problems. You, Jacob, have identified an instance of such thinking on the left, so I can't resist pointing to an example on the right, that being the degree to which many in the Tea Party movement are not only angry but wear their anger as a badge and constantly declare their victimization at the hands of the supposedly liberal establishment.

Jacob: So the pattern holds, once again, across political lines and issues. Hmm . . . are we starting to see a pattern of patterns?

Overall, the need to be restrained and cautious in the labels and accusations we use is surely an exercise that all sides of the sociopolitical spectrum can benefit from. At the 2010 "Rally to Restore Sanity," Jon Stewart said it this way:

> There are terrorists and racists and Stalinists and theocrats, but those are titles that must be earned. You must have the resume. Not being able to

distinguish between real racists and tea partiers, or real bigots and Juan Williams and Rich Sanchez is an insult—not only to those people, but to the racists themselves, who have put forth the exhausting effort it takes to hate.[11]

What about commonality?

Jacob: As a final note, while these discussions of difference are important, I also want to ask whether we can give equal time to how we are also similar, Phil. Can we put moments aside to celebrate our common heritage and our shared humanity? As a friend once reminded me, an exclusive focus on either commonalities or differences is, by definition, incomplete.

Phil: That's a great suggestion. I think that humans—as humans—have a great deal in common with one another. Indeed I think that commonalities outweigh differences by a long shot. A good diversity workshop will enable its participants to see precisely that; it will highlight how social practices that seem very different are not as different as they seem, and will thereby reveal groups of people that seem "other" to be composed of fellow human beings.

Jacob: Perhaps in the end, Phil, that which divides us is not as important as that which unites us. That's a remarkable thought to consider, given how polarized our communities are.

Phil: Yes. But it's also true that the suspicion some diversity activists harbor toward calls to commonality has a degree of reason behind it. Some calls to commonality don't *actually* welcome all groups, as in "all religions are welcome as long everyone keeps their religion private," "all ethnic groups are welcome, as long as they're not black," "all religions are welcome as long as they're Christian," and "all viewpoints are welcome as long as they're not socialist." So let's be sure that when we celebrate commonality we really mean it.

Jacob: Amen to that, Brother Phil!

Conclusion

We began this book spotlighting the barrage of jarring and aggressive statements issued by the U.S. media and government figures as one reason citizens appear to be having a harder time conversing about their differences in productive ways. Jon Stewart, at the aforementioned "Rally to Restore Sanity" in 2010, said much the same thing:

> The image of Americans that is reflected back to us by our political and media process is false. It is us through a fun house mirror, and not the good kind that makes you look slim in the waist and maybe taller, but the kind where you have a giant forehead, an ass shaped like a month-old pumpkin, and one eyeball. So, why would we work together? Why would you reach across the aisle to a pumpkin assed forehead eyeball monster? . . . Why would you work with Marxists actively subverting our Constitution or racists and homophobes who see no one's humanity but their own?[1]

The answer, of course, is that you probably wouldn't, unless and until you learn how distorted those images of your political opponents actually are. In the meantime, you talk about, read about, wonder about, and sometimes attack those who disagree with your core beliefs; and all the while "those people" lead parallel lives, at times saying negative things about *you* as well.

But what happens if we try talking to the eyeball monster? What happens when we invite the Marxist to grab lunch, or the fundamentalist to join your carpool to work? That's what the two of us wanted to know, a curiosity that led us to start talking with each other a lot, for a long time, about some of our core differences. At some level, we each sensed there was something exciting beyond the fun-house mirror.

Now, two years later, we have completed our dialogue experiment and reached some conclusions. In what follows, we first offer some personal insights in the form of individual responses and then turn to a review of four practical ways that dialogue across political lines may potentially change communities for the better.

Personal Responses to the Dialogue

Jacob: What a ride, Phil! In my thirty-three years of life, I don't know that I've ever had such an impactful conversation. Based on our experience together, I feel bad for other conservatives who haven't experienced an extended conversation with a liberal-leaning friend. What's funny is that after two years of talking, it feels like we've just begun to explore these issues—with other related questions coming up in my mind all the time. What I've perhaps enjoyed the most, Phil, are the surprising commonalities that arose during our conversations: from common commitments to moral principles, to your interest in sensible guidelines regarding sexually explicit media, to your concern with overaggressive accusations of racism.

At the same time, our differences were sharpened and clarified. While I learned a lot from your detailed explications of institutional and structural forces, for instance, you still gave it much more attention than I typically would. For you, the primary solutions to most societal problems seem to lie in rearranging that arena, with individual change being secondary. And you also made it abundantly clear that even if you knew God existed, you'd still wonder what gives Him the right to "tell you what to do"!

Before Phil takes a turn, let me make some brief suggestions to liberal readers of the book, especially those who are not religious, regarding how to talk with someone like me. First, when a religious conservative brings up God, religion, or scripture—try hard not to glaze over (good job, Phil!).

Perhaps you struggled with reading my words to that effect. If so, that's okay. Just understand that this is our "native tongue" and explore ways to translate between different meanings for words or concepts. Also, when we approach you to talk, please don't assume our only motivation is to convert you. Second, if we disagree about something especially important to you—from gay marriage to racism—understand that we have reasons for our convictions that go beyond what you might think initially.

Phil: Thank you, Jacob. I also had fun working on this book. Sometimes, in fact, I found it downright exhilarating. It *was* work, however. And I sometimes found myself pulling my hair out, muttering, "How could anyone possibly believe such a thing?" Each time that happened, however, all I had to do was read onward to find your claims motivated by compassion and a desire for truth. In the end, then, the work was well worth it.

Here are a few words meant especially for conservatives. Jacob, in our conversations together, did not—by my observation—try to move us toward discussion of whether or how systems or institutions might be changed. He's more than willing to consider ideas of that kind, but would much rather talk about individual beliefs and choices, and whether or not they should be altered. My inkling is that many conservatives feel the same way. Is that true of you as well? If so, then please know that I, too, believe that questions of personal behavior, responsibility, and belief are important. And many other liberals and leftists likewise agree. We just think other things are also important.

Next, does it seem to you that liberals and leftists overcriticize and overquestion, to the point where it seems they're ready to reject that which is good in tradition, along with that which is bad? If you feel that way, please realize that for the most part, when we criticize something it's because we honestly think it deserves criticism and we're trying to improve society as best we know how, not to deviously fulfill an immoral "agenda." Yes, we have lots of questions; but as Jacob has encouraged liberals to do for conservatives, try giving our questions a chance.

Finally, most liberals and leftists are not as radical as they're often portrayed, much less rabid revolutionaries. Also (dare I say it), being "radical" doesn't make someone a monster; sometimes it means they have a wild but great idea that simply hasn't caught on yet.

Practical Consequences of Dialogue

Phil and Jacob: Okay, so dialogue can cultivate deeper relationships. Some might yet ask, "Why does this even matter? So you found someone on the other side that you actually get along with—what's the big deal?" To answer that question fully, we now turn to some of the research on dialogue events spanning different settings, formats, and goals. In addition to referencing empirical work in this final section, we also cite student observations from the University of Illinois liberal-conservative dialogue course that Jacob cofacilitated. These cumulative findings identify at least four ways dialogue can potentially contribute to shaping communities for the better.

EXPANDED UNDERSTANDING

The first, most obvious benefit of healthy dialogue is that it generates better understanding. Fully hearing what someone else has to say naturally heightens one's insight into the nuance and richness of their understanding, leading those involved to view one another in "more complex and accurate ways."[2] This includes, first of all, a new awareness of common ground.

In our own dialogue, a good deal of common ground emerged. We agree, for instance, that morality exists independently of preference, that humans possess the potential for goodness (alongside much that needs to be resisted, tamed, or put to a higher calling), and that humans lack total freedom while still having the power and responsibility to choose the better over the worse.

Other commonalities were intertwined with meaningful differences. For instance, we agree on the importance of individual and institutional change (albeit of different kinds), holding media accountable (even if in different ways), the well-being of the family (but with distinct definitions), and changing certain aspects of tradition while preserving others (not the same ones).

The discovery of these commonalities confirmed our belief that any two persons who discuss views can, if they listen to each other with sincerity and openness, unearth kernels of rationality in each other's understandings. Moreover, they are each likely, to be led by that kind of exchange to see something more of the other's humanity. Indeed, the commonalities that tend to emerge in dialogue go beyond mere intellectual resonance to a felt emotional assurance of someone else's standing and value as a person. European philosopher Hans Georg Gadamer wrote that new interpretations gained in dialogue are more than simply fresh subjective perceptions; they instead constitute a way of *being differently* with the others involved.[3] Research has documented multiple ways that dialogue changes the "space" between individuals by bringing increased levels of comfort with the other, more feelings of connection and friendship, more ability to see the world from another perspective,[4] greater ease in communicating across differences, more interest in bridging differences, and new perceptions of common humanity.[5] Students in the University of Illinois liberal-conservative dialogue class remarked:

- "I now understand . . . far-left point of views a lot more. I don't agree with them, but I can *understand* . . .why they might feel as they do."
- "The dialogue made me more open to fears and concerns of the counter-group. It made me see them as a person and not just a view."
- "I have learned they aren't bad people, they just bump heads with me on certain topics."
- "Before this class, I went through the logic of conservatives and would think, 'They have to be *crazy!*' From this experience, it's great to know half of the world is *not nuts*. You don't get this on TV—both sides are goofy there. But from this class, I better understand now the conservative logic; I may not agree, but it makes more sense."[6]

New understanding, not new agreement per se, was the outcome of these dialogues. And indeed, because dialogue often clarifies beliefs and strengthens conviction, it may actually lead *away* from agreement between conversation partners. That clarification of true disagreement is a second kind of understanding generated within authentic dialogue.

As layers of assumptions and perceptions fell away, our dialogue revealed core differences between us. Without attempting a comprehensive list, these include: the ultimate source of morality and authority, the existence of God (and what the answer to that question entails for humans), whether or not the universe is guided by a plan, whether the natural order of the universe gives a special role to humans, the nature of the good (is it tragic or ultimately unified), and the nature of evil (and whether the idea of a devil leads to demonization among humans). As mentioned earlier, we also disagreed about the specific ways that institutions such as the media need to change, what counts as the proper or best family form, which traditions need to evolve or change, and which traditions need to be protected or reinstated.

One reason we are now able to offer this list of differences is that over time we were able to get past a problem faced by many dialogue participants: subtle differences in language and vocabulary that may disrupt communication. Certainly the students in Jacob's dialogue classes often seemed to be talking wholly different languages, with little awareness that basic terms such as rights, responsibility, change, progress, tradition, religion, and morality could have very different meanings. For those who made the effort to listen, however, the fact that the same words were being used in different ways soon became evident. And this, in turn, prompted opposing sides to understand each other better. Similarly, we struggled for a time with each other's different linguistic preferences and customs—exchanging literally thirty-five drafts of the introduction before settling on a format and language we both resonated with.

New Ability to Talk about Difficult Issues

A second practical benefit of dialogue is simply that it "exercises" an entirely new set of conversational muscles. After completing the Illinois dialogue course, students remarked:

- "It was like nothing I have experienced before."
- "[I learned] that it is possible to talk about politically relevant issues without being antagonistic or attacking."
- "Our class last week was . . . maybe the second time I saw people discuss gay marriage in a respectful way."

Why did the experience of dialogue feel so new for these students? One reason, we believe, is that our society provides so few examples of people disagreeing and not condemning each other, and thus doing so for the first time can feel strange. There are some good signs on the horizon, however. When, in January 2011, a member of the House of Representatives was critically wounded and many others killed, national leaders from both sides of the aisle responded by calling upon everyone to make a new commitment to civility in public discourse. Mark DeMoss, conservative creator of the "civility pledge," responded to President Obama's memorial speech with these words: "I have been encouraged by the words and disposition of our president—a man I did not vote for and disagree with on almost every policy issue. Still, I would defend him as a man I believe loves his family and his country, and wakes up each day desiring to do what he believes is best for both."[7] And Senator John McCain, after the same set of events, spoke in a similar vein:

> I disagree with many of the president's policies, but I believe he is a patriot sincerely intent on using his time in office to advance our country's cause. I reject accusations that his policies and beliefs make him unworthy to lead America or opposed to its founding ideals. And I reject accusations that Americans who vigorously oppose his policies are less intelligent, compassionate or just than those who support them.[8]

DeMoss and McCain demonstrate a crucial distinction: separating whether or not they agree with someone from what they think of him or her as a person. They appreciate the fact that questioning someone about even the most intense disagreements need not imply that person is thereby hateful, evil, or otherwise worthy of condemnation. This was epitomized by a placard at Jon Stewart's mock rally: "I disagree with you, but I'm pretty sure you're not Hitler."

Likewise, neither of us, even in our moments of greatest opposition, found the other to be truly crazy. Instead, we were each struck by the considerable coherence and good intention reflected in the views we were hearing. As Obama himself has suggested, "Challenging each other's ideas can renew our democracy. But when we challenge each other's motives, it becomes harder to see what we hold in common."[9] In the end, we found ourselves concluding that the "red-blue" divide may be less about who has the most noble or right desires and more about who *believes* one thing as opposed to another.

If this way of talking becomes more normal, those citizens who dislike adversarial conversation might be relieved to encounter the safety of exploration that genuine dialogue provides. By contrast, those accustomed to frequent debate might still see dialogue as a kind of kumbaya hand-holding feel-good show, with little substance or hard questions. They might also assume that participants in dialogue are not allowed to have strong positions or to share them with conviction. Our experience, however, suggests the reverse: that when you assume the best about someone and don't question their motives, the space for tough questions and direct sharing can dramatically expand.

Jacob: I want to jump in here and say that I've never been able to share so much detail of my beliefs, with so much conviction, as during our dialogue. It was a remarkable experience to share that much—and then to be asked for more—and this, with someone I knew disagreed with me! My prior math had gone something like this: "Oh, this person disagrees with me, so I need to figure out how to share my belief in a way that will help him/her see what I mean." But when I tried that approach, I found that being directly persuasive can be the least persuasive way to share something! After all, who likes a vacuum cleaner salesman? Rather than approach our friends, neighbors, and fellow community members with a "let's talk so I can change your mind" attitude, why not prioritize asking questions and showing an interest in their desires and beliefs? And then see where that takes you.

Similarly, I also learned far more about you, Phil, than I would have if you had merely been working your best professorial magic to try to convince, persuade, or debate me. And it was both refreshing and powerful to hear self-critique from you about liberals and to offer the same on my part—to let down my guard and admit things like, "Yeah, you're right, conservatives can be pretty stubborn about that."

Phil: Yes, Jacob, it's been quite a journey, worthwhile in many ways. I understand myself better, I understand the American political divide better, I'm more conscious of the ideas I share with conservatives, and I have more hope for the future. (And it wasn't tough for me, by the way, to critique liberals or my fellow leftists, perhaps because that's something we do, we critique one another, sometimes to a fault).

Jacob: Dialogue seems to increase people's confidence in sharing their true feelings and ideas (and not just with people they know agree with them). There is a strange cultural message out there claiming that there is something troubling or wrong about sharing what you believe (you should see the looks we Mormons sometimes get when we invite people to hear our message as missionaries; you would think we were spreading anthrax). Perhaps that message is a byproduct of the fact that we live in a world where everyone is out to convince everyone else of something—a world where, most of the time, we hear someone's ideas as part of a sales pitch. And thus it's understandable that we often protect ourselves by turning away from conversations and ideas that seem challenging.

Phil: Yes, and it seems to me, Jacob, that the guardedness you speak of helps explain why people so often lack the skill to talk to one another in situations of conflict. They lack practice.

Phil and Jacob: And so we ask: What if we lived in a world where everyone had something beautiful and precious to share, and no one had a monopoly on truth? Then again, what if this *is* the world we live in? We believe that each person does have something of value to offer. And we therefore believe that, by creating new dialogue spaces one conversation at a time, we-the-people can together move in the direction of what Glenn Tinder calls "the attentive society," meaning a place where "people listen seriously to those with whom they fundamentally disagree" and possess a "widespread willingness to give and receive assistance on the road to truth."[10]

FRAMING ISSUES IN A NEW WAY

We have made mention in this book of the fact that media and political leaders strategically deploy interpretive frames (e.g., philosophical frameworks, paradigms, narratives) as part of their political advocacy and commentary. These frames, which often operate beneath our awareness, have great power to determine outcomes. For example, suppose a new national security law that enhances the government's power of surveillance is proposed in Congress. If advocates of the bill succeed in framing the issue as "Are you in favor or protecting the nation or not?" then the bill is more likely to pass. If the frame that prevails instead emphasizes privacy issues, the bill is more likely to fail.

Fortunately, as illustrated in these chapters, there is also power in "reframing" an issue—that being the process of shifting the interpretive lens through which a question is viewed so people can see from a new angle, and thereby envision new possibilities. It is precisely this process that occurs naturally within healthy dialogue. As participants bring different frames to the table, juxtapose them with other frames, and realize entirely new ones, seismic shifts can result. To use Gadamer's language, a "fusion of horizons" is possible whenever two diverging horizons have been fully "put into play" through dialogue.[11] While such reframing does not magically dissolve underlying philosophical or ideological differences, it can create dramatically new perspectives. Indeed, a tangible power can emerge from this kind of experience, as participants become more aware of alternatives and thus better able to choose which frame they really believe and want.

The two of us experienced that very process in our work together. When the dialogue commenced, we were already aware of several dichotomous frames mentioned earlier, such as "preserving tradition vs. changing it," "embracing diversity vs. being prejudiced," etc. Then, as we critically examined these frames, we began to consider viable alternatives, such as "What exactly should be preserved in tradition and what ought to change?" and "What does it mean to be open, tolerant, and accepting?" Finally, as we explored questions raised by these new frames, we each came to new convictions as to where we stood, and why.

Alternative frames can function as fresh "centers of gravity" for public exchange. In addition to pulling citizen discourse away from intransigent culture-war ruts, the development of alternative frames could expand community exchanges to include a wider range of participants. Those shifts might even expand people's expectations of who is worth listening to on a particular issue. Conservative-leaning citizens, for instance, might be appreciated as potentially offering meaningful insights regarding institutional/ structural issues and the possibility of broad societal change. And liberal-leaning citizens might correspondingly be appreciated as having something valuable to say about individual-level processes and aspects of society needing preservation.

As noted earlier, even when participants gather for the explicit purpose of dialogue, conflicts between the different language or frames they bring to the table can prevent many from finding enough openness to connect. Disrupting these frames early in the dialogue, however, may gently spur participants to explore more openly the diverse views in play—helping to dissolve barriers that prevent people from engaging more fully in the conversation. Thus, a 2005 study conducted by George Bizer and Richard Petty found that even slight shifts in the "valence" of exchange—the degree to which issues are framed as oppositional or not—can have a significant effect on whether people lean toward resistance or openness in relation to a new political message.[12]

STARTLING COLLABORATIONS

"Okay, so some people have a great 'chat,' learn this and that, and see a few things differently. . . . So what? How can that help solve real-life problems?"

To answer that question, we need to remind ourselves that our current sociopolitical milieu accentuates frames that encourage a "winner-takes-all" approach to public judgment and predispose people to forms of engagement that do "not allow other perspectives to be incorporated into the final decision."[13] Such mindsets make collaboration on anything but the most rudimentary proposals difficult. One anti–domestic violence coalition in a local community, for example, nearly broke up when a Catholic hospital learned that Planned Parenthood was participating.

Because dialogue tends to uncover common ground, it can potentially lead to new collaborations that cross established political lines. Against this backdrop, Alison Kadlec and Will Friedman Public Agenda point out that an improved public discourse could create "an enormous range of possibilities for the advancement of . . . practices and policies" which may be achieved "simply for the price of improving our capacities and enlarging our opportunities for collaborative inquiry about common problems."[14] When it comes to the issue of domestic violence, for example, dialogue has the potential to help different citizens respond in unity, even while some frame the abuse as "an instantiation of traditional gender norms" while others frame it as "incompatible with biblical standards for relationships." Other topics ripe for collaboration include challenging excessive individualism, reducing gratuitous sex and violence in commercial media presentations, and creating new forms of (or methods to achieve) environmental protection.

We should not be naïve, however. Liberals and conservatives will not agree on gay marriage anytime soon (or ever). But, as illustrated by the adoption of the gay rights ordinance in Salt Lake City, the results of dialogue may yet surprise us. A 2005 Pew Research Center report on the "red/blue" divide argues that "numerous opportunities exist for building coalitions across party lines on many issues currently facing the nation"—coalitions that, in many cases, could "include some strange political bedfellows."[15] Kadlec and Friedman suggest that dialogue can create possibilities to "identify and pursue new, unforeseen and unexpected directions for working together," and lead people to develop "a greater appreciation of previously unknown shared interests that can form the basis of working agreements for moving forward on concrete public problems."[16] And the Boston-based Public Conversations Project points out that "relationships that evolve through dialogue hold previously unthinkable possibilities . . . for collaboration."[17]

In sum, dialogue is a potential catalyst for collaboration, for reframing, for new ways of disagreeing, and for better understanding. In spite of these potential benefits, substantial barriers still remain. To wit:

- Many people have little or no experience with dialogue.
- The media provides a steady stream of claims about what it is that different people and groups stand for or believe, thus prelabeling ideas and communities to the point that observers assume they've got "those people" figured out . . . hence they see no reason to bother talking with them.
- Many people are cynical or discouraged about the public sphere, to the point where they resort mostly to grumbling and complaining, rather than attempting some positive form of action.

On a brighter note, anger sometimes prompts fresh analysis that then gives rise to new ideas and energy for change. Thus MSNBC commentator Joe Scarborough, after complaining about the "war on words" and the "angry voices" that currently dominate public discourse, goes on to suggest dialogue as a potential alternative. He first challenges government leaders to seek out the "voices of . . . rational Americans who show respect to their neighbors, who raise their families, who go to work, and who play by the rules." And he then speaks directly to the general public: "It's time for *you*, you quiet Americans to respond. Not with angry words or hateful commentaries or setting your hair on fire . . . but rather . . . with reasonable voices and a rational debate."[18]

We agree. We believe it is time to stand against distorted images. We believe it is time for each of us to learn more about the people around us. And we believe that there is good to be found in those people. Speaking at the Tucson memorial service mentioned earlier, President Obama noted: "For all our imperfections, we are full of decency and goodness, and . . . the forces that divide us are not as strong as those that unite us."[19] And Senator John McCain, in a response to the same shooting, spoke in similar terms: "We Americans have different opinions on how best to serve [the country] . . . but we should be mindful . . . that our differences . . . are smaller than we sometimes imagine them to be." He concluded, "We are Americans and fellow human beings, and that shared distinction is so much more important than the disputes that invigorate our noisy, rough-and-tumble political culture."[20]

These views are optimistic, but maybe they should be. Maybe what unites us is truly stronger than we think, just as perhaps our differences are "smaller than we imagine them to be." That's something you might explore and test for yourself. For indeed, this book is presented not as the end of the conversation—but just the beginning. Why not explore those possibilities for yourself by putting down this book (in just a second) and picking up your phone. The Marxist neighbor and fundamentalist coworker are waiting for your call. When you meet, consider opening your conversation with something general: "So what do you really care about most in life . . . and why is that?" Then, hold your expectations in check and listen. Pay attention to what you agree with and don't agree with, what feels right, and what makes you uncomfortable. Then start asking specific questions—one at a time—and look for what comes up. Before it's over, don't be surprised if this person begins raising questions for you too. You'll know what to do from there.

Notes

Introduction

1. Chris Rovzar, "Rush Limbaugh: 'There's Going to Be a Retard Summit at the White House,'" *New York*, February 3, 2010, http://nymag.com/daily/intel/2010/02/rush_limbaugh_theres_going_to.html (accessed January 5, 2012).
2. Karin Tanabe, "Charles Barkley Calls GOP Field 'Idiots,'" azcentral.com, December 21, 2011, http://www.azcentral.com/news/articles/2011/12/21/20111221charles-barkley-calls-republicans-idiots-politico.html (accessed January 10, 2012).
3. *Hardball with Chris Matthews* (transcript), MSNBC, July 27, 2011, http://www.msnbc.msn.com/id/43928001/ns/msnbc_tv-hardball_with_chris_matthews/t/hardball-chris-matthews-wednesday-july/ (accessed January 5, 2012).
4. Anne Coulter, *If Democrats Had Any Brains, They'd Be Republicans* (New York: Crown Forum Publishers, 2007), 165.
5. Phil Neisser, *United We Fall: Ending America's Love Affair with the Political Center* (Santa Barbara, CA: Praeger, 2008).
6. Morgan Fiorina, Samuel Abrams, and Jeremy Pope, *Culture War? The Myth of a Polarized America* (New York: Longman, 2004), 78, 102.
7. "Jon Stewart Speech: Transcript," *TBD Arts*, http://www.tbd.com/blogs/tbd-arts/2010/10/jon-stewart-speech-transcript-3955.html (accessed January 23, 2011).
8. James Davidson Hunter, *Culture Wars: The Struggle to Define America. Making Sense of the Battles Over the Family, Art, Education, Law, and Politics* (New York: HarperCollins, 1991), 290.
9. Ibid., 30.

10. D. Conor Seyle and Matthew L. Newman, "A House Divided? The Psychology of Red and Blue America," *American Psychologist* 61, (2006): 577.

11. Ibid.

12. David Bohm, *On Dialogue*, Lee Nicol, ed. (London: Routledge, 1996); Peter Kühnlein, Hannes Rieser, and Henk Zeevat, eds., *Perspectives on Dialogue in the New Millennium*, Pragmatics & Beyond New Series (Amsterdam: John Benjamins Publishing Co., 2003); Nancy Rodenborg and Nancy Huynh, "On Overcoming Segregation: Social Work and Intergroup Dialogue," *Social Work with Groups* 29, no. 1 (2006): 27–44.

13. David Schoem and Sylvia Hurtado, eds., *Intergroup Dialogue: Deliberative Democracy in School, College, Community and Workplace* (Anne Arbor: University of Michigan Press, 2001); Lenny Traubman, "Our Jewish-Palestinian Living Room Dialogue Group in California," http://traubman.igc.org/dg -prog.htm (accessed January 23, 2011).

14. Sandy Heierbacher, quoted on the resource page of the National Coalition for Dialogue and Deliberation website, http://ncdd.org/rc/item/1501 (accessed February 16, 2011).

15. Liyakatali Takim, "From Conversion to Conversation: Interfaith Dialogue in Post 9-11 America," *Muslim World* 94, no. 3 (2004): 343–55.

16. Colin Knox and Joanne Hughes, "Crossing the Divide: Community Relations in Northern Ireland," *Journal of Peace Research* 33 (1996): 83–98; Elisabeth Porter, "Creating Dialogical Spaces in Northern Ireland," *International Feminist Journal of Politics* 2, no. 2 (2000): 163–84.

17. Mohammed Abu-Nimer, "Education for Coexistence and Arab-Jewish Encounters in Israel," *Journal of Social Issues* 60, no. 2 (2004): 405–22; Ben Mollov and Chaim Lavie, "Culture, Dialogue, and Perception Change in the Israeli-Palestinian Conflict," *International Journal of Conflict Management* 12, no. 1 (2001): 69–87.

18. Phil, a political scientist, had published *United We Fall*, which details the alarming deterioration of American citizens' basic ability to disagree in productive ways and calls upon people to more fully embrace disagreement as a valuable practice. And Jacob, a community psychologist, had helped create and evaluate a college-level dialogue class for liberal and conservative students and also collaborated with researcher Nathan Todd on a series of interviews exploring the divergent narratives of liberal and conservative citizens (see Jacob Hess, Danielle Rynczak, Joe Minarik, and Joycelyn Landrum-Brown, "Alternative Settings for Liberal-Conservative Exchange: Examining an Undergraduate Dialogue Course," *Journal of Community and Applied Social Psychology* 20, no. 2 [2010]: 156–66; Jacob Hess and Nathan Todd, "From Culture War to Difficult Dialogue: Exploring Distinct Frames for Citizen Exchange about Social Problems," *Journal of Public Deliberation* 5, no.1, article 3 [2009]: 1–27.); "What Is Dialogue? Definitions from Leaders in the Field," National Coalition for Dialogue and Deliberation, http://ncdd.org/rc/item/1501 (accessed January 16, 2012).

19. Although the word "leftist" is used in specific ways at some points, it is mostly used interchangeably with liberal" and "progressive" throughout the text.

20. There will be religious conservatives that, when finding out Jacob is writing as a Mormon, may put the book aside, assuming he could not speak well on behalf of other conservative believers and certainly not for them. And indeed, I (Jacob) don't pretend to speak for all conservative believers, given the wide range of understandings that exist regarding God's plan for His children. In some cases, those differences do figure prominently in my discussions with Phil. In most instances, however—especially on the level of basic values, my efforts to articulate core commitments will, I believe, largely reaffirm and satisfy other conservative religionists, including orthodox Christians. To my broader conservative family, I would ask you—like our liberal brothers and sisters—to hear me out before passing judgment (offering the same consideration, of course, to Phil).

21. Seyle and Newman, "A House Divided?," 577–79.

22. Ibid.

23. David Davenport, "Back to the Town Hall: Why Conservatives Should Embrace Deliberative Democracy," *Hoover Digest: Research and Opinion on Public Policy* (2008): 97. Common Sense California is an initiative of the Davenport Institute for Public Engagement and Civic Leadership at Pepperdine University's School of Public Policy.

24. Hess and Todd, "From Culture War."

25. In Sandy Heierbacher, "Taking Our Work to the Next Level: Addressing Challenges Facing the Dialogue and Deliberation Community," *International Journal of Public Participation* 3, no. 1 (2009): 1–19.

26. Nicolas C. Burbules, "The Limits of Dialogue as a Critical Pedagogy," in *Revolutionary Pedagogies: Cultural Politics, Education, and the Discourse of Theory*, Peter Trifonas, ed. (London: Routledge, 2000), 251–73; L. M. Sanders, "Against Deliberation," *Political Theory* 25 (1997): 347–64.

27. Alison Kadlec and Will Friedman, "Deliberative Democracy and the Problem of Power," *Journal of Public Deliberation* 3, no. 1, article 8 (2007): 7.

28. Paulo Freire, *Pedagogy of the Oppressed* (New York: Herder and Herder, 1970), 70.

29. Abu-Nimer, "Education for Coexistence and Arab-Jewish Encounters in Israel,"; Mollov and Lavie, "Culture, Dialogue, and Perception Change," 69–87.

30. Mark DeMoss, "Don't Expect Civility," *Politico*, January 17, 2011, http://www.politico.com/news/stories/0111/47677.html#ixzz1EX3flhKc (accessed January 31, 2011).

31. Thomas Schwandt, "Farewell to Criteriology," *Qualitative Inquiry* 2 (1996): 67.

32. Hess, Rynczak, Minarik, and Landrum-Brown, "Alternative Settings for Liberal-Conservative Exchange," 156–66.

Chapter 1. Differing Takes on Power and Authority
1. Matthew 18:3–5 (King James Version).
2. Brigham Young, *Journal of Discourses* (Liverpool: F. D. Richards, 1855), 9:150.
3. Michel Foucault, *The Archeology of Knowledge* (New York: Routledge, 1962).
4. Ephesians 6:12 (King James Version).

Chapter 2. Big Government, Big Media, Big Business, and Big Religion
1. Charley Reese, "545 People Responsible for All of America's Woes," *Stonewall County Courier* (Aspermont, Texas), September 19, 1985 (updated by Reese in 2009), http://www.apfn.org/APFN/woes.htm (accessed July 30, 2009).
2. Ezra Taft Benson, "Born of God," *Ensign* (July 1989): 2.
3. "Gallup: Conservatives Outnumber Liberals 2:1, Church Attendance Rising," Secular News Daily, June 28, 2010, http://www.secularnewsdaily.com/2010/06/28/gallup-conservatives-outnumber-liberals-21-church-attendance-rising/ (accessed January 29, 2011).
4. William J. Bennett, *The Devaluing of America: The Fight for Our Culture and Our Children* (New York: Touchstone, 1992), especially chapter 1: "Introduction: The Culture Wars."
5. Ephesians 6:12 (King James Version).
6. "Sexualization of Girls," American Psychological Association, http://www.apa.org/pi/wpo/sexualization.html (accessed January 9, 2011).
7. University of Michigan Health System, "Television and Children," *Your Child: Development and Behavior Resources; A Guide to Information and Support to Parents*, http://www.med.umich.edu/yourchild/topics/tv.htm (accessed February 26, 2011).
8. "Religion," *Dictionary.com*, http://dictionary.reference.com/browse/religion (accessed January 30, 2011).
9. William McKenzie, "Ready for Some Football but it Feels Like a Pagan Ritual," *DallasNews.com*, January 31, 2011, http://www.dallasnews.com/opinion/columnists/william-mckenzie/20110131-william-mckenzie-ready-for-some-football-but-it-feels-like-a-pagan-ritual.ece (accessed January 31, 2011).
10. Sharlene Nagy Hesse-Biber, *The Cult of Thinness* (USA: Oxford University Press, 2006), 4, 10.
11. "Protect the Truth," http://www.protectthetruth.org/truthcampaign.htm (accessed February 26, 2011).
12. "Fight the New Drug," http://www.fightthenewdrug.org (accessed February 26, 2011).
13. Gary Marcus, *The Birth of the Mind* (New York: Perseus, 2004), 45, 148, emphasis added.
14. Mitch Daniels, "Transcript: GOP Response From Gov. Mitch Daniels," National Public Radio (January 24, 2012), http://www.npr.org/2012/01/24/145812869/transcript-gop-response-from-gov-mitch-daniels, (accessed January 29, 2012).

Chapter 3. What to Make of Values and Morality

1. Brent Slife, *Managing Inescapable Values in Psychotherapy* (Los Angeles: Counseling Program, University of Southern California, 2000).

2. Charles Taylor, *Sources of the Self: The Making of the Modern Identity* (Harvard University Press, 1992), 15–16, 28.

3. Aristotle, *Politics by Aristotle*, Benjamin Jowett, trans. (New York: Oxford University Press, 1945).

4. Taylor, *Sources of the Self*.

5. Jonathan Haidt and Jesse Graham, "When Morality Opposes Justice: Conservatives Have Moral Intuitions that Liberals May not Recognize," *Social Justice Research* 20, no. 1 (2007): 98–116.

6. Jonathan Haidt, "Jonathan Haidt on the Moral Roots of Liberals and Conservatives," TED Talks (March 2008), http://www.ted.com/talks/jonathan _haidt_on_the_moral_mind.html (accessed April 25, 2010).

7. Hess and Todd, "From Culture War" 1–27.

8. Genesis 1:26–27 (King James Version).

9. Revelation 12:7 (King James Version).

10. *The Book of Mormon*, 2 Nephi 2:17.

11. *The Book of Mormon*, 2 Nephi 2:11, 22–25.

12. James 1:27 (King James Version).

13. *The Book of Mormon*, Alma 7:7, 11–13.

14. There are many illustrations in the Bible, or instance, Isaiah 1:18 (King James Version): "Come let us reason together. . . ."

15. Richard N. Williams, "Faith, Reason, Knowledge, and Truth," *Brigham Young University Speeches* (February 1, 2000), http://speeches.byu.edu/reader /reader.php?id=1600 (accessed on February 27, 2011).

16. *The Book of Mormon*, Alma 32.

17. Mark DeMoss, "Don't Expect Civility," *Politico* (January 17, 2011), http://www.politico.com/news/stories/0111/47677.html#ixzz1EX3fIhKc (accessed January 31, 2011).

18. Joseph Smith Jr., *"Joseph Smith History." In The Pearl of Great Price,* 1(8–17) *(Salt Lake City:* The Church of Jesus Christ of Latter-day Saints, 1851/1981).

19. James 1:5 (King James Version).

20. Smith, *"Joseph Smith History."*

21. Ibid.

22. Exodus 33:11 (King James Version).

23. Galatians 5:22 (King James Version).

24. Donald Q. Canon, "The King Follett Discourse: Joseph Smith's Greatest Sermon in Historical Perspective," *BYU Studies* 18, vol. 2 (1978): 179–92, http://byustudies.byu.edu/showTitle.aspx?title=5320.

25. James Perloff, *The Case Against Darwin: Why the Evidence Should Be Examined*, (Refuge Books, 2002).

26. Miiamaaria Saarela et al., "The Compassionate Brain: Humans Detect Intensity of Pain from Another's Face," *Cerebral Cortex* 17, no. 1 (February 2006): 230–37, http://cercor.oxfordjournals.org/content/17/1/230.full (accessed January 21, 2011).

Chapter 4. Traditional Gender Roles: Blessing, Oppressing, or What?

1. "The Family: A Proclamation to the World," the First Presidency and Council of the Twelve Apostles of the Church of Jesus Christ of Latter-day Saints, 1995, http://lds.org/library/display/0,4945,161-1-11-1,00.html (accessed December 20, 2010).
2. Matthew 23:11 (King James Version).
3. The song is "More Beautiful You" (2009) by Johnny Diaz.
4. Barack Obama, "Remarks by the President at a Father's Day Event" (The White House: Office of the Press Secretary, June 21, 2010), http://www.whitehouse.gov/the-press-office/remarks-president-a-fathers-day-event (accessed January 31, 2011).
5. Ibid.
6. Ibid.
7. Doctrine and Covenants 121:39 (Church of Jesus Christ of Latter-day Saints, 1835/1981).
8. Unpublished manuscript, with permission, emphasis in the original.
9. Eliza R. Snow, "Oh, my Father," *Hymns* (Salt Lake City: The Church of Jesus Christ of Latter-day Saints, 1985), no. 292.
10. Jacob Z. Hess, Nicole Elaine Allen, and Nathan R. Todd, "Interpreting Community Accountability: Citizen Views of Responding to Domestic Violence (or Not)," *Qualitative Report* 16, no. 6 (2011).
11. Camreeno360, "Why Are American men Depicted So Badly in Shows and Movies?" (Gametrailers.com, Dec 30, 2008), http://forums.gametrailers.com/thread/why-are-american-men-depicted-/563820 (accessed January 20, 2012).
12. Hess and Todd, "From Culture War," 13.
13. Mary Pipher, *Reviving Ophelia: Saving the Selves of Adolescent Girls* (New York: Ballantine Books, 1994).

Chapter 5. Sexual Orientation Battles: Can We Disagree and Not Hate Each Other?

1. Jacob Hess, Discourse analysis study of online comments in response to Proposition 8's passage, (working paper). Excerpts taken from comment pages of the *San Francisco Chronicle*, *San Diego Union Tribune*, *New York Times*, *USA Today*, *Wall Street Journal*, *Deseret News*, and *Salt Lake Tribune*.
2. See Public Conversations Project, "Getting Started: PCP's First Dialogues," http://www.publicconversations.org/who/firstdialogues (accessed January 23, 2011).
3. Barack Obama, "Notre Dame Commencement Address" (The White House: Office of the Press Secretary, May 17, 2009), http://www.whitehouse.gov/video/President-Obama-Notre-Dame-Commencement (accessed June 1, 2011).
4. Antoine Lutz et al., "Regulation of the Neural Circuitry of Emotion by Compassion Meditation: Effects of Meditative Expertise," *PLoS ONE* , no. 3 (2008): e1897, http://www.plosone.org/article/info%3Adoi%2F10

.1371%2Fjournal.pone.0001897 (accessed March 2, 2011); Lee Osterhout et al., "Second-language Learning and Changes in the Brain," *Journal of Neurolinguistics* 21, no. 6 (2008): 509–21; Kimberly Goldapple et al., "Modulation of Cortical-limbic Pathways in Major Depression: Treatment-specific Effects of Cognitive Behavior Therapy," *Archives of General Psychiatry* 61 (2004): 34–41.

5. Doug Haldeman, "Gay Rights, Patient Fights: The Implications of Sexual Orientation Conversion Therapy," *Professional Psychology: Research and Practice* 33, no. 3 (2002): 260–64.

6. A great essay on this subject is John Corvino's classic, "Homosexuality: The Nature and Harm Arguments," in *The Philosophy of Sex: Contemporary Readings*, Alan Soble, ed. (Lanham, MD: Rowman and Littlefield, 1997), 137–48.

7. Bill Bishop, *The Big Sort: Why the Clustering of Like-minded America Is Tearing Us Apart* (Boston, MA: Houghton Mifflin Harcourt, 2008).

8. Neisser, *United We Fall.*

9. Matt Canham, Derek P. Jensen, and Rosemary Winters, "Salt Lake City Adopts Pro-gay Statutes—with LDS Church Support," *Salt Lake Tribune*, November 11, 2009.

10. Ibid.

11. Ibid.

12. Ibid.

Chapter 6. Ongoing Racial Tension: Inevitable or Escapable?

1. Thomas Sugrue, *The Origins of the Urban Crisis* (Princeton, NJ: Princeton University Press, 1996).

2. Carter Wilson, *Racism: From Slavery to Advanced Capitalism* (Thousand Oaks, CA: Sage, 1996).

3. Shehnaz Jagpal, *Racial Inequality in the United States: Analyzing the Wealth Gap* (master's thesis, Georgetown University, 2003), posted at http://aladinrc .wrlc.org/bitstream/1961/4127/1/etd_sj87.pdf (accessed January 21, 2012).

4. The phrase is that of Shelby Steele, a thoughtful conservative whose work has influenced me a good deal, even though I think he is all wrong about poverty and welfare. See Shelby Steele, *A Dream Deferred: The Second Betrayal of Black Freedom in America* (New York: HarperCollins, 1998).

5. Private correspondence, with permission.

6. Dr. Mikhail Lyubansky, private correspondence, with permission.

7. Dr. Gregory A. Miller, E-mail communication, University of Illinois at Urbana-Champaign, with permission.

8. Bruce A. Jacobs, *Race Manners: Navigating the Minefield between Black and White Americans* (New York: Arcade Books, 2007).

9. Studs Terkel, "C. P. Ellis," in *Race, Class, and Gender in the United States: An Integrated Study*, 5th ed., Paula S. Rothenberg, ed. (New York: Worth Publishers, 2000).

10. 1st Corinthians 13 (King James Version).

11. "Jon Stewart Speech: Transcript," *TBD Arts.*

Conclusion

1. "Jon Stewart Speech: Transcript," *TBD Arts*.
2. John Gastil and James Dillard "Increasing Political Sophistication Through Public Deliberation," *Political Communication* 16 (1999): 3–23.
3. Hans Georg Gadamer, *Truth and Method*, 2nd revised ed., Joel Weinsheimer and Donald G. Marshall, trans. (New York: Continuum International Publishing Group, 2004).
4. Alison Yeakley, "The Nature of Prejudice Change: Positive and Negative Change Processes Arising from Intergroup Contact Experiences," *Dissertation Abstracts International* 59, 10-A (1999).
5. Biren Nagda, "Fostering Meaningful Racial Engagement Through Intergroup Dialogues," *Group Processes & Intergroup Relations* 6, no. 1 (2003): 111–28.
6. Hess, Rynczak, Minarik, and Landrum-Brown, "Alternative Settings for Liberal-Conservative Exchange," 156–66.
7. DeMoss, "Don't Expect Civility."
8. John McCain, "After the Shootings, Obama Reminds the Nation of the Golden Rule," op-ed, *Washington Post*, January 16, 2011, http://www.washingtonpost.com/wp-dyn/content/article/2011/01/14/AR2011011403871.html (accessed January 25, 2011).
9. Michael A. Fletcher, "At National Prayer Breakfast, Obama Warns Against 'Erosion of Civility,'" *Washington Post*, February 4, 2010, http://www.washingtonpost.com/wp-dyn/content/article/2010/02/04/AR2010020401728.html (accessed February 18, 2010).
10. E. J. Dionne and Michael Cromartie, "Modernist, Orthodox, or Flexidox: Why the Culture War Debate Endures," in *Is There a Culture War?: A Dialogue on Values and American Public Life*, James Davidson Hunter and Alan Wolfe, eds. (Washington, DC: Brooking Institution Press, 2006), 8.
11. Ibid.
12. George Y. Bizer and Richard E. Petty, "How We Conceptualize Our Attitudes Matters: The Effects of Valence Framing on the Resistance of Political Attitudes," *Political Psychology* 26 (2005): 553–68.
13. Seyle and Newman, "A House Divided?" 577.
14. Kadlec and Friedman, "Deliberative Democracy," 23.
15. Pew Research Center for the People and the Press, "The 2005 Political Typology: Beyond Red vs. Blue," (Washington, DC, 2005), 2.
16. Kadlec and Friedman, "Deliberative Democracy," 14–15.
17. Maggie Herzig and Laurie Chasin, "Fostering Dialogue Across Divides: A Nuts and Bolts Guide from the Public Conversations Project" (Watertown, MA: Public Conversations Project, 2006), http://www.publicconversations.org/resources/fostering-dialogue-across-divides (accessed January 12, 2011).
18. Mark Finkelstein, "Dems Will Love Morning Joe's Odd Manifesto Against 'Angry Voices,'" *NewsBusters*, September 20, 2010, http://newsbusters.org/blogs/mark-finkelstein/2010/09/20/morning-joes-odd-manifesto-against-angry-voices-sounds-lot-obama-s. (accessed March 2, 2011).

19. Barack Obama, "Remarks by the President at a Memorial Service for the Victims of the Shooting in Tucson, Arizona" (The White House: Office of the Press Secretary, January 12, 2011), http://www.whitehouse.gov /the-press-office/2011/01/12/remarks-president-barack-obama-memorial -service-victims-shooting-tucson (accessed March 1, 2011).

20. John McCain, "After the Shootings, Obama Reminds the Nation of the Golden Rule," (Washington Post, January 16, 2011), http://www.washing tonpost.com/wp-dyn/content/article/2011/01/14/AR2011011403871.html, (accessed January 20, 2012).

Selected Bibliography

Abu-Nimer, Mohammed. "Education for Coexistence and Arab-Jewish Encounters in Israel." *Journal of Social Issues* 60, no. 2 (2004): 405–22.

American Psychological Association. "Sexualization of Girls." http://www.apa.org/pi/wpo/sexualization.html (accessed January 9, 2011).

Aristotle, *Politics by Aristotle*. Benjamin Jowett, trans. New York: Oxford University Press, 1945.

Bennett, William J. *The Devaluing of America: The Fight for Our Culture and Our Children*. New York: Touchstone, 1992.

Benson, Ezra Taft. "Born of God," *Ensign* (July 1989).

Bishop, Bill. *The Big Sort: Why the Clustering of Like-minded America Is Tearing Us Apart*. Boston, MA: Houghton Mifflin Harcourt, 2008.

Bizer, George, and Richard Petty. "How We Conceptualize Our Attitudes Matters: The Effects of Valence Framing on the Resistance of Political Attitudes." *Political Psychology* 26 (2005): 553–68.

Bohm, David. *On Dialogue*. Lee Nicol, ed. London: Routledge, 1996.

Burbules, Nicholas C. "The Limits of Dialogue as a Critical Pedagogy." In *Revolutionary Pedagogies: Cultural Politics, Education, and the Discourse of Theory*. Peter Trifonas, ed. London: Routledge, 2000.

Canham, Matt, Derek P. Jensen, and Rosemary Winters. "Salt Lake City Adopts Pro-gay Statutes—with LDS Church Support." *Salt Lake Tribune*, November 11, 2009.

Corvino, John. "Homosexuality: The Nature and Harm Arguments." In *The Philosophy of Sex: Contemporary Readings*, Alan Soble, ed. Lanham, MD: Rowman and Littlefield, 1997.

Coulter, Anne. *If Democrats Had Any Brains, They'd Be Republicans* New York: Crown Forum Publishers, 2007.

Daniels, Mitch. "Transcript: GOP Response From Gov. Mitch Daniels," National Public Radio (January 24, 2012), http://www.npr.org/2012/01/24/145812869/transcript-gop-response-from-gov-mitch-daniels, (accessed January 29, 2012).

Davenport, David. "Back to the Town Hall: Why Conservatives Should Embrace Deliberative Democracy." *Hoover Digest: Research and Opinion on Public Policy* (2008): 97.

DeMoss, Mark. "Don't Expect Civility." *Politico* (January 17, 2011). http://www.politico.com/news/stories/0111/47677.html#ixzz1EX3fIhKc (accessed January 31, 2011).

Dionne, E. J., and Michael Cromartie. "Modernist, Orthodox, or Flexidox: Why the Culture War Debate Endures." In *Is There a Culture War?: A Dialogue on Values and American Public Life*, James Davidson Hunter and Alan Wolfe, eds. Washington, DC: Brooking Institution Press, 2006.

Finkelstein, Mark. "Dems Will Love Morning Joe's Odd Manifesto Against 'Angry Voices.'" *NewsBusters*, September 20, 2010. http://newsbusters.org/blogs/mark-finkelstein/2010/09/20/morning-joes-odd-manifesto-against-angry-voices-sounds-lot-obama-s (accessed March 2, 2011).

Fiorina, Morgan, Samuel Abrams, and Jeremy Pope. *Culture War? The Myth of a Polarized America.* New York: Longman, 2004.

First Presidency and Council of the Twelve Apostles of the Church of Jesus Christ of Latter-day Saints. "The Family: A Proclamation to the World," 1995. http://lds.org/library/display/0,4945,161-1-11-1,00.html (accessed December 20, 2010).

Fletcher, Michael A. "At National Prayer Breakfast, Obama Warns Against 'Erosion of Civility.'" *Washington Post*, February 4, 2010. http://www.washingtonpost.com/wp-dyn/content/article/2010/02/04/AR2010020401728.html (accessed February 18, 2010).

Foucault, Michel. *The Archeology of Knowledge.* New York: Routledge, 1962.

Freire, Paulo. *Pedagogy of the Oppressed.* New York: Herder and Herder, 1970.

Gadamer, Hans Georg. *Truth and Method*, 2nd revised ed. Joel Weinsheimer and Donald G. Marshall, trans. New York: Continuum International Publishing Group, 2004.

Gastil, John, and James Dillard. "Increasing Political Sophistication Through Public Deliberation." *Political Communication* 16 (1999): 3–23.

Goldapple, Kimberly, Z. Segal, C. Garson, M. Lau, P. Bieling, S. Kennedy, and H. Mayberg. "Modulation of Cortical-limbic Pathways in Major Depression: Treatment-specific Effects of Cognitive Behavior Therapy." *Archives of General Psychiatry* 61 (2004): 34–41.

Goodstein, Laurie. "Founder of 'Civility Project' Calls It Quits." *New York Times Politics and Government Blog.* http://thecaucus.blogs.nytimes.com/2011/01/12/founder-of-civility-project-calls-it-quits/ (accessed January 12, 2011).

Haidt, Jonathan. "Jonathan Haidt on the Moral Roots of Liberals and Conservatives." TED Talks, March 2008. http://www.ted.com/talks/jonathan_haidt_on_the_moral_mind.html (accessed April 25, 2010).

Haidt, Jonathan, and Jesse Graham. "When Morality Opposes Justice: Conservatives Have Moral Intuitions that Liberals May not Recognize." *Journal Social Justice Research* 20, no. 1 (2007): 0885-7466.

Haldeman, Doug. "Gay Rights, Patient Fights: The Implications of Sexual Orientation Conversion Therapy." *Professional Psychology: Research and Practice* 33, no. 3 (2002): 260–64.

Hardball with Chris Matthews (transcript), MSNBC, July 27, 2011, http://www .msnbc.msn.com/id/43928001/ns/msnbc_tv-hardball_with_chris_ matthews/t/hardball-chris-matthews-wednesday-july/ (accessed January 5, 2012).

Heierbacher, Sandy. National Coalition for Dialogue & Deliberation website resource page. http://ncdd.org/rc/item/1501 (accessed February 16, 2011).

———. "Taking our Work to the Next Level: Addressing Challenges Facing the Dialogue and Deliberation Community," *The International Journal of Public Participation* 3, no. 1, (2009): 1–19.

Herzig, Maggie, and Laurie Chasin. "Fostering Dialogue Across Divides: A Nuts and Bolts Guide from the Public Conversations Project." Watertown, MA: Public Conversations Project, 2006. http://www.publicconversations.org /resources/guides (accessed January 14, 2012).

Hesse-Biber, Sharlene Nagy. *The Cult of Thinness*. USA: Oxford University Press, 2006.

Hess, Jacob, and Nathan Todd. "From Culture War to Difficult Dialogue: Exploring Distinct Frames for Citizen Exchange about Social Problems." *Journal of Public Deliberation* 5, no. 1, article 3 (2009): 1–27.

Hess, Jacob, Danielle Rynczak, Joe Minarik, and Joycelyn Landrum-Brown. "Alternative Settings for Liberal-Conservative Exchange: Examining an Undergraduate Dialogue Course." *Journal of Community and Applied Social Psychology* 20, no. 2 (2010): 156–66.

Hess, Jacob Z., Nicole Elaine Allen, and Nathan R. Todd. "Interpreting Community Accountability: Citizen Views of Responding to Domestic Violence (or Not)." *Qualitative Report* 16, no. 6 (2011).

Hunter, James Davison. *Culture Wars: The Struggle to Define America. Making Sense of the Battles Over the Family, Art, Education, Law, and Politics*. New York: HarperCollins, 1991.

Jacobs, Bruce A. *Race Manners: Navigating the Minefield between Black and White Americans*. New York: Arcade Books, 2007.

Kadlec, Alison, and Will Friedman. "Deliberative Democracy and the Problem of Power." *Journal of Public Deliberation* 3, no. 1, article 8 (2007): 7, 23.

Knox, Colin, and Joanne Hughes. "Crossing the Divide: Community Relations in Northern Ireland." *Journal of Peace Research* 33 (1996): 83–98.

Kühnlein, Peter, Hannes Rieser, and Henk Zeevat, eds. *Perspectives on Dialogue in the New Millennium*. Amsterdam: John Benjamins Publishing Co., 2003.

Lakoff, George. *Moral Politics: How Liberals and Conservatives Think*. Chicago: University of Chicago Press, 2002.

Lutz, Antoine, J. Brefczynski-Lewis, T. Johnstone, and R. J. Davidson. "Regulation of the Neural Circuitry of Emotion by Compassion Meditation: Effects

of Meditative Expertise." *PLoS ONE* 3, no. 3 (2008): e1897. http://www
.plosone.org/article/info%3Adoi%2F10.1371%2Fjournal.pone.0001897
(accessed March 2, 2011).

Marcus, Gary. *The Birth of the Mind.* New York: Perseus, 2004.

McCain, John. "After the Shootings, Obama Reminds the Nation of the Golden
Rule," op-ed., *Washington Post*, January 16, 2011. http://www.washington
post.com/wp-dyn/content/article/2011/01/14/AR2011011403871.html (accessed January 25, 2011).

McKenzie, William. "Ready for Some Football but it Feels Like a Pagan Ritual."
Dallas News.com, January 31, 2011. http://www.dallasnews.com/opinion
/columnists/william-mckenzie/20110131-william-mckenzie-ready-for
-some-football-but-it-feels-like-a-pagan-ritual.ece (accessed January 31, 2011).

Miller, Gregory. E-mail communication (with permission). University of Illinois,
Urbana-Champaign.

Mollov, Ben, and Chaim Lavie. "Culture, Dialogue, and Perception Change in
the Israeli-Palestinian Conflict." *International Journal of Conflict Management*
12, no. 1 (2001): 69–87.

Nagda, Biren. "Fostering Meaningful Racial Engagement Through Intergroup
Dialogues." *Group Processes & Intergroup Relations* 6, no. 6 (2003): 111–28.

Neisser, Phil. *United We Fall: Ending America's Love Affair with the Political Center.*
Santa Barbara: Praeger, 2008.

Obama, Barack. "Notre Dame Commencement Address." The White House:
Office of the Press Secretary, May 17, 2009. http://www.whitehouse.gov
/video/President-Obama-Notre-Dame-Commencement (accessed June 1,
2011).

———. "Remarks by the President at a Father's Day Event." The White House:
Office of the Press Secretary, June 21, 2010. http://www.whitehouse.gov
/the-press-office/remarks-president-a-fathers-day-event (accessed January
31, 2011).

———. "Remarks by the President at a Memorial Service for the Victims of
the Shooting in Tucson, Arizona." The White House: Office of the Press
Secretary, January 12, 2011. http://www.whitehouse.gov/the-press-office
/2011/01/12/remarks-president-barack-obama-memorial-service-victims
-shooting-tucson (accessed March 1, 2011).

Osterhout, Lee, A. Poliakovb, K. Inouea, J. McLaughlina, G. Valentinea, I.
Pitkanena, C. Frenck-Mestred, and J. Hirschensohnc. "Second-language
Learning and Changes in the Brain." *Journal of Neurolinguistics* 21, no. 6
(2008): 509–21.

Perloff, James. *The Case Against Darwin: Why the Evidence Should Be Examined.*
(Burlington, MA: Refuge Books, 2002).

Pew Research Center for the People and the Press. "The 2005 Political Typology:
Beyond Red vs. Blue" Washington, DC, 2005. Event transcript.

Pipher, Mary. *Reviving Ophelia: Saving the Selves of Adolescent Girls.* New York:
Ballantine Books, 1994.

Porter, Elisabeth. "Creating Dialogical Spaces in Northern Ireland." *International
Feminist Journal of Politics* 2, no. 2 (2000): 163–84.

Public Conversations Project. "Getting Started: PCP's First Dialogues." http:// www.publicconversations.org/who/firstdialogues (accessed January 23, 2011).

Reese, Charley. "545 People Responsible for All of America's Woes." *Stonewall County Courier* (Aspermont, Texas), September 19, 1985. http://www.apfn .org/APFN/woes.htm (accessed July 30, 2009).

Rodenborg, Nancy, and Nancy Huynh. "On Overcoming Segregation: Social Work and Intergroup Dialogue." *Social Work with Groups* 29, no. 1 (2006): 27–44.

Rovzar, Chris. "Rush Limbaugh: 'There's Going to Be a Retard Summit at the White House,'" *New York*, February 3, 2010, http://nymag.com/daily/intel /2010/02/rush_limbaugh_theres_going_to.html (accessed January 5, 2012).

Saarela, M. V., Y. Hlushchuk, A. C. de C. Williams, M. Schürmann, E. Kalso, and R. Hari. "The Compassionate Brain: Humans Detect Intensity of Pain from Another's Face." *Cerebral Cortex* 17, no. 1 (February 2006): 230– 37. http://cercor.oxfordjournals.org/content/17/1/230.full (accessed January 21, 2011).

Sanders, L. M. "Against Deliberation." *Political Theory* 25 (1997): 347–64.

Schoem, David, and Sylvia Hurtado, eds. *Intergroup Dialogue: Deliberative Democracy in School, College, Community and Workplace.* Anne Arbor: University of Michigan Press, 2001.

Schwandt, Thomas. "Farewell to Criteriology." *Qualitative Inquiry* 2 (1996): 67.

Secular News Daily. "Gallup: Conservatives Outnumber Liberals 2:1, Church Attendance Rising," June 28, 2010. http://www.secularnewsdaily.com /2010/06/28/gallup-conservatives-outnumber-liberals-21-church-attendance -rising/ (accessed January 29, 2011).

Seyle, D. Conor, and Matthew L. Newman. "A House Divided? The Psychology of Red and Blue America." *American Psychologist* 61 (2006): 577.

Slife, Brent. *Managing Inescapable Values in Psychotherapy.* Los Angeles: Counseling Program, University of Southern California, 2000.

Smith, Joseph, Jr. *Joseph Smith History, the Pearl of Great Price.* Salt Lake City: The Church of Jesus Christ of Latter-day Saints, 1851/1981.

Snow, Eliza R. "Oh, my Father." *Hymns.* Salt Lake City: The Church of Jesus Christ of Latter-day Saints, 1985.

Steele, Shelby. *A Dream Deferred: The Second Betrayal of Black Freedom in America.* New York: HarperCollins, 1998.

Stewart, Jon. "Jon Stewart Speech: Transcript." *TBD Arts.* October 30, 2010. http://www.tbd.com/blogs/tbd-arts/2010/10/jon-stewart-speech -transcript-3955.html (accessed January 23, 2011).

Sugrue, Thomas. *The Origins of the Urban Crisis.* Princeton, NJ: Princeton University Press, 1996.

Takim, Liyakatali. "From Conversion to Conversation: Interfaith Dialogue in Post 9-11 America." *Muslim World* 94, no. 3 (2004): 343–55.

Tanabe, Karin. "Charles Barkley Calls GOP Field 'Idiots,'" azcentral.com, December 21, 2011, http://www.azcentral.com/news/articles/2011/12/21/201 11221charles-barkley-calls-republicans-idiots-politico.html (accessed January 10, 2012).

Taylor, Charles. *Sources of the Self: The Making of the Modern Identity*. Cambridge, MA: Harvard University Press, 1992.

Terkel, Studs. "C. P. Ellis." In *Race, Class, and Gender in the United States: An Integrated Study*, 5th ed., Paula S. Rothenberg, ed. (New York: Worth Publishers, 2000).

Traubman, Lenny. *Jewish-Palestinian Living Room Dialogue* (documentary). Exhibition booth at American Psychological Association (San Francisco: APA Annual Convention, August 17–20, 2007).

University of Michigan Health System. "Television and Children." *Your Child: Development and Behavior Resources; A Guide to Information and Support to Parents*. http://www.med.umich.edu/yourchild/topics/tv.htm (accessed February 26, 2011).

"What Is Dialogue? Definitions from Leaders in the Field," National Coalition for Dialogue and Deliberation, http://ncdd.org/rc/item/1501 (accessed January 16, 2012).

Williams, Richard N. "Faith, Reason, Knowledge, and Truth," February 1, 2000. http://speeches.byu.edu/reader/reader.php?id=1600.

Wilson, Carter. *Racism: From Slavery to Advanced Capitalism*. Thousand Oaks, CA: Sage, 1996.

Yeakley, Alison. "The Nature of Prejudice Change: Positive and Negative Change Processes Arising from Intergroup Contact Experiences." *Dissertation Abstracts International* 59, no 10 (1999): 3970.

Young, Brigham. *Journal of Discourses*. Liverpool: F. D. Richards, 1855.

Index

About the Authors

Phil Neisser teaches political theory at the State University of New York at Potsdam, where he also serves as the Associate Dean of Arts and Sciences. Neisser earned his MA at Georgetown University and his PhD at the University of Massachusetts–Amherst. He is the author of *United We Fall: Ending America's Love Affair with the Political Center* (Praeger, 2008), coeditor of *Tales of the State: Narrative in Contemporary U.S. Politics and Public Policy* (1997), and the author of essays and book chapters on a variety of subjects. In 2000 he received a SUNY Potsdam Presidential Award for Excellence in Teaching.

Jacob Hess is research director at Utah Youth Village, a nonprofit for abused children in the Rocky Mountain region. After graduating from Brigham Young University, Jacob studied in the clinical-community psychology doctoral program at the University of Illinois, Urbana-Champaign. While there, he was invited by Joycelyn Landrum-Brown with the UIUC Program on Intergroup Relations to help develop and cofacilitate a liberal-conservative dialogue course for undergraduates, the first of its kind in the nation. Jacob also joined Nathan Todd and Nicole Allen in interview research, comparing narratives of liberal and conservative citizens. Since completing his PhD dissertation research on contrasting narratives of anti-depressant treatment in 2009, Jacob has been conducting long-term treatment outcome studies and developing in-home, public health interventions for depression.